ASEBA — Achenbach System of Empirically Based Assessment

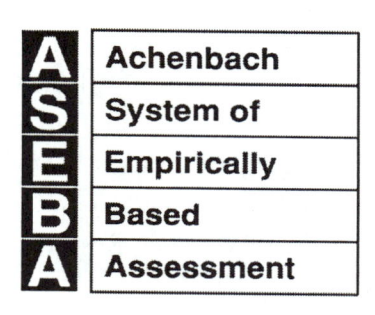

Manual for the ASEBA Preschool Forms & Profiles

- **Child Behavior Checklist for Ages 1½ – 5**
- **Language Development Survey**
- **Caregiver – Teacher Report Form**

An Integrated System of Multi-informant Assessment

Thomas M. Achenbach, University of Vermont & Leslie A. Rescorla, Bryn Mawr College

Ordering Information

This *Manual* and other ASEBA materials can be ordered from:

> ASEBA
> 1 South Prospect Street
> Burlington, VT 05401-3456

> Fax: 802-264-6433
> E-mail: mail@ASEBA.org
> Web: www.ASEBA.org

Proper bibliographic citation for this *Manual*:

Achenbach, T. M., & Rescorla, L. A. (2000). *Manual for the ASEBA Preschool Forms & Profiles*. Burlington, VT: University of Vermont, Research Center for Children, Youth, & Families.

Related Books

Achenbach, T.M., & McConaughy, S.H. (2007). *School-Based Practitioners' Guide for the Achenbach System of Empirically Based Assessment (ASEBA)* (5th ed.). Burlington, VT: University of Vermont, Research Center for Children, Youth, & Families.

Achenbach, T.M., Newhouse, P.A., & Rescorla, L.A. (2004). *Manual for the ASEBA Older Adult Forms & Profiles*. Burlington, VT: University of Vermont, Research Center for Children, Youth, & Families.

Achenbach, T.M., Newhouse, P.A., & Rescorla, L.A. (2007). *Guide for ASEBA Instruments for Adults/18-59 and Older Adults/60-90+* (2nd ed.). Burlington, VT: University of Vermont, Research Center for Children, Youth, & Families.

Achenbach, T.M., Pecora, P.J., & Wetherbee, K.M. (2007). *Child and Family Service Workers' Guide for the Achenbach System of Empirically Based Assessment (ASEBA)* (5th ed.). Burlington, VT: University of Vermont, Research Center for Children, Youth, & Families.

Achenbach, T.M., & Rescorla, L.A. (2001). *Manual for the ASEBA School-Age Forms & Profiles*. Burlington, VT: University of Vermont, Research Center for Children, Youth, & Families.

Achenbach, T.M., & Rescorla, L.A. (2003). *Manual for the ASEBA Adult Forms & Profiles*. Burlington, VT: University of Vermont, Research Center for Children, Youth, & Families.

Achenbach, T.M., & Rescorla, L.A. (2007). *Mental Health Practitioners' Guide for the Achenbach System of Empirically Based Assessment (ASEBA)* (5th ed.). Burlington, VT: University of Vermont, Research Center for Children, Youth, & Families.

Achenbach, T.M., & Rescorla, L.A. (2007). *Multicultural Guide for the ASEBA School-Age Forms & Profiles*. Burlington, VT: University of Vermont, Research Center for Children, Youth, & Families.

Achenbach, T.M., & Rescorla, L.A. (2007). *Multicultural Supplement to the Manual for the ASEBA School-Age Forms & Profiles*. Burlington, VT: University of Vermont, Research Center for Children, Youth, & Families.

Achenbach, T.M., & Rescorla, L.A. (2007). *Multicultural Understanding of Child and Adolescent Psychopathology: Implications for Mental Health Assessment*. New York: Guilford Press.

Achenbach, T.M., & Ruffle, T.M. (2007). *Medical Practitioners' Guide for the Achenbach System of Empirically Based Assessment (ASEBA)* (5th ed.). Burlington, VT: University of Vermont, Research Center for Children, Youth, & Families.

McConaughy, S.H., & Achenbach, T.M. (2001). *Manual for the Semistructured Clinical Interview for Children and Adolescents* (2nd ed.). Burlington, VT: University of Vermont, Research Center for Children, Youth, & Families.

McConaughy, S.H., & Achenbach, T.M. (2004). *Manual for the Test Observation Form for Ages 2-18*. Burlington, VT: University of Vermont, Research Center for Children, Youth, & Families.

> Copyright 2000 T.M. Achenbach & L.A. Rescorla. All rights reserved.
> Unauthorized reproduction prohibited by law.
> ISBN 978-0-938565-68-0   Library of Congress 00-131-596
> Printed in the United States of America 14 13 12 11 10 9 8 7

User Qualifications

The ASEBA preschool forms are designed to be self-administered by respondents who have at least fifth grade reading skills. The Child Behavior Checklist for Ages 1½-5 and the Language Development Survey (CBCL/1½-5-LDS) are to be completed by parents and others who see children in home-like settings. The Caregiver-Teacher Report Form (C-TRF) is to be completed by daycare providers and preschool teachers who have known a child in daycare, preschool, or similar settings for at least 2 months. If a respondent has difficulty completing a form, it can be read aloud by an interviewer who writes the respondent's answers on the form. The respondent should also have a copy of the form to look at while the interviewer reads each item.

When a form is given to a respondent, the user should explain that its aim is to obtain a picture of the child's behavior as the respondent sees it. It is important to tell respondents that the forms are designed to describe many different children. If some items do not seem applicable to a particular child, respondents should still rate the items, but they should also write explanations for their responses. For example, a respondent who lacks opportunities to observe the behavior described by a particular problem item should rate the item *0* to indicate *Not true (as far as you know)*, but may wish to write "No chance to observe."

A person familiar with the form should be available to answer questions about it. Answers to questions should be objective and factual, rather than probing or interpretive.

Whenever possible, it is desirable to have at least two adults independently complete separate forms describing the child's behavior in each setting, such as home, daycare, and preschool. As detailed in this *Manual*, the profiles scored from the forms should then be compared to identify consistencies and inconsistencies in how the child is seen by different informants. Systematic comparisons between reports from different respondents are facilitated by ASEBA computer software.

If a child has a disability or is in a special setting for children with disabilities, respondents should be told to base their ratings on expectations for typical peers of the child's age, i.e., children who do not have disabilities. This is necessary to provide appropriate comparisons with the norms for the ASEBA scales.

To make proper use of the ASEBA forms, the data should be scored on the appropriate profiles. Completion of hand-scored profiles requires that the instructions in Appendix A be carefully followed. The ASEBA computer software provides instructions that can be followed by users familiar with basic computer procedures. The profiles from all respondents should be compared with each other and with other relevant data. Users should therefore have access to multiple sources of data about the child and must be trained in the theory and methodology of standardized assessment, as well as in work with children and families. The training required will differ according to the specific applications of the ASEBA forms, but graduate training of at least the Master's degree level or two years of residency in pediatrics, psychiatry, or family practice is usually necessary. No amount of prior training, however, can substitute for professional maturity and a thorough knowledge of the procedures and cautions presented in the *Manual*.

All users should understand that ASEBA instruments are designed to provide standardized descriptions of functioning. No scores on ASEBA scales should be automatically equated with a particular diagnosis or disorder. Instead, the responsible professional will integrate ASEBA data with other types of data to provide comprehensive evaluations of functioning.

Preface

There is growing awareness of the need for more systematic assessment of maladaptive behavior among preschoolers. In response to the need for more systematic and useful assessment, we have made substantial improvements in our assessment instruments for preschoolers. This *Manual* provides essential information about using and scoring the ASEBA preschool instruments and about the new database on which they rest. It also provides extensive guidelines and illustrations of practical and research applications for helping users achieve their objectives most effectively.

To enable users to quickly learn about the ASEBA preschool forms, Chapters 1 through 5 provide basic information in a practical format without technical details. Chapters 6 through 11 document the research basis for the ASEBA preschool instruments. Chapter 12 presents ways to use the ASEBA instruments in new research, while Chapter 13 provides answers to commonly asked questions. The Reader's Guide following this preface offers an overview of the *Manual*'s contents to aid users in quickly locating the material they seek.

The versions of the ASEBA preschool instruments presented here offer the following innovative features:

1. Both the CBCL and C-TRF now span ages 1½-5.

2. The Language Development Survey (LDS) is now included with the CBCL to identify language delays.

3. The scoring scales and norms are based on new national samples.

4. Syndrome scales have been revised on the basis of new, larger samples that were analyzed via more advanced factor analytic methodology designed to coordinate CBCL and C-TRF scales.

5. DSM-oriented scales have been constructed from ASEBA items rated as very consistent with DSM-IV diagnostic categories.

6. ASEBA software now compares scores for empirically based and DSM-oriented scales on any combination of up to eight CBCL and C-TRF forms per child.

The innovations in the ASEBA preschool instruments are fruits of long-term programmatic research and practical experience. Many colleagues throughout the world have contributed ideas, data, findings, and other ingredients to this effort. For their help with this particular phase of the work, we especially thank the following people: Janet Arnold, Rachel Bérubé, Ken Britting, Christine Chase, Sarah Cochran, Levent Dumenci, Rick Goode, Michelle Hayes, James Hudziak, David Jacobowitz, Stephanie McConaughy, Thomas Ruffle, Catherine Stanger, Frank Verhulst, Denise Vignoe, Dan Walter, and Stephen Zubrick.

We also thank the psychiatrists and psychologists from nine cultures who rated the consistency of ASEBA preschool items with DSM-IV diagnostic categories to provide the basis for our new DSM-oriented scales. Their names and affiliations are listed in our report of that effort (Achenbach, Dumenci, & Rescorla, 2000), which is available at our website: www.ASEBA.org

READER'S GUIDE

I. **Introductory Material Needed by Most Readers**
   A. Features of ASEBA Preschool Forms .... Chapter 1
   B. Hand-Scored Profiles .... Chapter 2
   C. Computerized Scoring and Cross-Informant Comparisons .... Chapter 3
   D. DSM-Oriented Scales .... Chapter 4
   E. Practical Applications .... Chapter 5

II. **Construction of Scales for ASEBA Preschool Forms**
   A. Syndrome and LDS Scales .... Chapter 6
   B. Internalizing, Externalizing, and Total Problems Scales ..... Chapter 7

III. **Statistical Data on Reliability and Validity**
   A. Reliability, Cross-Informant Agreement, and Stability .... Chapter 8
   B. Validity .... Chapter 9
   C. Item Scores .... Chapter 10

IV. **Relations of New Scales to Previous Versions** .... Chapter 11

V. **Research Use** .... Chapter 12

VI. **Answers to Commonly Asked Questions** .... Chapter 13

VII. **Instructions for Hand Scoring the Profiles** .... Appendix A

VIII. **Factor Loadings of Items on Syndrome Scales** .... Appendix B

IX. **Mean Scale Scores for Normative Samples** .... Appendix C

X. **Mean Scale Scores for Matched Referred and Nonreferred Samples** .. Appendix D

XI. **Correlations Among Scales** .... Appendix E

XII. **Tabulations of Problem Item Scores** .... Appendix F

CONTENTS

User Qualifications iii
Preface iv
Reader's Guide v

1. **Features of ASEBA Preschool Forms** 1
   The *Child Behavior Checklist for Ages 1½-5* (CBCL/1½-5) 1
   The *Language Development Survey* (LDS) 4
   The *Caregiver-Teacher Report Form for Ages 1½-5* (C-TRF) 4
   Achenbach System of Empirically Based Assessment (ASEBA) 4
   Structure of this *Manual* 9
   Summary 9

2. **Hand-Scored Profiles for ASEBA Preschool Forms** 11
   Syndrome Scales of the CBCL/1½-5 11
   Internalizing and Externalizing Groupings of CBCL/1½-5 Syndromes 13
   CBCL/1½-5 Total Problems Score 14
   Language Development Survey 14
   Syndrome Scales of the C-TRF 16
   Summary 18

3. **Computerized Scoring and Cross-Informant Comparisons** 19
   Kenny Randall, Age 30 Months 19
       Computer-Scored CBCL/1½-5 Profile 19
   Cross-informant Comparisons of Problem Item Scores 21
   Cross-informant Correlations 25
   Cross-informant Comparisons of Syndrome Scale Scores Via Bar Graphs 25
   Clinical Evaluation of Kenny 28
       Diagnostic Conclusions and Recommendations 28
   Summary 29

4. **DSM-Oriented Scales for Scoring ASEBA Preschool Forms** 30
   Constructing DSM-oriented Scales 30
   Profiles of DSM-oriented Scales 31
   Profiles and Cross-informant Comparisons of DSM-oriented Scales 32
   Guidelines for Using DSM-oriented Scales 32
       High Scores on Multiple Scales 35
       Cross-Informant Differences in Scale Scores 35
       Severity of Problems on DSM-Oriented Scales 35
   Summary 35

CONTENTS

5. Practical Applications of ASEBA Preschool Forms 37
  Guidelines for Practical Applications 37
    Use ASEBA Forms Routinely 37
    Obtain Reports from Multiple Informants Whenever Feasible 37
    Use ASEBA Data to Guide Interviews 38
    Use ASEBA Data in the Diagnostic Process 38
    Use ASEBA Forms for Assessing Service Delivery and Outcomes 38
  Mental Health and Developmental Service Settings 39
    Having Both Parents Fill Out CBCLs 40
    Interviewing Parents 42
    Diagnostic Issues 42
  Educational Settings 43
    Identifying Problems 43
    Planning Interventions 44
    Case Example in Head Start: Tyrone Jenkins, Age 5 44
  Medical Settings 47
    Case Example in an HMO: Lily Chang, Age 4 48
  Child and Family Service Settings 50
    Case Example in Foster Care: Luisa Solano, Age 2 51
  Forensic Applications 53
    Child Abuse 53
  Summary 53

6. Construction of Syndrome and LDS Scales 55
  Statistical Derivation of the Syndromes 55
    Factor Analysis of Item Scores 55
    CBCL/1½-5 Samples 56
    C-TRF Samples 56
    Items Analyzed 56
    Factor-Analytic Methods 57
    Results of the Factor Analyses 58
  Construction of Syndrome Scales 58
    Normative Samples 58
    Selection of Nonreferred Children for Norms 60
  Assigning Normalized T Scores 62
    Truncation of Lower T Scores at 50 62
    Assigning T Scores Above 70 (98th Percentile) 64
    Mean T Scores 64
  Borderline and Clinical Ranges 65
  Norms for DSM-oriented Scales 65
  Norms for the LDS 65
    Length of Phrases 67
    Vocabulary Scores 67
  Summary 67

CONTENTS

7. Internalizing, Externalizing, and Total Problems Scales 69
   Derivation of Internalizing and Externalizing Groupings of Syndromes 69
      Arrangement of Internalizing and Externalizing Syndromes on Profiles 70
   Assignment of Internalizing, Externalizing, and Total Problems T Scores 70
   Normal, Borderline, and Clinical Ranges 71
   Relations Between Internalizing and Externalizing Scores 72
      Distinguishing Between Internalizing and Externalizing Patterns 72
   Summary 73

8. Reliability, Cross-Informant Agreement, and Stability 74
   Test-retest Reliability of Scale Scores 74
      CBCL and C-TRF 74
      LDS 77
   Cross-informant Agreement 77
      Cross-Informant Correlations 77
      Relative Risk Odds Ratios (ORs) 79
      Mothers' vs. Fathers' Mean Scale Scores 79
   Stabilities of Scale Scores 79
   Summary 79

9. Validity of the ASEBA Preschool Scales 82
   Content Validity of the Problem Items 82
      Selection of CBCL Items 82
      Selection of C-TRF Items 82
      Associations of CBCL and C-TRF Items with Referral Status 83
   Content Validity of the LDS 83
   Criterion-related Validity of Problem Scores 83
      CBCL and C-TRF Samples Analyzed 84
      Multiple Regression Analyses of Problem Scale Scores 84
      Referral Status Differences in Problem Scale Scores 86
      Demographic Differences in Problem Scale Scores 86
   Classification of Children According to Clinical Cutpoints 86
      Odd Ratios (ORs) 90
      Discriminant Analyses Using Problem Scores 92
   Probability of Particular Total Problems Scores Being
   from the Referred vs. Nonreferred Samples 93
   Criterion-related Validity of LDS Scores 93
      Correlations with Test Scores 93
      Classification of Children as Delayed vs. Not Delayed 94
   Construct Validity of ASEBA Problem Scales 96
      Correlations with Other Measures of Problems 96
   Construct Validity of the LDS 100
   Summary 100

CONTENTS

10. Problem Item Scores 101
   Referral Status Differences in Problem Item Scores 101
      Effect Sizes 101
   Demographic Differences in Problem Scores 105
      Gender Differences 105
      Age Differences 105
      SES Differences 105
      Ethnic Differences 105
   Graphs of Prevalence Rates 105
   Summary 116

11. Relations Between the New ASEBA Scales and Previous Versions 117
   Changes in Syndrome Scales 117
   Internalizing and Externalizing 118
   Total Problems Scale 118
   Statistical Relations Between the New ASEBA Scales and Previous Versions 118
      DSM-Oriented Scales 118
   Summary 120

12. Research Use of ASEBA Preschool Forms 121
   Guidelines for Use of ASEBA Forms in Research 121
      Use of Raw Scores vs. *T* Scores 122
      Standardization of Scale Scores within Research Samples 122
      Developmental Perspectives on Longitudinal Research 123
   Epidemiological Research 124
      Population Studies 124
   Diagnostic and Taxonomic Research 125
      Diagnosis of Behavioral/Emotional Problems 125
      Assessment and Taxonomy 125
      The DSM-Oriented ASEBA Scales 126
      Classification of Children with Language Delays 126
   Etiological Research 127
   Outcome Research 128
      Groups at Risk 128
      Outcomes of Services 129
      Experimental Intervention Studies 129
   Cross-cultural Research 130
   Research on Child Abuse 130
   Research on Parental Characteristics 130
   Research on Medical Conditions 132
   Summary 132

CONTENTS

13. Answers to Commonly Asked Questions 134
    Questions about the CBCL/1½-5 and C-TRF Forms 134
    Questions about Scoring the CBCL/1½-5 and C-TRF 136
    Questions about the CBCL/1½-5 and C-TRF Profiles 137
    Relations of the CBCL/1½-5 and C-TRF Preschool Forms to
        the School-age CBCL and TRF 140
    Questions about the LDS 141
    Questions about Scoring the LDS 141
    Questions about Interpreting the LDS 142

References 143

Appendix

A. Instructions for Hand Scoring the ASEBA Preschool Forms 149

B. Loadings of Items on Syndrome Scales in Final Weighted Least Squares Factor Analyses of Tetrachoric Correlations 151

C. Problem Scale Scores for Normative Samples 153

D. Mean CBCL Scale Scores for Matched Referred Children and Nonreferred Children 155

E. Pearson Correlations Among *T* Scores 159

F. Scores for Referred and Nonreferred Children on Each Problem Item ... 161

Index 173

Chapter 1
Features of ASEBA Preschool Forms

This *Manual* is designed to help people assess preschoolers in easy and cost-effective ways. By using ASEBA forms, you can quickly obtain standardized ratings of diverse aspects of behavioral, emotional, and social functioning. In addition, unlike many standardized forms, these forms also request explanatory details, plus open-ended descriptions of the best things about the child and greatest concerns about the child. Each form can be filled out in about 10 to 15 minutes.

THE *CHILD BEHAVIOR CHECKLIST FOR AGES 1½-5* (CBCL/1½-5)

The CBCL/1½-5—a revision of the CBCL/2-3 (Achenbach, 1992)—is completed by parents, parent surrogates, and others who see children in family settings. Figure 1-1 shows the CBCL/1½-5 completed for 2-year-old Anna Fernandez by her mother. A Spanish version of the CBCL/1½-5 is also available, but English was the main language in Anna's home, and her mother preferred completing the English version of the CBCL/1½-5. As shown in Figure 1-1, the CBCL/1½-5 requests demographic information about the child and asks respondents to indicate their name and their relationship to the child, such as mother, father, foster parent, or other relationship. Information about the parents' occupations is requested as a basis for scoring socioeconomic status, in case the user wishes to do so. The respondent is then asked to rate 99 problem items as *0* for *not true* of the child, *1* for *somewhat or sometimes true*, and *2* for *very true or often true*, based on the preceding 2 months. For several items, respondents are asked to provide descriptions of the problems. In addition, item *100* requests respondents to write in any additional problems that were not previously listed. Several problem items of the CBCL/1½-5 differ in minor ways from those of the CBCL/2-3. In addition, CBCL/2-3 items *51* and *79*, which were found to be ineffective, were changed to: *51. Shows panic for no good reason*, and *79. Rapid shifts between sadness and excitement*.

Following the items to be rated, the CBCL/1½-5 provides open-ended items (bottom of page 2) that ask the respondent to describe any illnesses or disabilities that the child has, what concerns the respondent most about the child, and the best things about the child. When people complete the CBCL/1½-5, they thus provide not only ratings that are scored on the scales to be described later, but also descriptive information specific to the child who is being assessed. This descriptive information provides users with a picture of the child in the respondent's own words. Users can then consider such information, along with scores on items and scales, for discussion with parents and others.

For respondents whose reading skills are poor or who may be unable to fill out the CBCL/1½-5 for other reasons, the following procedure is recommended:

An interviewer hands the respondent a copy of the form while retaining a second copy. The interviewer says: "I'll read you the questions on this form and I'll write down your answers." Respondents who can read well enough will typically start answering questions without waiting for each one to be read. However, for respondents who cannot read well, this procedure avoids embarrassment and inaccuracies, while at the same time maintaining standardization like that for respondents who complete the form independently.

ASEBA FEATURES

CHILD BEHAVIOR CHECKLIST FOR AGES 1½ - 5

Please print. Be sure to answer all items.

For office use only
ID #

CHILD'S FULL NAME: Anna Maria Fernandez

CHILD'S GENDER: ☐ Boy ☒ Girl
CHILD'S AGE: 2
CHILD'S ETHNIC GROUP OR RACE: Latina

PARENTS' USUAL TYPE OF WORK, even if not working now. *Please be specific—for example, auto mechanic, high school teacher, homemaker, laborer, lathe operator, shoe salesman, army sergeant.*

FATHER'S TYPE OF WORK: X-ray technician
MOTHER'S TYPE OF WORK: secretary

TODAY'S DATE: Mo. 8 Date 8 Yr. 00
CHILD'S BIRTHDATE: Mo. 3 Date 3 Yr. 98

THIS FORM FILLED OUT BY: (print your full name) Daniela Fernandez

Please fill out this form to reflect *your* view of the child's behavior even if other people might not agree. Feel free to write additional comments beside each item and in the space provided on page 2. **Be sure to answer all items.**

Your relationship to child:
☒ Mother ☐ Father ☐ Other (specify):

Below is a list of items that describe children. For each item that describes the child *now or within the past 2 months*, please circle the **2** if the item is **very true** or **often true** of the child. Circle the **1** if the item is **somewhat or sometimes true** of the child. If the item is **not true** of the child, circle the **0**. Please answer all items as well as you can, even if some do not seem to apply to the child.

0 = Not True (as far as you know)   1 = Somewhat or Sometimes True   2 = Very True or Often True

- ⓪ 1 2   1. Aches or pains (without medical cause; *do not* include stomach or headaches)
- 0 ① 2   2. Acts too young for age
- 0 ① 2   3. Afraid to try new things
- ⓪ 1 2   4. Avoids looking others in the eye
- 0 ① 2   5. Can't concentrate, can't pay attention for long
- 0 ① 2   6. Can't sit still, restless, or hyperactive
- ⓪ 1 2   7. Can't stand having things out of place
- 0 1 ②   8. Can't stand waiting; wants everything now
- ⓪ 1 2   9. Chews on things that aren't edible
- 0 ① 2   10. Clings to adults or too dependent
- 0 ① 2   11. Constantly seeks help
- ⓪ 1 2   ᵃ12. Constipated, doesn't move bowels (when not sick)
- 0 ① 2   13. Cries a lot
- ⓪ 1 2   14. Cruel to animals
- 0 ① 2   15. Defiant
- 0 ① 2   16. Demands must be met immediately
- ⓪ 1 2   17. Destroys his/her own things
- ⓪ 1 2   18. Destroys things belonging to his/her family or other children
- ⓪ 1 2   ᵃ19. Diarrhea or loose bowels (when not sick)
- ⓪ 1 2   20. Disobedient
- 0 1 ②   21. Disturbed by any change in routine
- 0 ① 2   ᵃ22. Doesn't want to sleep alone
- 0 ① 2   23. Doesn't answer when people talk to him/her
- 0 1 ②   ᵃ24. Doesn't eat well (describe): won't eat solid foods
- 0 ① 2   25. Doesn't get along with other children
- 0 ① 2   26. Doesn't know how to have fun; acts like a little adult
- ⓪ 1 2   27. Doesn't seem to feel guilty after misbehaving
- ⓪ 1 2   ᵃ28. Doesn't want to go out of home
- 0 1 ②   29. Easily frustrated

- ⓪ 1 2   30. Easily jealous
- ⓪ 1 2   31. Eats or drinks things that are not food—*don't* include sweets (describe): _____
- 0 ① 2   32. Fears certain animals, situations, or places (describe): Sometimes afraid of going out of home
- 0 1 ②   33. Feelings are easily hurt
- ⓪ 1 2   34. Gets hurt a lot, accident-prone
- ⓪ 1 2   35. Gets in many fights
- ⓪ 1 2   36. Gets into everything
- 0 1 ②   37. Gets too upset when separated from parents
- ⓪ 1 2   ᵃ38. Has trouble getting to sleep
- ⓪ 1 2   39. Headaches (without medical cause)
- ⓪ 1 2   40. Hits others
- ⓪ 1 2   41. Holds his/her breath
- 0 1 ②   42. Hurts animals or people without meaning to
- 0 1 ②   43. Looks unhappy without good reason
- 0 1 ②   44. Angry moods
- 0 ① 2   45. Nausea, feels sick (without medical cause)
- ⓪ 1 2   46. Nervous movements or twitching (describe): _____
- ⓪ 1 2   47. Nervous, highstrung, or tense
- 0 ① 2   ᵃ48. Nightmares
- ⓪ 1 2   ᵃ49. Overeating
- ⓪ 1 2   50. Overtired
- ⓪ 1 2   ᵃ51. Shows panic for no good reason
- ⓪ 1 2   ᵃ52. Painful bowel movements (without medical cause)
- ⓪ 1 2   53. Physically attacks people
- ⓪ 1 2   54. Picks nose, skin, or other parts of body (describe): _____

Be sure you have answered all items. Then see other side.

Copyright 2000 T. Achenbach & L. Rescorla
ASEBA, University of Vermont, 1 S. Prospect St., Burlington, VT 05401-3456 Web: http://Checklist.uvm.edu
UNAUTHORIZED REPRODUCTION IS ILLEGAL   7-28-00 Edition

Figure 1-1. Page 1 of the CBCL/1½ -5. Superscript *a* = items that differ from C-TRF items.

ASEBA FEATURES

Please print your answers. Be sure to answer all items.

0 = Not True (as far as you know)   1 = Somewhat or Sometimes True   2 = Very True or Often True

(0) 1 2	55.	Plays with own sex parts too much
(0) 1 2	56.	Poorly coordinated or clumsy
(0) 1 2	57.	Problems with eyes (without medical cause) (describe): _____
0 (1) 2	58.	Punishment doesn't change his/her behavior
0 1 (2)	59.	Quickly shifts from one activity to another
(0) 1 2	60.	Rashes or other skin problems (without medical cause)
0 (1) 2	61.	Refuses to eat
(0) 1 2	62.	Refuses to play active games
(0) 1 2	63.	Repeatedly rocks head or body
0 (1) 2	[a]64.	Resists going to bed at night
(0) 1 2	[a]65.	Resists toilet training (describe): _____
0 (1) 2	66.	Screams a lot
(0) 1 2	67.	Seems unresponsive to affection
(0) 1 2	68.	Self-conscious or easily embarrassed
0 (1) 2	69.	Selfish or won't share
(0) 1 2	70.	Shows little affection toward people
(0) 1 2	71.	Shows little interest in things around him/her
(0) 1 2	72.	Shows too little fear of getting hurt
0 (1) 2	73.	Too shy or timid
(0) 1 2	[a]74.	Sleeps less than most children during day and/or night (describe): _____
(0) 1 2	[a]75.	Smears or plays with bowel movements
(0) 1 2	76.	Speech problem (describe): _____
(0) 1 2	77.	Stares into space or seems preoccupied
0 (1) 2	78.	Stomachaches or cramps (without medical cause)

(0) 1 2	[a]79.	Rapid shifts between sadness and excitement
(0) 1 2	80.	Strange behavior (describe): _____
0 1 (2)	81.	Stubborn, sullen, or irritable
0 1 (2)	82.	Sudden changes in mood or feelings
(0) 1 2	83.	Sulks a lot
0 (1) 2	[a]84.	Talks or cries out in sleep
0 1 (2)	85.	Temper tantrums or hot temper
(0) 1 2	86.	Too concerned with neatness or cleanliness
0 (1) 2	87.	Too fearful or anxious
0 1 (2)	88.	Uncooperative
(0) 1 2	89.	Underactive, slow moving, or lacks energy
0 (1) 2	90.	Unhappy, sad, or depressed
(0) 1 2	91.	Unusually loud
0 (1) 2	92.	Upset by new people or situations (describe): goes to room when visitors come
(0) 1 2	93.	Vomiting, throwing up (without medical cause)
0 (1) 2	[a]94.	Wakes up often at night
(0) 1 2	95.	Wanders away
0 1 (2)	96.	Wants a lot of attention
(0) 1 2	97.	Whining
(0) 1 2	98.	Withdrawn, doesn't get involved with others
0 (1) 2	99.	Worries
	100.	Please write in any problems the child has that were not listed above.
0 1 2		_____
0 1 2		_____
0 1 2		_____

Please be sure you have answered all items. Underline any you are concerned about.

Does the child have any illness or disability (either physical or mental)? ☒ No ☐ Yes—Please describe:

What concerns you most about the child? She seems unhappy and gets upset easily. Also seems angry a lot.

Please describe the best things about the child: Very cute and loving.

Figure 1-1 (cont.). Page 2 of the CBCL/1½-5. Superscript *a* = items that differ from C-TRF items.

THE *LANGUAGE DEVELOPMENT SURVEY* (LDS)

Delayed language is a common cause for concern about young children's development and behavior. Behavioral and emotional problems may arise from language delays that interfere with peer relations and with responsiveness to adult expectations. Conversely, behavioral and emotional problems may interfere with learning language.

It is often difficult for professionals to directly evaluate the language of children under 3, because the children may be shy with strangers or may resist structured testing. This is especially true of children who have behavioral or emotional problems. Even when testing succeeds, it typically samples only a narrow range of children's language. Parents' reports of their children's everyday speech are therefore essential for evaluating early language development. To maximize the value of parents' reports, standardized formats are needed for obtaining data that can be directly compared with data for normative samples of children.

To make it easy to obtain parents' reports of their children's speech, pages 3 and 4 of the CBCL/1½-5 include the LDS (Rescorla, 1989), as shown in Figure 1-2 for Anna Fernandez. The LDS should be completed by parents of all children under 3, as well as by parents of children over 3 who are suspected of having language delays. Page 3 asks questions about the child's birth history and ear infections, as well as about speech problems among family members, all of which may be related to language delays. Page 3 also requests the respondent to report the child's best multi-word phrases. Page 4 lists 310 words that are among the first learned by most children. The respondent is asked to circle the words that the child uses spontaneously. Spaces are also provided to enter additional words used by the child. Chapter 2 describes the basis for determining whether language development is below the normal range for a child's age.

THE *CAREGIVER-TEACHER REPORT FORM FOR AGES 1½-5* (C-TRF)

The C-TRF is completed by daycare providers, teachers, and others who see a child in a group of at least four children. Figure 1-3 shows the C-TRF completed for Anna Fernandez by her preschool teacher. As shown in Figure 1-3, the C-TRF requests demographic information about the child, plus information about the role of the respondent in relation to the child (i.e., caregiver or teacher), how well the respondent knows the child, and the context in which the respondent sees the child. The C-TRF has many of the same problem items as the CBCL/1½-5 but it substitutes items pertinent to group situations for items that are specific to family situations. Like the CBCL/1½-5, the C-TRF asks respondents to rate each item as *0, 1,* or *2* based on the preceding 2 months. The C-TRF also has open-ended items that encourage respondents to describe the child, including the best things about the child. To improve the version of the C-TRF that was previously normed for ages 2-5 (Achenbach, 1997), we have made minor changes in a few items.

ACHENBACH SYSTEM OF EMPIRICALLY BASED ASSESSMENT (ASEBA)

The CBCL/1½-5 and C-TRF are components of the ASEBA. Developed through decades of research and practical experience, ASEBA forms are designed to capture both the similarities and differences in how children function under different conditions and with different interaction partners. For example, 2-year-old Anna may behave differently at home, in daycare, and in preschool. Within each of these settings, Anna may also behave differently in the presence of different adults, such as her mother

ASEBA FEATURES

LANGUAGE DEVELOPMENT SURVEY FOR AGES 18-35 MONTHS

For office use only
ID #

The Language Development Survey assesses children's word combinations and vocabulary. By carefully completing the Language Development Survey, you can help us obtain an accurate picture of your child's developing language. *Please print your answers. Be sure to answer all items.*

I. Was your child born earlier than the usual 9 months after conception?

☒ No ☐ Yes—how many weeks early? _____ weeks early.

II. How much did your child weigh at birth? __6__ pounds __5__ ounces or _____ grams.

III. How many ear infections did your child have before age 24 months?

☐ 0-2 ☐ 3-5 ☒ 6-8 ☐ 9 or more

IV. Is any language beside English spoken in your home?

☐ No ☒ Yes—please list the languages: __Spanish__

V. Has anyone in your family been slow in learning to talk?

☒ No ☐ Yes—please list their relationships to your child; for example, brother, father:

VI. Are you worried about your child's language development?

☒ No ☐ Yes—why? _____

VII. Does your child spontaneously say words in any language? (not just imitates or understands words)?

☐ No ☒ Yes—if yes, please complete item VIII and page 4.

VIII. Does your child combine 2 or more words into phrases? For example: "more cookie," "car bye-bye."

☐ No ☒ Yes—please print 5 of your child's longest and best phrases or sentences.
For each phrase that is not in English, print the name of the language.

1. __Baby go bye-bye__
2. __Daddy come home__
3. __more milk__
4. __no juice__
5. __Anna want ice cream__

Be sure you have answered all items. Then see other side.

Figure 1-2. Language Development Survey (page 3 of CBCL/1½-5).

ASEBA FEATURES

Please circle each word that your child says SPONTANEOUSLY (not just imitates or understands). If your child says non-English versions of words on the list, circle the English word and write the first letter of the language (e.g., S for Spanish). Please include words even if they are not pronounced clearly or are in "baby talk" (for example: "baba" for bottle).

FOODS
- (1.) apple
- 2. banana
- (3.) bread **S**
- 4. butter
- 5. cake
- (6.) candy **S**
- 7. cereal
- 8. cheese
- 9. coffee
- 10. cookie
- (11.) crackers
- (12.) drink
- (13.) egg
- (14.) food
- 15. grapes
- (16.) gum
- 17. hamburger
- 18. hotdog
- (19.) ice cream
- (20.) juice
- (21.) meat
- (22.) milk
- 23. orange
- 24. pizza
- 25. pretzel
- (26.) raisins
- (27.) soda
- 28. soup
- 29. spaghetti
- 30. tea
- 31. toast
- 32. water

TOYS
- (33.) ball
- (34.) balloon
- (35.) blocks
- (36.) book
- 37. crayons
- (38.) doll
- (39.) picture
- (40.) present
- (41.) slide
- (42.) swing
- (43.) teddy bear

OUTDOORS
- 44. flower
- (45.) house
- (46.) moon
- (47.) rain **S**
- 48. sidewalk
- 49. sky
- 50. snow
- 51. star
- (52.) street
- (53.) sun
- (54.) tree

ANIMALS
- 55. bear
- 56. bee
- (57.) bird
- (58.) bug
- 59. bunny
- (60.) cat
- 61. chicken
- (62.) cow
- (63.) dog
- 64. duck
- 65. elephant
- (66.) fish
- 67. frog
- 68. horse
- 69. monkey
- (70.) pig
- (71.) puppy
- 72. snake
- 73. tiger
- 74. turkey
- 75. turtle

BODY PARTS
- (76.) arm
- 77. belly button
- (78.) bottom
- (79.) chin
- (80.) ear **S**
- 81. elbow
- (82.) eye
- (83.) face
- (84.) finger
- (85.) foot
- (86.) hair
- (87.) hand
- (88.) knee
- (89.) leg
- 90. mouth
- 91. neck
- (92.) nose
- 93. teeth
- 94. thumb
- 95. toe
- 96. tummy

VEHICLES
- (97.) bike
- (98.) boat
- (99.) bus
- (100.) car
- 101. motorcycle
- 102. plane
- 103. stroller
- (104.) train
- (105.) trolley
- 106. truck

ACTIONS
- (107.) bath
- (108.) breakfast
- (109.) bring
- (110.) catch
- 111. clap
- (112.) close
- (113.) come
- 114. cough
- 115. cut
- 116. dance
- 117. dinner
- 118. doodoo
- 119. down
- (120.) eat
- 121. feed
- 122. finish
- 123. fix
- 124. get
- 125. give
- (126.) go
- 127. have
- (128.) help
- 129. hit
- 130. hug
- 131. jump
- 132. kick
- (133.) kiss
- 134. knock
- 135. look
- 136. love
- 137. lunch
- 138. make
- (139.) nap
- 140. open
- 141. outside
- 142. pattycake
- 143. peekaboo
- (144.) peepee
- 145. push
- 146. read
- 147. ride
- 148. run
- (149.) see
- 150. show
- 151. shut
- 152. sing
- 153. sit
- (154.) sleep
- 155. stop
- 156. take
- 157. throw
- 158. tickle
- 159. up
- (160.) walk
- (161.) want
- 162. wash

HOUSEHOLD
- 163. bathtub
- (164.) bed
- 165. blanket
- (166.) bottle **S**
- 167. bowl
- 168. chair
- 169. clock
- 170. crib
- (171.) cup
- (172.) door
- (173.) floor
- (174.) fork
- (175.) glass
- (176.) knife
- 177. light
- 178. mirror
- 179. pillow
- 180. plate
- 181. potty
- 182. radio
- 183. room
- 184. sink
- (185.) soap
- 186. spoon
- 187. stairs
- 188. table
- 189. telephone
- 190. towel
- (191.) trash
- (192.) T.V.
- 193. window

PERSONAL
- (194.) brush
- (195.) comb
- 196. glasses
- 197. key
- 198. money
- 199. paper
- 200. pen
- 201. pencil
- 202. penny
- 203. pocketbook
- 204. tissue
- 205. tooth brush
- 206. umbrella
- 207. watch

PLACES
- (208.) church
- (209.) home
- 210. hospital
- 211. library
- 212. park
- (213.) school
- 214. store
- 215. zoo

MODIFIERS
- (216.) all gone
- 217. all right
- (218.) bad
- (219.) big
- 220. black
- 221. blue
- 222. broken
- 223. clean
- 224. cold
- 225. dark
- 226. dirty
- 227. dry
- (228.) good
- 229. happy
- 230. heavy
- (231.) hot
- 232. hungry
- 233. little
- 234. mine
- (235.) more
- 236. nice
- 237. pretty
- 238. red
- 239. stinky
- 240. that
- 241. this
- 242. tired
- 243. wet
- 244. white
- 245. yellow
- (246.) yucky

CLOTHES
- 247. belt
- (248.) boots
- (249.) coat
- 250. diaper
- 251. dress
- 252. gloves
- 253. hat
- 254. jacket
- 255. mittens
- 256. pajamas
- 257. pants
- 258. shirt
- 259. shoes
- 260. slippers
- 261. sneakers
- (262.) socks
- 263. sweater

OTHER
- 264. any letter
- 265. away
- 266. booboo
- (267.) byebye
- 268. excuse me
- 269. here
- (270.) hi, hello
- (271.) in
- (272.) me
- 273. meow
- (274.) my
- 275. myself
- (276.) nightnight
- (277.) no
- 278. off
- (279.) on
- (280.) out
- 281. please
- 282. Sesame St.
- (283.) shut up
- (284.) thank you
- 285. there
- 286. under
- 287. welcome
- 288. what
- 289. where
- (290.) why
- 291. woofwoof
- (292.) yes
- (293.) you
- 294. yumyum
- 295. any number

PEOPLE
- 296. aunt
- (297.) baby
- (298.) boy
- (299.) daddy
- 300. doctor
- (301.) girl
- (302.) grandma **S**
- (303.) grandpa **S**
- 304. lady
- 305. man
- (306.) mommy
- (307.) own name
- (308.) pet name
- 309. uncle
- (310.) name of TV or story character

Other words your child says, including non-English words:
_____
_____
_____
_____

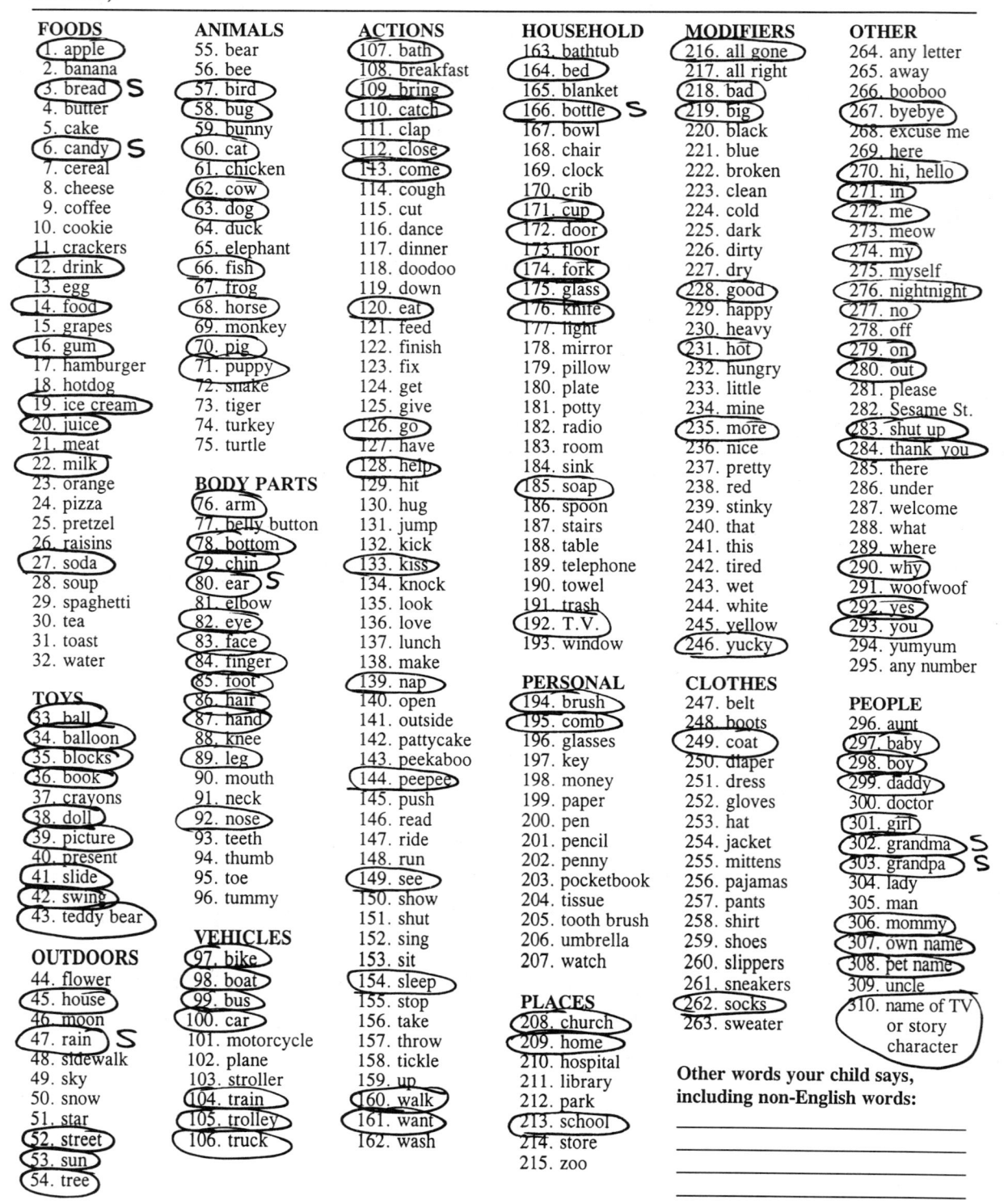

Figure 1-2 (cont.). Language Development Survey (page 4 of CBCL/1½-5).

ASEBA FEATURES

Please print — **CAREGIVER-TEACHER REPORT FORM FOR AGES 1½ - 5** — For office use only ID#

CHILD'S FULL NAME: First **Anna** Middle **M.** Last **Fernandez**

GENDER: ☐ Boy ☑ Girl
CHILD'S AGE: **2**
CHILD'S ETHNIC GROUP OR RACE: **Latina**

TODAY'S DATE: Mo. **8** Date **15** Yr. **00**
CHILD'S BIRTHDATE: Mo. **3** Date **3** Yr. **98**

PARENTS' USUAL TYPE OF WORK, even if not working now. *Please be specific—for example, auto mechanic, high school teacher, homemaker, laborer, lathe operator, shoe salesman, army sergeant.*

FATHER'S TYPE OF WORK: **Technician**
MOTHER'S TYPE OF WORK: **Secretary**

THIS FORM FILLED OUT BY: (print your full name) **Melissa Cortes**

Please fill out this form to reflect *your* view of the child's behavior even if other people might not agree. Feel free to write additional comments beside each item and in the space provided on page 2. *Be sure to answer all items.*

Your role at the school or care facility:
☑ primarily educational (teacher) ☐ primarily care (caregiver)

Your training for this position: **Bachelor's Degree**

Name & address of school or care facility: **Hillside Preschool 411 James Ct, Middletown California**

Your experience in child care or early education: **3** years.

I. What kind of a facility is it? (Please be specific, e.g., home day care, day care center, nursery school, preschool, school readiness class, Early Childhood Special Education, Headstart, Kindergarten, etc.) **Preschool**

II. What is the average number of children in the child's group or class? **9** children in the child's group or class.

III. How many hours per week does this child spend at the facility? **20** hours per week.

IV. For how many months have you known this child? **4** months.

V. How well do you know him/her? 1. ☐ Not well   2. ☐ Moderately well   3. ☑ Very well

VI. Has he/she ever been referred for a special education program or special services?
☐ Don't know   0. ☑ No   1. ☐ Yes - what kind and when?

Below is a list of items that describe children. For each item that describes the child *now or within the past 2 months*, please circle the **2** if the item is *very true or often true* of the child. Circle the **1** if the item is *somewhat or sometimes true* of the child. If the item is *not true* of the child, circle the **0**. Please answer all items as well as you can, even if some do not seem to apply to the child.

0 = Not True (as far as you know)   1 = Somewhat or Sometimes True   2 = Very True or Often True

(0) 1 2 1. Aches or pains (without medical cause; *do not* include stomach or headaches)
0 (1) 2 2. Acts too young for age
0 1 (2) 3. Afraid to try new things
(0) 1 2 4. Avoids looking others in the eye
0 1 (2) 5. Can't concentrate, can't pay attention for long
0 (1) 2 6. Can't sit still, restless, or hyperactive
(0) 1 2 7. Can't stand having things out of place
0 1 (2) 8. Can't stand waiting; wants everything now
(0) 1 2 9. Chews on things that aren't edible
0 1 (2) 10. Clings to adults or too dependent
0 1 (2) 11. Constantly seeks help
0 (1) 2 ᵃ12. Apathetic or unmotivated
0 1 (2) 13. Cries a lot
(0) 1 2 14. Cruel to animals
(0) 1 2 15. Defiant
0 (1) 2 16. Demands must be met immediately
(0) 1 2 17. Destroys his/her own things
(0) 1 2 18. Destroys property belonging to others
0 (1) 2 ᵃ19. Daydreams or gets lost in his/her thoughts
(0) 1 2 20. Disobedient
0 1 (2) 21. Disturbed by any change in routine

(0) 1 2 ᵃ22. Cruelty, bullying, or meanness to others
0 (1) 2 23. Doesn't answer when people talk to him/her
0 (1) 2 ᵃ24. Difficulty following directions
0 (1) 2 25. Doesn't get along with other children
0 1 (2) 26. Doesn't know how to have fun; acts like a little adult
(0) 1 2 27. Doesn't seem to feel guilty after misbehaving
(0) 1 2 ᵃ28. Disturbs other children
0 1 (2) 29. Easily frustrated
0 (1) 2 30. Easily jealous
(0) 1 2 31. Eats or drinks things that are not food—*do not* include sweets (describe): _____
0 1 (2) 32. Fears certain animals, situations, or places other than daycare or school (describe): **Afraid to go on swings, monkey bars, trikes**
0 1 (2) 33. Feelings are easily hurt
(0) 1 2 34. Gets hurt a lot, accident-prone
(0) 1 2 35. Gets in many fights
0 (1) 2 36. Gets into everything
0 (1) 2 37. Gets too upset when separated from parents

Copyright 1997 T. Achenbach
ASEBA, University of Vermont, 1 S. Prospect St., Burlington, VT 05401-3456 Web: http://Checklist.uvm.edu
Be sure you have answered all items. Then see other side.
UNAUTHORIZED REPRODUCTION IS ILLEGAL   7-28-00 Edition

Figure 1-3. Page 1 of the C-TRF. Superscript *a* = items that differ from CBCL/1½-5 items.

ASEBA FEATURES

Please print. Be sure to answer all items.

0 = Not True (as far as you know)   1 = Somewhat or Sometimes True   2 = Very True or Often True

0 (1) 2 [a]38. Explosive and unpredictable behavior	(0) 1 2 71. Shows little interest in things around him/her
(0) 1 2 39. Headaches (without medical cause)	(0) 1 2 72. Shows too little fear of getting hurt
(0) 1 2 40. Hits others	(0) 1 2 73. Too shy or timid
(0) 1 2 41. Holds his/her breath	(0) 1 2 [a]74. Not liked by other children
0 1 (2) 42. Hurts animals or people without meaning to	0 (1) 2 [a]75. Overactive
0 1 (2) 43. Looks unhappy without good reason	(0) 1 2 76. Speech problem (describe): _____
0 1 (2) 44. Angry moods	
(0) 1 2 45. Nausea, feels sick (without medical cause)	0 1 (2) 77. Stares into space or seems preoccupied
(0) 1 2 46. Nervous movements or twitching (describe): _____	0 (1) 2 78. Stomachaches or cramps (without medical cause)
	(0) 1 2 [a]79. Overconforms to rules
(0) 1 2 47. Nervous, highstrung, or tense	(0) 1 2 80. Strange behavior (describe): _____
0 (1) 2 [a]48. Fails to carry out assigned tasks	
0 (1) 2 [a]49. Fears daycare or school	0 1 (2) 81. Stubborn, sullen, or irritable
(0) 1 2 50. Overtired	0 1 (2) 82. Sudden changes in mood or feelings
0 (1) 2 [a]51. Fidgets	(0) 1 2 83. Sulks a lot
(0) 1 2 [a]52. Gets teased by other children	(0) 1 2 [a]84. Teases a lot
(0) 1 2 53. Physically attacks people	0 1 (2) 85. Temper tantrums or hot temper
0 (1) 2 54. Picks nose, skin, or other parts of body (describe): Picks scabs	(0) 1 2 86. Too concerned with neatness or cleanliness
	0 1 (2) 87. Too fearful or anxious
	0 1 (2) 88. Uncooperative
(0) 1 2 55. Plays with own sex parts too much	(0) 1 2 89. Underactive, slow moving, or lacks energy
(0) 1 2 56. Poorly coordinated or clumsy	0 1 (2) 90. Unhappy, sad, or depressed
(0) 1 2 57. Problems with eyes without medical cause (describe): _____	(0) 1 2 91. Unusually loud
	0 (1) 2 92. Upset by new people or situations (describe): Looks anxious when strangers come to class
(0) 1 2 58. Punishment doesn't change his/her behavior	
0 1 (2) 59. Quickly shifts from one activity to another	(0) 1 2 93. Vomiting, throwing up (without medical cause)
(0) 1 2 60. Rashes or other skin problems (without medical cause)	(0) 1 2 [a]94. Unclean personal appearance
	0 (1) 2 95. Wanders away
0 1 (2) 61. Refuses to eat	0 1 (2) 96. Wants a lot of attention
0 (1) 2 62. Refuses to play active games	(0) 1 2 97. Whining
(0) 1 2 63. Repeatedly rocks head or body	(0) 1 2 98. Withdrawn, doesn't get involved with others
0 (1) 2 [a]64. Inattentive, easily distracted	(0) 1 2 99. Worries
(0) 1 2 [a]65. Lying or cheating	100. Please write in any problems the child has that were not listed above.
0 (1) 2 66. Screams a lot	
(0) 1 2 67. Seems unresponsive to affection	(0) 1 2 _____
(0) 1 2 68. Self-conscious or easily embarrassed	0 1 2 _____
0 (1) 2 69. Selfish or won't share	0 1 2 _____
(0) 1 2 70. Shows little affection toward people	

Please be sure you have answered all items. Underline any you are concerned about.

Does the child have any illness or disability (either physical or mental)? ☑ No ☐ Yes—Please describe:

What concerns you most about the child? Seems fearful and unhappy can't concentrate on tasks. Jumps from one thing to another

Please describe the best things about the child: Very pretty child, very loving with dolls.

Figure 1-3 (cont.). Page 2 of the C-TRF. Superscript *a* = items that differ from CBCL/1½-5 items.

vs. her father vs. her grandmother at home, and with different daycare providers or teachers in other settings. To enable users to document both the similarities and differences in how Anna appears to different adults, the CBCL/1½-5 and C-TRF can be completed by all the relevant adults. As described in Chapter 2, profiles scored from each form can then be compared to pinpoint similarities and differences. Such comparisons can help users identify consistencies in Anna's functioning across situations and interaction partners, as well as discrepancies that may reveal the idiosyncratic effects or perceptions of particular interaction partners. The findings can then be used to identify areas where help may be needed and to plan appropriate interventions.

STRUCTURE OF THIS *MANUAL*

The early chapters of this *Manual* are designed to help you start using the ASEBA preschool forms as quickly as possible. Thus, Chapter 2 teaches you about the profiles on which the data are scored, and Chapter 3 teaches you about cross-informant comparisons for pinpointing similarities and differences among reports by different respondents. Chapter 4 presents scales comprising problems that are consistent with diagnostic categories of the fourth edition of the American Psychiatric Association's (1994) *Diagnostic and Statistical Manual* (DSM-IV). To help you see how the forms are used in various settings, Chapter 5 presents guidelines for practical applications, as well as cases illustrating applications in contexts such as Head Start, medical, and child and family service settings.

For readers who want to understand how the scoring scales and norms were developed, Chapters 6 and 7 present the research basis. Data on reliability, cross-informant agreement, and longer term stability are presented in Chapter 8. Validity data for the CBCL/1½-5, LDS, and C-TRF are presented in Chapter 9, while data on the prevalence and discriminative power of each problem item are presented in Chapter 10. To facilitate comparisons with previous editions of the scales scored from the CBCL/1½-5 and C-TRF, Chapter 11 presents relations between the previous scales and the current scales.

To assist readers who are interested in research, Chapter 12 focuses on research applications, including suggestions for new research and guidelines for statistical use of data from the preschool forms. Our website offers periodic updates on ASEBA research from around the world at http://ASEBA.uvm.edu.

Chapter 13 provides answers to commonly asked questions. If you have a question about the forms, the profiles, or their applications, look for the answer in Chapter 13.

Instructions for hand scoring the forms are provided in Appendix A, while computer scoring instructions accompany the computer software, which is described in Chapter 3. Appendix B lists the factor loadings of the problem items that comprise the ASEBA preschool syndromes. Appendix C displays scale scores for the normative samples, Appendix D displays scores for demographically similar clinical and nonclinical samples, and Appendix E displays correlations among scales. Appendix F lists the percentage of *1* and *2* scores and the mean scores for each problem item by gender and referral status.

SUMMARY

At low cost, the CBCL/1½-5 and C-TRF enable users to quickly obtain standardized ratings, and descriptive details of children's functioning, as seen by parents, parent surrogates, caregivers, and preschool teachers. The CBCL/1½-5 also includes the Language Development Survey (LDS) for identifying children whose language development is delayed.

To help users document different adults' perceptions of a child, each of the relevant adults can complete the CBCL/1½-5 or C-TRF. Profiles scored from each form can be used to pinpoint similarities and differences in problems reported from various perspectives. The findings can then be used to identify areas where help may be needed and to plan appropriate interventions.

The early chapters of this *Manual* are designed to help readers start using the ASEBA preschool forms as quickly as possible. Later chapters present the research basis for the scales, plus norms, psychometric data, comparisons with previous versions of the scales, research applications, and answers to commonly asked questions.

Chapter 2
Hand-Scored Profiles for ASEBA Preschool Forms

In this chapter, we describe and illustrate the hand-scored profiles for displaying item and scale scores obtained from the ASEBA forms.

To make it easy to see the specific problems reported for a child, each problem's score is displayed on a profile. Figure 2-1 shows a hand-scored profile that displays the scores obtained by 2-year-old Anna Fernandez on the CBCL/1½-5 completed by her mother. (Appendix A provides instructions for transferring the scores from the CBCL/1½-5 and C-TRF to hand-scored profiles. Instructions for computer-scored profiles accompany the computer software.)

SYNDROME SCALES OF THE CBCL/1½-5

A syndrome is a set of problems that tend to co-occur. To determine which ASEBA problem items tend to occur together to form syndromes, we performed statistical analyses of CBCL/1½-5 and C-TRF forms completed for large numbers of children. These analyses are described in Chapter 6. Based on our findings, we constructed syndrome scales comprising the problem items that tend to occur together.

As you can see in Figure 2-1, there are seven syndrome scales. Reading from left to right, the scales are designated as *Emotionally Reactive, Anxious/Depressed, Somatic Complaints, Withdrawn, Sleep Problems, Attention Problems,* and *Aggressive Behavior.* The title of each scale summarizes the kinds of problems that form the syndrome. Beneath the name of the scale, you can see the 0, 1, or 2 score that Anna's mother gave to each item of the scale. To the right of the 0, 1, or 2 score is the number that the item has on the CBCL/1½-5. And to the right of the item number is an abbreviated version of the item's wording on the CBCL/1½-5.

As an example, look at the top item in the *Emotionally Reactive* scale, which is the leftmost scale on the profile in Figure 2-1. The score on the item is 2. The item's number on the CBCL/1½-5 is 21 and the abbreviated version of the item is *Disturbed By Change*. The full wording of the item is *Disturbed by any change in routine*. The total score for each syndrome scale is computed by summing the scores of 1 and 2 for all the items of the scale. For example, on the Emotionally Reactive syndrome scale in Figure 2-1, you can see that two items received scores of 1 from Ms. Fernandez, while two items received scores of 2, for a total syndrome scale score of 6.

To see how Anna's score of 6 compares with scores obtained by normative samples of children, you circle the 6 in the column of numbers above the title of the scale. By looking to the left of the graphic display, you can see that Anna's score on the Emotionally Reactive scale corresponds to the 93rd percentile of the normative sample. This means that 93% of the children in the normative sample (i.e., children who had not been referred for mental health services in the preceding 12 months) received scores equal to or lower than Anna's score. By obtaining the total score for each syndrome scale and circling the score in the column of numbers in the graphic display, you can see how the child compares with the normative sample on each scale. By drawing a line to connect the circled scores, you can form a profile that highlights the syndromes on which the child has low scores, intermediate scores, and high scores.

Notice the broken lines printed across the graphic display in Figure 2-1. These broken lines demarcate a borderline clinical range spanning from the 93rd to the 97th percentile of the normative sample of nonreferred children.

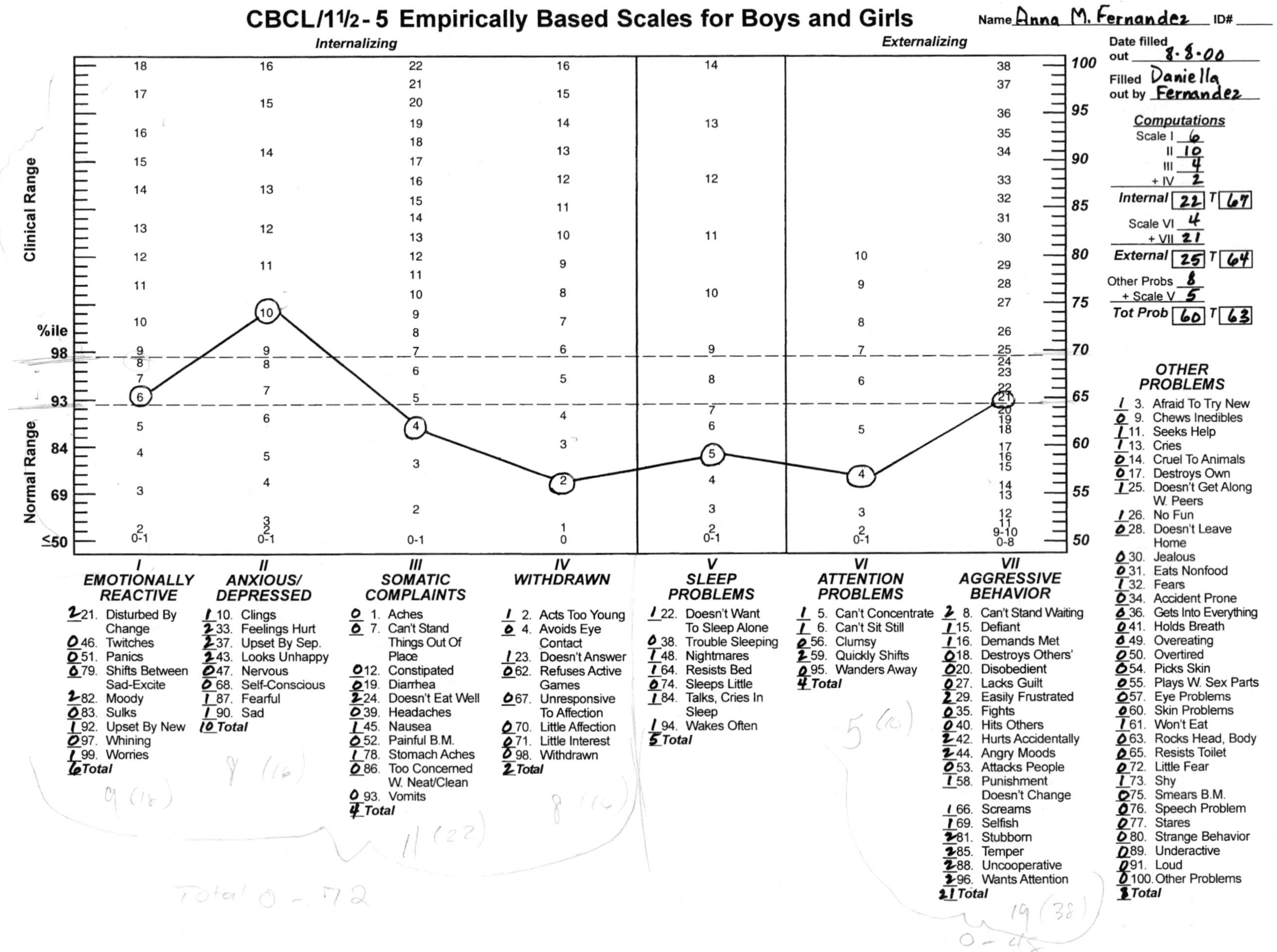

Figure 2-1. Hand-scored CBCL/1½-5 profile for Anna Fernandez. (T scores for Internalizing, Externalizing, and Total Problems scores listed at right side of profile are not shown.)

Scores in the borderline range are high enough to be of concern, but are not so clearly deviant as scores that are above the top broken line. Scores above the top broken line (i.e., above the 97th percentile) indicate that the person who completed the CBCL/1½-5 reported enough problems to be of clinical concern. Scores below the bottom broken line are in the normal range. As Figure 2-1 shows, Ms. Fernandez's ratings placed Anna in the borderline range on the Emotionally Reactive syndrome, in the clinical range on the Anxious/Depressed syndrome, and in the normal range on the Somatic Complaints syndrome.

The righthand side of the profile in Figure 2-1 displays *T* scores for each syndrome. *T* scores are standard scores that have a similar meaning for each scale, even though the distributions of raw scores differ among the scales. For example, Anna's raw score for the Emotionally Reactive syndrome was 6, while her raw score for the Aggressive Behavior syndrome was 21. However, by looking to the right of the graphic display, you can see that both these very different raw scores were equivalent to a *T* score of 65. A particular *T* score indicates the same degree of elevation on each scale relative to normative samples of peers. (Chapter 6 explains *T* scores and their relations to percentiles in more detail.)

It is important to obtain data from additional sources before drawing conclusions about a child's need for help. Whenever possible, users should have the CBCL/1½-5 completed by two or more adults who know the child, such as both parents or a parent and another relative. On hand-scored profiles, results from two or more informants can be compared by drawing lines to reflect the scale scores from each informant on the same profile. For example, if Anna's father and grandmother had each completed a CBCL/1½-5, lines reflecting their scale scores could be drawn on the same profile form as was used for Anna's mother's scores. You could then see at a glance whether the three family members differed much in how they scored Anna on any of the syndromes. In addition, if the child attends daycare or preschool, users should obtain parents' permission to have the C-TRF completed by daycare providers and preschool teachers. Chapter 3 explains computerized comparisons among multiple informants.

INTERNALIZING AND EXTERNALIZING GROUPINGS OF CBCL/1½-5 SYNDROMES

In addition to the syndrome scales, the CBCL/1½-5 can be scored in terms of two broad groupings of syndromes. One grouping, designated as *Internalizing*, consists of the four syndromes on the left side of the profile shown in Figure 2-1. This grouping is called "Internalizing," because it comprises problems that are mainly within the self. The second grouping, designated as *Externalizing*, consists of the two syndromes on the right side of the profile. This grouping is called "Externalizing" because it comprises problems that mainly involve conflicts with other people and with their expectations for the child. Chapter 7 explains how the Internalizing and Externalizing groupings were derived. (The Sleep Problems syndrome is not included in either the Internalizing or Externalizing grouping.)

The Internalizing score is easily computed by summing the scores for the four Internalizing syndromes, as shown under the heading *Computations* to the right of the profile in Figure 2-1. The Externalizing score is then computed by summing the scores for the two Externalizing syndromes, as shown under the *Computations* heading in Figure 2-1. Although not shown in Figure 2-1, *T* scores for the Internalizing and Externalizing scores are listed in a box to the right of the Computations boxes. These *T* scores indicate how elevated the child's Internalizing and Externalizing scores are on a scale similar to that for the *T* scores shown for the syndromes. For example, a *T* score of 70 for Internalizing is at the 98th percentile, just as it is for the syndrome scales and for Externalizing. By looking at a child's *T* scores for Internalizing and Externalizing, you can obtain a global picture of whether the child's problems tend to be concentrated in either, both, or neither of these broad areas.

Broken lines in the *T* score box to the right of the profile indicate the borderline range for Internalizing and Externalizing. The borderline range spans *T* scores of 60 to 63 (83rd to 90th percentile). This is lower than the borderline range for the syndromes, because the Internalizing and Externalizing groupings encompass more numerous and diverse problems than each syndrome scale. *T* scores above 63 are in the clinical range. Because the problems on each syndrome scale are less numerous and diverse than those in the Internalizing and Externalizing groupings, the syndrome scales warrant more conservative (i.e., higher) cutpoints for the borderline and clinical ranges than do the Internalizing and Externalizing groupings.

CBCL/1½-5 TOTAL PROBLEMS SCORE

The *Total Problems* score is the sum of the 0-1-2 scores on the 99 specific problem items of the CBCL/1½-5, plus the highest score (1 or 2) on any additional problems entered by the respondent for the open-ended item *100*. Item *100* has space for entering and scoring up to three problems that are not listed among items 1-99. Even if a respondent has entered as many as three additional problems, only one score of 1 or 2 is included in the Total Problems score in order to limit the impact of idiosyncratic problems on children's total scores. Thus, a child's Total Problems score can range from 0 (if the respondent scored every problem 0) to 200 (if the respondent scored every problem 2).

As shown under the heading *Computations* in Figure 2-1, the Total Problems score is readily computed by summing the scores for Internalizing, Externalizing, the Sleep Problems syndrome, and the other problems that are not on any of the syndromes. Although not shown in Figure 2-1, *T* scores for Total Problems scores are in a box to the right of the Computations boxes, with the *T* scores for Internalizing and Externalizing. As with the Internalizing and Externalizing scales, the borderline range for Total Problems spans *T* scores of 60 to 63 (83rd to 90th percentile) and the clinical range is above the *T* score of 63. These are lower than the borderline and clinical ranges for the syndromes, because the Total Problems score encompasses more numerous and diverse items than the syndrome scales.

LANGUAGE DEVELOPMENT SURVEY

The LDS provides two measures of children's language development. The first is the average length of the multi-word phrases written by the informant on page 3. For example, Anna's mother wrote down five multi-word phrases. The second measure, derived from the vocabulary list on page 4, is the number of words that the child is reported to use spontaneously. Anna's mother circled 110 words.

Figure 2-2 displays the scoring form for the LDS. By looking at the left side of Figure 2-2, you can see the instructions for scoring the average length of the phrases reported for the child. In item 2, the first five boxes have the numbers 3, 3, 2, 2 and 4. These numbers indicate that Anna's mother reported two 3-word phrases, two 2-word phrases, and one 4-word phrase. The sum of $3 + 3 + 2 + 2 + 4 = 14$, which is written in the box to the right of the = sign. To obtain the average length of Anna's phrases, 14 is divided by 5, i.e., the number of phrases that were reported: $14 \div 5 = 2.80$, which is written in the box in item 3. In the

HAND-SCORED PROFILES 15

Scoring Form for Language Development Survey (LDS) for Ages 18-35 Months

For Children 24-35 Months: Calculate Average Length of Phrases

1. On LDS page 3, item VIII, count the number of words in each phrase, as follows:
   a) Compound words such as "byebye," "nightnight," "alldone," "booboo," "no-no," and "lookie-look" count as <u>one</u> word when computing words per phrase.
   b) The rote phrases "thank you," "excuse me," and "shut up" count as <u>one</u> word in computing words per phrase.
   c) Contractions such as "can't" and "I'll" also count as <u>one</u> word.
   d) All compound words, rote phrases, and contractions <u>when used alone</u> are excluded when computing the mean length of phrases, because they are not considered valid phrases.
   e) If informant provides fewer than five valid phrases, compute average length of phrases using those provided.
   f) If informant provides more than five valid phrases, use only the first five.

2. Including non-English phrases, count the number of words in each valid phrase; then enter each number in a box below and sum these numbers:

   $\boxed{3} + \boxed{3} + \boxed{2} + \boxed{2} + \boxed{4} = \boxed{14}$

3. Divide this sum by the number of valid phrases to obtain the average length of phrases: $\boxed{2.8}$
4. Identify the column corresponding to child's age in the table below.
5. Circle the numbers corresponding to the child's average length of phrases.
6. The percentile for the U.S. national normative sample is shown to the left and right of the box.
7. Scores ≤ 20th percentile suggest delayed phrase development.

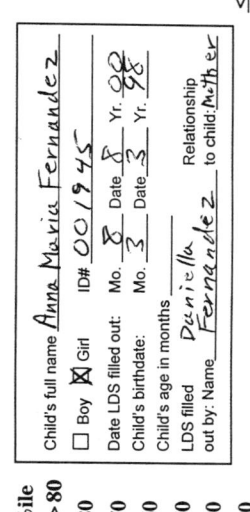

%ile	Boys & Girls	Boys & Girls	%ile
>80	>5.00	>5.40	>80
80	4.35-5.00	4.97-5.40	70
70	3.61-4.34	4.41-4.96	60
60	3.21-3.60	4.01-4.40	50
50	3.01-3.20	3.61-4.00	40
40	(2.76-3.00)	3.25-3.60	30
30	2.35-2.75	2.81-3.24	≤20
≤20	1.00-2.34	1.00-2.80	
	24-29 mos.	30-35 mos.	

For Children 18-35 months: Calculate Vocabulary Score

1. On LDS page 4, count the number of vocabulary words endorsed, including non-English words and words added by the respondent, up to a maximum of 315 words.
2. Enter vocabulary score here: $\boxed{110}$
3. In the table below, locate the column of scores for the child's age and gender.
4. Circle the numbers in the column corresponding to the child's vocabulary score.
5. The percentile for the U.S. national normative sample is shown to the left and right of the box.
6. Scores ≤ 15th percentile suggest delayed vocabulary development.

%ile	Boys	Girls	Boys	Girls	Boys	Girls	%ile
>85	195-315	237-315	294-315	297-315	307-315	311-315	>85
85	151-194	192-236	291-293	294-296	304-306	308-310	80
80	143-150	159-191	281-290	285-293	293-303	307	75
75	126-142	142-158	237-280	276-284	282-292	305-306	70
70	116-125	131-141	217-236	274-275	276-281	303-304	65
65	92-115	127-130	206-216	265-273	275	297-302	60
60	82-91	110-126	186-205	238-264	265-274	296	55
55	69-81	103-109	162-185	225-237	239-264	280-295	50
50	59-68	94-102	144-161	215-224	224-238	273-279	45
45	51-58	82-93	130-143	163-214	204-223	270-272	40
40	50	68-81	112-129	135-162	194-203	267-269	35
35	36-49	55-67	103-111	130-134	172-193	231-266	30
30	30-35	50-54	91-102	121-129	139-171	200-230	25
25	22-29	39-49	73-90	(109-120)	123-138	157-199	20
20	11-21	25-38	40-72	84-108	88-122	115-156	≤15
≤15	0-10	0-24	0-39	0-83	0-87	0-114	
	18-23 mos.		24-29 mos.		30-35 mos.		

Child's full name **Anna Maria Fernandez**
☐ Boy ☒ Girl ID# **00/945**
Date LDS filled out: Mo. **8** Date **8** Yr. **98**
Child's birthdate: Mo. **3** Date **3** Yr. **98**
Child's age in months
LDS filled out by: Name **Daniella Fernandez** Relationship to child: **mother**

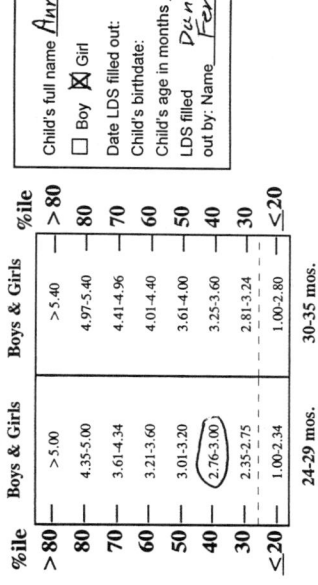

7-28-00 Edition-603

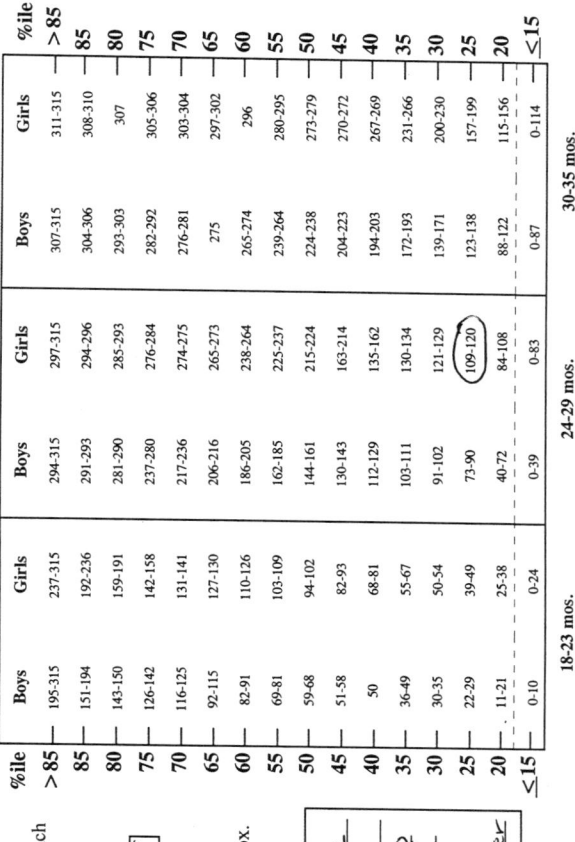

Figure 2-2. LDS Scoring Form for Anna Fernandez.

table at the lower left side of Figure 2-2, the numbers 2.76-3.00 are circled to indicate where Anna's score of 2.80 falls for ages 24-29 months. By looking to the left or right of the table, you can see that Anna's score is at the 40th percentile. Scores below the broken line (≤20th percentile) suggest delayed phrase development.

On the right side of Figure 2-2, you can see the instructions for scoring the vocabulary reported for the child. Because Anna's mother circled 110 words, 110 is written in the box in item 2. In the table at the lower right side of Figure 2-2, the numbers 109-120 are circled to indicate where Anna's score falls for 24- to 29-month-old girls. By looking to the left or right of the table, you can see that Anna's score is at the 25th percentile. Scores below the broken line (≤15th percentile) suggest delayed vocabulary development.

There is considerable variation in how many words children acquire before 24 months of age. It is therefore prudent to wait until at least 24 months before deciding whether a child has a significant expressive language delay. The information provided on the LDS (page 3 of the CBCL/1½-5) indicates possible risk factors for language delays, such as early birth, low birthweight, multiple ear infections, different languages being spoken at home, and close biological relatives who have been slow in learning to talk.

Delayed language may sometimes be associated with behavioral/emotional problems reported on pages 1 and 2 of the CBCL/1½-5. Certain kinds of behavioral/emotional problems may interfere with the development of language. Behavioral/emotional problems may also result from disorders that include communication problems, such as autism, hearing loss, or neurological dysfunction. On the other hand, language delays may lead to behavioral/emotional problems in children who are frustrated by or teased about their inability to speak. In any event, comprehensive assessment should include evaluation of language development.

SYNDROME SCALES OF THE C-TRF

Figure 2-3 shows a profile scored from the C-TRF completed for 2-year-old Anna Fernandez by her preschool teacher. As you can see from Figure 2-3, there are six syndrome scales. The syndrome scales are the same as for the CBCL/1½-5, except that no Sleep Problems syndrome is scored from the C-TRF. Like the CBCL/1½-5 profile, the C-TRF profile shows the 0, 1, and 2 scores given each item by the person who completed the form. The scores of the items on each syndrome are summed to yield the total score for the syndrome scale. In the graphic display, you circle the number corresponding to each syndrome scale and then draw a line connecting the circled numbers to form a profile.

By looking to the left of the graphic display, you can see the percentile corresponding to Anna's score on each syndrome scale. The broken lines printed across the profile indicate the borderline clinical range, which spans from the 93rd to the 97th percentile (T scores of 65 to 69). As you can see in Figure 2-3, Anna obtained scores in the normal range on the Somatic Problems and Withdrawn syndromes, in the borderline range on the Emotionally Reactive, Attention Problems, and Aggressive Behavior syndromes, and in the clinical range on the Anxious/Depressed syndrome. You can compute Internalizing, Externalizing, and Total Problems scores by following procedures like those described for the CBCL/1½-5 profile.

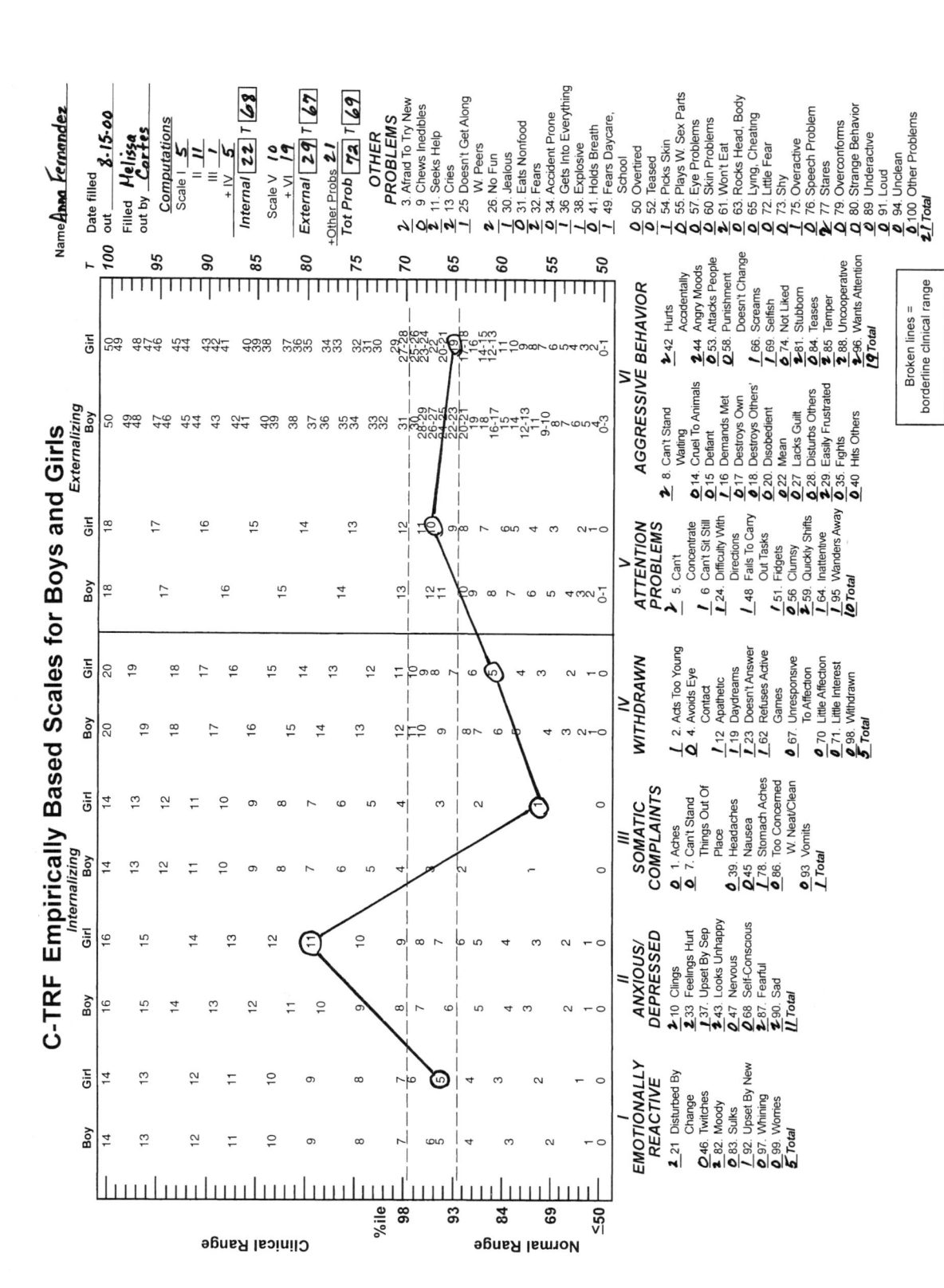

Figure 2-3. Hand-scored C-TRF profile for Anna Fernandez. (*T* scores for Internalizing, Externalizing, and Total Problems scores listed at right side of profile are not shown.)

SUMMARY

Syndromes of co-occurring problems were derived from statistical analyses of CBCL/1½-5 and C-TRF forms completed for large numbers of children. Hand-scored and computer-scored profiles are available for displaying children's scores on each syndrome in relation to scores for national normative samples of peers. This chapter illustrated profiles for Anna Fernandez that were hand-scored from the CBCL/1½-5 completed by her mother and the C-TRF completed by her preschool teacher.

Language development is a common cause for concern about young children. The LDS requests information on possible risk factors for language delay, including premature birth, ear infections, different languages being spoken at home, and relatives who have been slow to talk. The scoring form for the LDS enables you to compare scores for children's multi-word phrases and expressive vocabulary with scores for a national normative sample of children. You can therefore evaluate children both in terms of behavioral/emotional problems and language development in relation to national norms.

Chapter 3
Computerized Scoring and Cross-Informant Comparisons

Chapter 2 illustrated hand-scored profiles for the ASEBA preschool forms. Because the preschool forms are easily scored by hand, the hand-scored profiles are practical for users who assess small numbers of children. However, for users who assess large numbers of children, users who prefer computers, and users who wish to systematically compare CBCL/1½-5 and C-TRF scores, ASEBA Windows® software can be far more efficient and cost-effective than hand-scoring.

Software for scoring ASEBA forms is available on a CD-ROM that includes procedures for comparing data from up to eight forms per child. For preschoolers, this can include any combination of CBCL/1½-5 and C-TRF forms. For example, if 2-year-old Anna's mother, father, and grandmother each filled out a CBCL/1½-5 and Anna's daycare provider and two preschool teachers each filled out a C-TRF, data from all six forms could be entered via the preschool module on the ASEBA CD-ROM. If two other people filled out ASEBA forms for Anna, or if some respondents filled out ASEBA forms to describe Anna on multiple occasions, these additional forms could be compared as well.

The CD-ROM that includes entry and scoring of the preschool forms also includes the Assessment Data Manager (ADM). The ADM enables you to manage and compare data entered from multiple sources via modules for ASEBA forms. As illustrated in the following sections, the ADM prints profiles from forms completed by each informant. It also prints side-by-side comparisons of the 0-1-2 scores obtained from each informant on the problem items; correlations between scores obtained from each pair of informants; graphs that vividly compare syndrome scores from all informants; and narrative reports of the findings. In addition, the ADM enables you to enter other kinds of data for analysis in relation to ASEBA scores. The case of Kenny Randall will be used to illustrate computerized scoring and cross-informant comparisons of the preschool forms.

KENNY RANDALL, AGE 30 MONTHS

Ms. Randall contacted Dr. Barbara Winter on the advice of the director of Kenny's preschool. Kenny's teachers noticed that he did not interact with other children and that he seemed to talk mainly to himself. Ms. Randall told Dr. Winter that Kenny interacted with his parents and his 12-month-old sister, Carla, but that he was shy with new people and did not interact much even with his grandparents, who lived nearby. Dr. Winter asked each parent to complete the CBCL/1½-5 and a developmental history form prior to their visit. She also obtained Ms. Randall's permission to send C-TRF forms to Kenny's teachers.

Computer-Scored CBCL/1½-5 Profile

Figure 3-1 shows the profile scored from the CBCL/1½-5 completed by Ms. Randall. As you can see from the center of Figure 3-1, Ms. Randall's ratings on the Withdrawn syndrome placed Kenny well above the top broken line on the profile. This means that Ms. Randall reported more problems on the Withdrawn scale than were reported by parents of 97% of nonreferred children in the national normative sample. By looking beneath the title *Withdrawn*, you can see that Kenny's total score for the Withdrawn syndrome was 10, his T score was 82, and his percentile was >97, i.e., above the 97th percentile for the normative sample. The C printed to the right of the T score indicates that the T score is in the clinical range. For

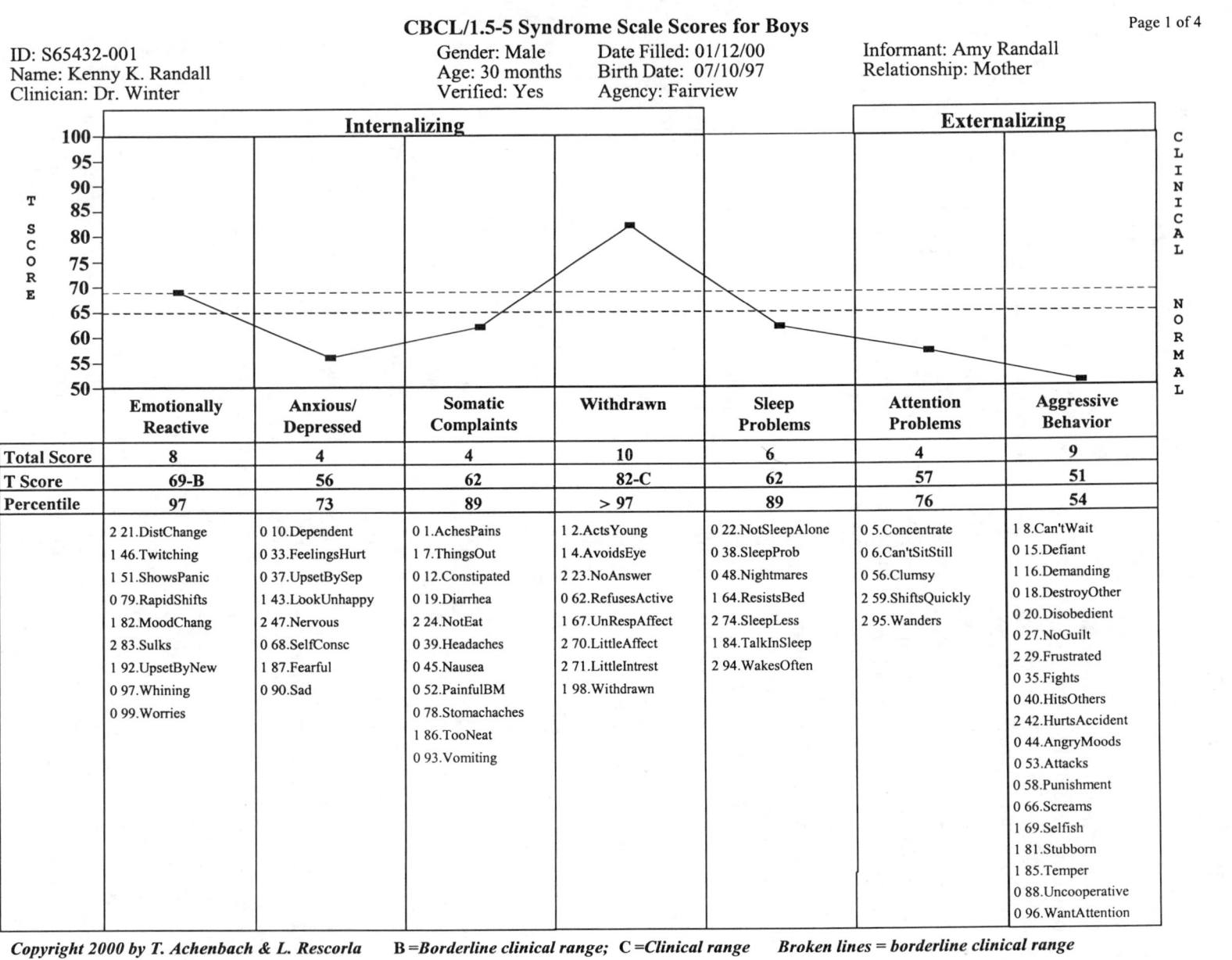

Figure 3-1. CBCL/1½-5 computer-scored syndrome profile for Kenny Randall.

scores that are in the borderline range (between the two broken lines), B is printed next to the *T* score. By looking at the items printed below these numbers, you can see that Ms. Randall gave scores of *2 (very true or often true)* to the following items: *23. Doesn't answer when people talk to him/her; 70. Shows little affection toward people;* and *71. Shows little interest in things around him/her.* She also gave scores of *1* to the following items: *2. Acts too young for age; 4. Avoids looking others in the eye; 67. Seems unresponsive to affection;* and *98. Withdrawn, doesn't get involved with others.*

By looking again at the graphic display in the top portion of Figure 3-1, you can see that Ms. Randall's ratings placed Kenny in the normal range (below the broken lines) on all the other syndrome scales, except Emotionally Reactive, which was in the borderline range.

Figure 3-2 shows the second page of the printout scored from Ms. Randall's CBCL/1½-5. The second page displays Kenny's score for Internalizing (in the clinical range, above the top broken line), Externalizing (in the normal range, below the bottom broken line), and Total Problems (in the borderline range). An additional page, detailed in Chapter 4, displays a profile of DSM-oriented scales scored from the ASEBA forms. As will be discussed in Chapter 4, Ms. Randall's ratings placed Kenny in the clinical range on the DSM-oriented Pervasive Developmental Problems scale.

Beneath each bar in the graphic display in Figure 3-2 are the Total Score, *T* score, and percentile for that scale. By looking at the box to the right of the graphic display, you can see a list of items headed *Other Problems*. These are problem items that were not strongly enough associated with any syndrome to be included in the syndrome scales. However, each problem may be important in its own right, and their scores are all included in the Total Problems score for the CBCL/1½-5.

In response to the open-ended questions following the scored items, both of Kenny's parents indicated that he had no illnesses or disabilities. They both indicated concerns about his lack of communicative language and his failure to interact with other children. For the best things about Kenny, Ms. Randall described him as energetic, playful, and as having a good sense of humor. Mr. Randall described him as fun, active, knowledgeable about the world, and well-coordinated.

On the LDS, both parents reported five multi-word phrases, with an average length of 3.80 words, which was at the 50th percentile for Kenny's age. Among the phrases was "Doesn't open Ben," which Ms. Randall said was one of the few instances of Kenny's saying something informative to another child. Mr. Randall noted that Kenny could accurately repeat long passages from his favorite books. On the vocabulary portion of the LDS, Ms. Randall circled 260 words, while Mr. Randall circled 245 words, both of which were at the 55th percentile for boys of Kenny's age. According to both the average length of phrases and number of vocabulary words reported on the LDS, Kenny's speech development was not delayed. Figure 3-3 displays a narrative report summarizing the results of the CBCL and LDS completed by Ms. Randall.

CROSS-INFORMANT COMPARISONS OF PROBLEM ITEM SCORES

To help you identify specific problem items on which the informants agreed or disagreed, the ASEBA software prints side-by-side comparisons of the 0-1-2 scores given to the problem items by each informant. As Figure 3-4 shows, the printout lists problem items according to their syndrome scales. For syndromes that have counterparts on both the CBCL/1½-5 and C-TRF, the

ID: S65432-001
Name: Kenny K. Randall
Clinician: Dr. Winter

CBCL/1.5-5 Internalizing, Externalizing, Total Problems, Other Problems for Boys

Gender: Male
Age: 30 months

Date Filled: 01/12/00
Birth Date: 07/10/97
Agency: Fairview

Informant: Amy Randall
Relationship: Mother

Page 2 of 4

Other Problems

2 3.AfraidOfNew	0 72.LittleFear
1 9.ChewNonfood	1 73.Shy
0 11.SeeksHelp	0 75.SmearsBM
0 13.Cries	1 76.SpeechProb
0 14.CruelAnimal	1 77.Stares
0 17.DestroyOwn	1 80.StrangeBehav
2 25.NotGetAlong	0 89.Underactive
1 26.NoFun	0 91.Loud
1 28.OutOfHome	0 100.OtherProb
0 30.Jealous	
0 31.EatNonFood	
0 32.Fears	
0 34.GetsHurt	
0 36.GetIntoThings	
0 41.HoldsBreath	
0 49.Overeating	
0 50.Overtired	
0 54.PicksSkin	
0 55.SexParts	
0 57.EyeProb	
0 60.SkinProb	
0 61.Won'tEat	
1 63.RocksHead	
0 65.ResistToilet	

	Internalizing Problems	Externalizing Problems	Total Problems
Total Score	26	13	57
T Score	71-C	51	62-B
Percentile	> 97	54	89

B = *Borderline clinical range*; C = *Clinical range*   Broken lines = *borderline clinical range*

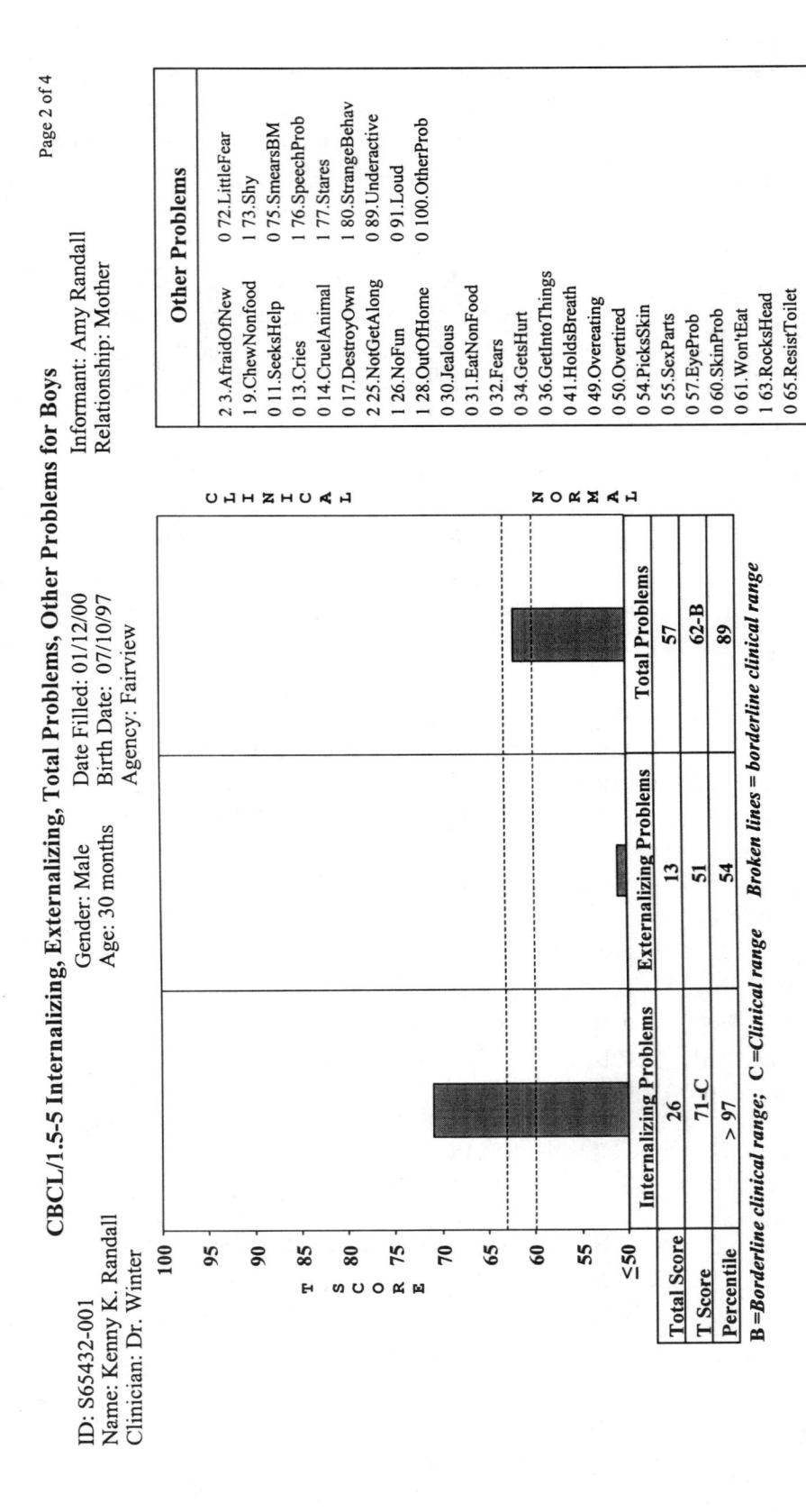

Figure 3-2. CBCL/1½-5 computer-scored Internalizing, Externalizing, and Total Problems profile for Kenny Randall.

ID: S65432-001
Name: Kenny Randall
Date of Birth: 07/10/97
Age: 30 months
Gender: Male
Date of Evaluation: 01/12/00
Informant Name: Amy Randall

The Child Behavior Checklist for Ages 1.5-5 (CBCL/1.5-5) was completed by Amy Randall, Kenny's mother, to obtain her perceptions of Kenny's problems.

On the CBCL/1.5-5 problem scales, Kenny's Total Problems score was in the borderline clinical range (83rd to 90th percentiles) for boys aged 1.5 to 5. His Internalizing score was in the clinical range (above the 90th percentile) and his Externalizing score was in the normal range. His scores on the Anxious/Depressed, Somatic Complaints, Sleep Problems, Attention Problems, and Aggressive Behavior syndromes were in the normal range. His score on the Withdrawn syndrome was in the clinical range (above the 97th percentile). His score on the Emotionally Reactive syndrome was in the borderline clinical range (93th to 97th percentiles). These results indicate that Kenny's mother reported more problems than are typically reported by parents of boys aged 1.5 to 5, particularly emotional problems and withdrawn behavior.

On the Language Development Survey for Ages 18-35 Months, Kenny's score for Average Length of Phrases was at the 50th percentile, which suggests normal phrase development for children aged 30-35 months. Kenny's Vocabulary score was at the 55th percentile, which suggests normal vocabulary development for children aged 30-35 months.

Figure 3-3. Narrative report summarizing the results of the CBCL and LDS for Kenny Randall.

printout lists the items that have counterparts on both instruments. The Sleep Problems syndrome is scored only from the CBCL/1½-5. In addition to the items that are scored on syndromes, Figure 3-4 shows that the scores from all informants for Other Problems items (those that do not belong to syndromes) are also listed side-by-side, following the items listed for the syndromes. For Kenny, the scores are listed from the CBCL/1½-5 completed by his mother and his father, followed by scores from the C-TRF completed by his morning teacher and then scores from the C-TRF completed by his afternoon teacher.

As you can see in Figure 3-4, both parents endorsed most of the same problems on the Withdrawn syndrome. Both teachers also endorsed most of the same items as Kenny's parents on the Withdrawn syndrome. However, the teachers endorsed numerous other items, some of which are on both the CBCL/1½-5 and C-TRF, while others are only on the C-TRF. Of the items that are on both forms, you can see in Figure 3-4 that the teachers endorsed the following items that were not endorsed by Kenny's parents: *5. Can't concentrate, can't pay attention for long; 6. Can't sit still, restless, or hyperactive;* and *32. Fears certain animals,*

Cross-Informant Comparison - Problem Items Common to the CBCL/CTRF/1.5-5 Page 1 of 4

ID: S65432 Name: Kenny K. Randall Gender: Male Birth Date: 07/10/97 Comparison Date: 01/31/00

Form	Eval ID	Age	Informant Name	Relationship	Date	Form	Eval ID	Age	Informant Name	Relationship	Date
C151	001	30m	Amy Randall	Mother	01/12/00						
C152	002	30m	Robert Randall	Father	01/13/00						
T153	003	30m	Beatrice Jackson	Teacher {F}	01/18/00						
T154	004	30m	Linda James	Teacher {F}	01/19/00						

	C15 1	C15 2	T15 3	T15 4	5	6	7	8
Emotionally Reactive								
21.DistChange	2	1	2	1				
46.Twitching	1	0	0	0				
82.MoodChang	1	2	1	2				
83.Sulks	2	1	0	0				
92.UpsetByNew	1	1	2	1				
97.Whining	0	0	0	1				
99.Worries	0	0	0	0				
Anxious/Depressed								
10.Dependent	0	0	0	0				
33.FeelingsHurt	0	0	0	0				
37.UpsetBySep	0	0	0	0				
43.LookUnhapp	1	0	0	0				
47.Nervous	2	2	1	2				
68.SelfConsc	0	0	0	0				
87.Fearful	1	1	2	1				
90.Sad	0	0	0	0				
Somatic Complaints								
1.AchesPains	0	0	0	0				
7.ThingsOut	1	2	2	2				
39.Headaches	0	0	0	0				
45.Nausea	0	0	0	0				
78.Stomachache	0	0	0	0				
86.TooNeat	1	0	1	2				
93.Vomiting	0	0	0	0				
Withdrawn								
2.ActsYoung	1	2	2	1				
4.AvoidsEye	1	1	2	2				
23.NoAnswer	2	2	2	1				
62.RefusesActiv	0	0	1	2				
67.UnRespAffec	1	0	1	2				
70.LittleAffect	2	1	0	1				
71.LittleIntrest	2	1	2	2				
98.Withdrawn	1	1	1	2				

	C15 1	C15 2	T15 3	T15 4	5	6	7	8
Attention Problems								
5.Concentrate	0	0	2	2				
6.Can'tSitStill	0	0	2	2				
56.Clumsy	0	0	0	0				
59.ShiftsQuickly	2	2	2	1				
95.Wanders	2	2	2	1				
Aggressive Behavior								
8.Can'tWait	1	2	2	2				
15.Defiant	0	0	0	0				
16.Demanding	1	2	1	2				
18.DestroyOther	0	0	0	0				
20.Disobedient	0	0	0	0				
27.NoGuilt	0	1	1	1				
29.Frustrated	2	2	1	0				
35.Fights	0	0	0	0				
40.HitsOthers	0	0	0	0				
42.HurtsAcciden	2	2	0	1				
44.AngryMoods	0	0	0	0				
53.Attacks	0	0	0	0				
58.Punishment	0	0	2	1				
66.Screams	0	0	0	1				
69.Selfish	1	1	0	0				
81.Stubborn	1	2	2	1				
85.Temper	1	1	2	1				
88.Uncooperativ	0	0	1	2				
96.WantAttentio	0	0	0	0				
CBCL/1.5-5 only: Sleep Problems								
22.NotSleepAlo	0	0	-	-				
38.SleepProb	0	0	-	-				
48.Nightmares	0	0	-	-				
64.ResistsBed	1	1	-	-				
74.SleepLess	2	1	-	-				
84.TalkInSleep	1	1	-	-				
94.WakesOften	2	2	-	-				

	C15 1	C15 2	T15 3	T15 4	5	6	7	8
Other Problems								
3.AfraidOfNew	2	1	2	1				
9.ChewNonfood	1	1	1	0				
11.SeeksHelp	0	0	0	0				
13.Cries	0	0	0	0				
25.NotGetAlong	2	2	2	1				
26.NoFun	1	0	2	1				
30.Jealous	0	0	0	0				
31.EatNonFood	0	1	0	0				
32.Fears	0	0	2	2				
34.GetsHurt	0	0	0	0				
36.GetIntoThing	0	0	1	0				
41.HoldsBreath	0	0	0	0				
50.Overtired	0	0	0	0				
54.PicksSkin	0	0	0	0				
55.SexParts	0	0	0	0				
57.EyeProb	0	0	0	0				
60.SkinProb	0	0	0	0				
61.Won'tEat	0	0	1	0				
63.RocksHead	1	0	1	1				
72.LittleFear	0	0	1	0				
73.Shy	1	2	1	2				
76.SpeechProb	1	1	2	1				
77.Stares	1	1	2	1				
80.StrangeBeha	1	1	2	1				
89.Underactive	0	0	0	0				
91.Loud	0	0	0	0				

{F}=Female {M}=Male

Figure 3-4. Cross-informant comparisons of item scores for Kenny Randall.

situations or places, other than daycare or school. In addition, one or both teachers endorsed several items that are on the C-TRF but not on the CBCL/1½-5, such as *24. Difficulty following directions* and *64. Inattentive, easily distracted.*

Comments written in the open-ended sections of the C-TRF indicated that the teachers were concerned about Kenny's repetitive speech and about out-of-context remarks that he made from conversations occurring weeks earlier. What concerned the teachers most was Kenny's failure to play with other children and his lack of sustained attention. In response to the C-TRF question regarding the best things about Kenny, the teachers wrote that he seemed smart and was very cute.

CROSS-INFORMANT CORRELATIONS

To help you evaluate the degree of agreement among various informants, ASEBA software prints correlations between problem item scores obtained from each pair of informants. By looking at the top portion of the large box in the center of Figure 3-5, you can see the degree of agreement between Kenny's mother and father, between each parent and each teacher, and between each teacher.

Under the heading *Cross-Informant Agreement*, you can see that agreement between Kenny's parents' ratings is described as *Above Average*. By looking under the heading *Q Corr*, you can see that the actual correlation between their ratings was .78. The *Q* correlation reflects the degree to which the 82 items that are common to the CBCL/1½-5 and C-TRF received similar scores of *0, 1,* and *2* from two raters, such as Kenny's mother and father. The *Q* correlation can range from -1.00, which indicates maximum disagreement in the scores assigned by two raters, to +1.00, which indicates perfect agreement between two raters. (*Q* correlations are computed by applying the formula for the Pearson correlation to pairs of scores on a set of items, such as the 0-1-2 ratings of CBCL/1½-5 items by Kenny's mother vs. his father.)

By looking under the columns headed *Reference Group* in Figure 3-5, you can see the 25th percentile, mean, and 75th percentile correlations found in a reference group of parents. Because the correlation of .78 between Ms. and Mr. Randall's ratings was above the 75th percentile found in the reference group of parents, it is considered to be above average. If the correlation had been below average (i.e., below the 25th percentile), the practitioner could seek to determine why the parents' ratings agreed less well than the ratings of most parents of preschoolers. For example, by interviewing the parents, the practitioner might learn that their poor agreement reflected possibilities such as the following: one parent had little contact with the child; one parent over- or under-reported problems; or one parent evoked certain problem behavior.

CROSS-INFORMANT COMPARISONS OF SYNDROME SCALE SCORES VIA BAR GRAPHS

Following the page of correlations between item scores from each pair of informants, the ASEBA software prints bar graphs that compare the syndrome scores obtained from each informant. By looking at Figure 3-6, you can see the syndromes on which all informants scored Kenny in the clinical range, such as the Withdrawn syndrome in the left middle portion of the printout. You can also compare scores obtained from multiple informants on each of the other syndromes. For example, on the Attention Problems syndrome (to the right of the Withdrawn syndrome), both parents scored Kenny in the normal range, whereas both teachers scored him in the clinical range. This indicated that Kenny was consistently perceived as having considerably more attention problems at school

Cross-Informant Comparison - CBCL/CTRF/1.5-5 Cross-Informant Correlations Page 2 of 4

ID: S65432 Name: Kenny K. Randall Gender: Male Birth Date: 07/10/97 Comparison Date: 01/31/00

Form	Eval ID	Age	Informant Name	Relationship	Date
C151	001	30m	Amy Randall	Mother	01/12/00
C152	002	30m	Robert Randall	Father	01/13/00
T153	003	30m	Beatrice Jackson	Teacher {F}	01/18/00
T154	004	30m	Linda James	Teacher {F}	01/19/00

Form	Eval ID	Age	Informant Name	Relationship	Date

Q Correlations Between Problem Item Scores

Forms	Informants	Cross-Informant Agreement	Q Corr	Reference Group 25th %ile	Mean	75th %ile
C151 x C152	Mother x Father	Above average	0.78	0.38	0.51	0.61
C151 x T153	Mother x Teacher {F}	Above average	0.55	0.08	0.23	0.38
C151 x T154	Mother x Teacher {F}	Above average	0.45	0.08	0.23	0.38
C152 x T153	Father x Teacher {F}	Above average	0.57	0.08	0.23	0.38
C152 x T154	Father x Teacher {F}	Above average	0.49	0.08	0.23	0.38
T153 x T154	Teacher {F} x Teacher {F}	Above average	0.71	0.26	0.46	0.62

{F}=Female {M}=Male nc = *not calculated due to insufficient data*

Copyright 2000 by T. Achenbach & L. Rescorla, ASEBA, University of Vermont, 1 South Prospect St., Burlington, VT 05401-3456, http://ASEBA.uvm.edu

Figure 3-5. Cross-informant correlations for Kenny Randall.

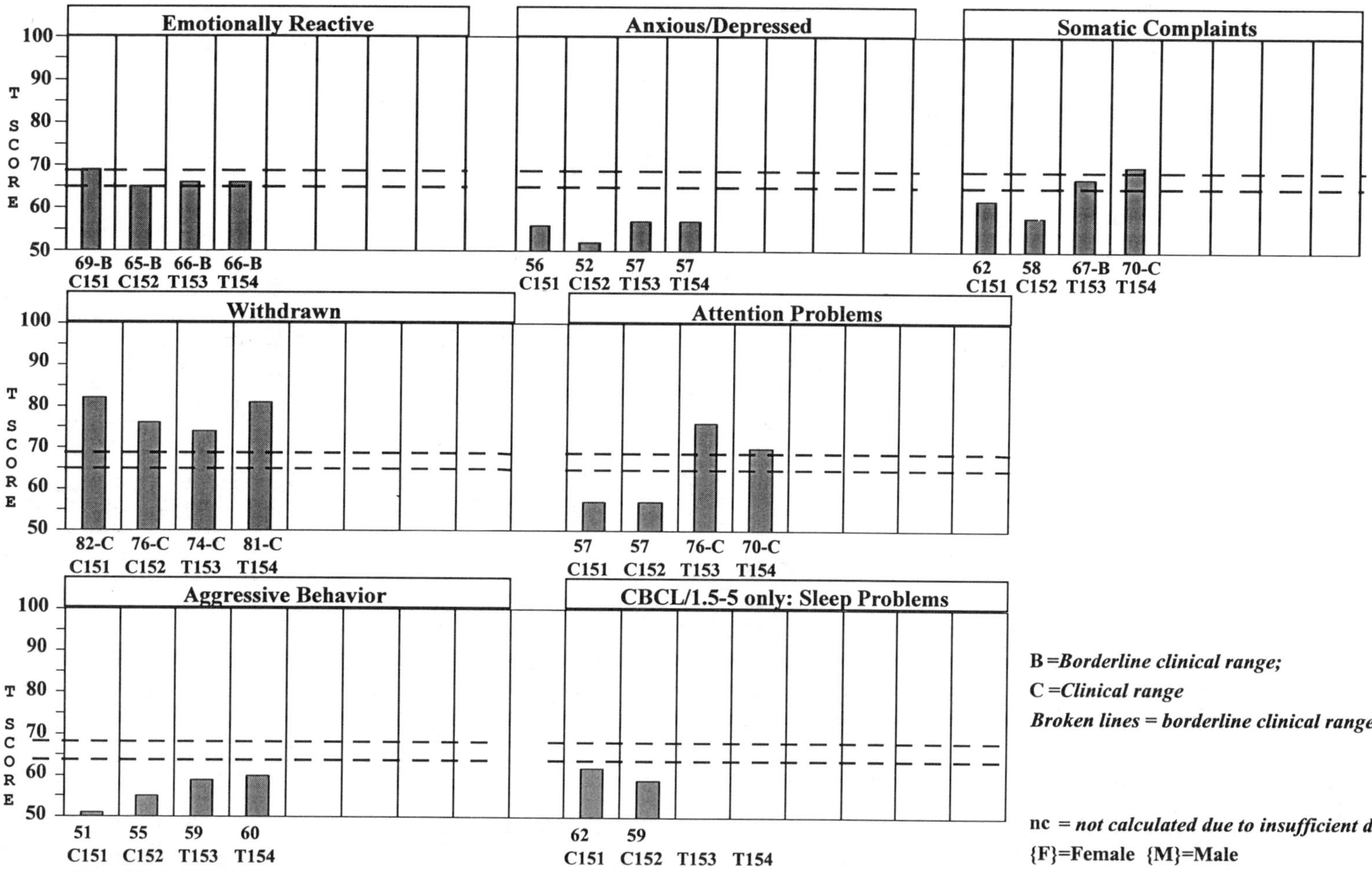

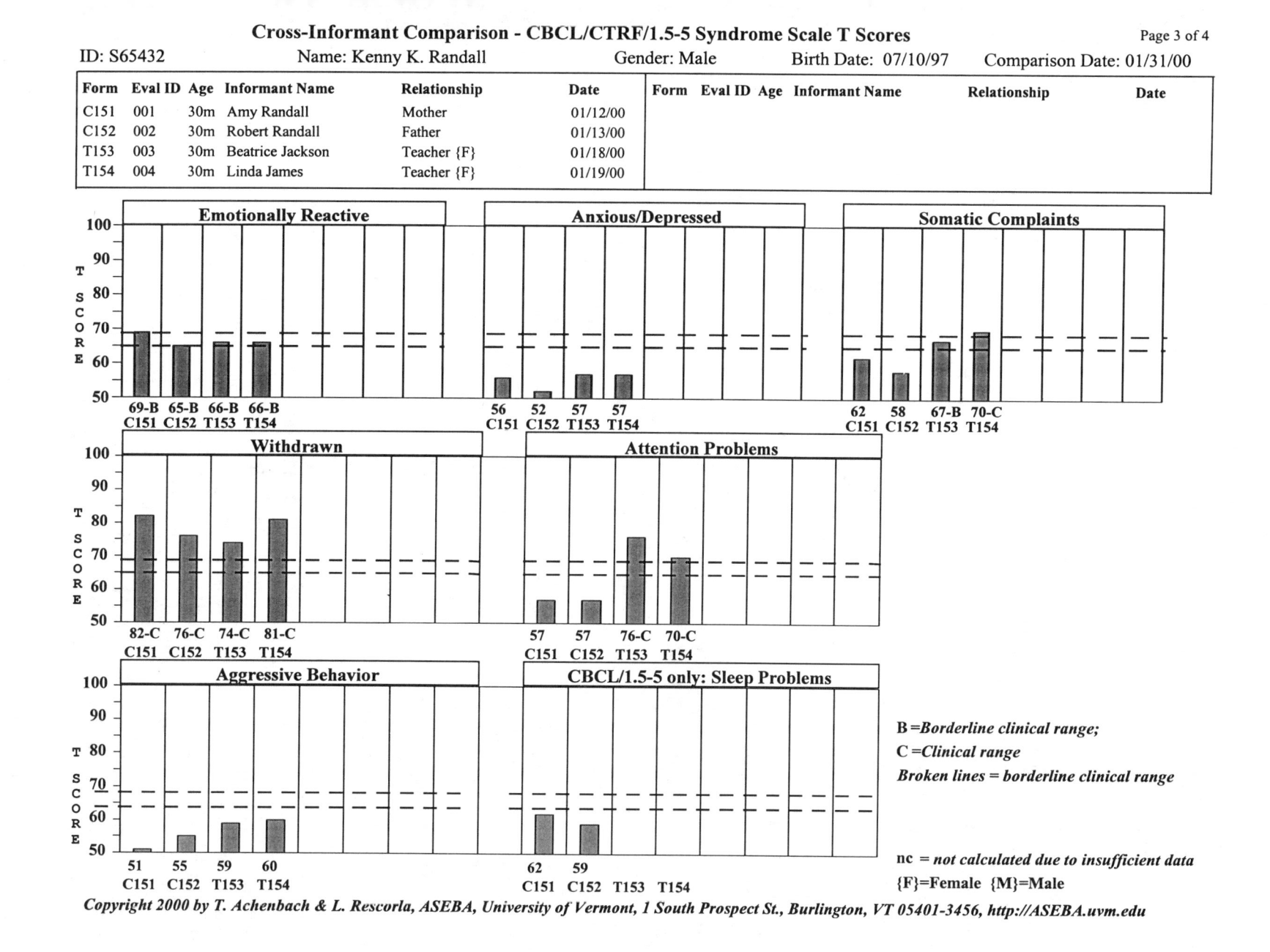

Figure 3-6. Cross-informant comparisons of syndrome scores for Kenny Randall.

than at home. Figure 3-6 also shows that all four informants scored him in the borderline range on the Emotionally Reactive syndrome.

CLINICAL EVALUATION OF KENNY

After reviewing the CBCL/1½-5 and C-TRF forms and profiles, Dr. Winter interviewed Mr. and Ms. Randall. She asked them if they had any questions or comments about the forms they had completed. Ms. Randall said that she had rated item 92. *Upset by new people or situations* as 2 and had written that Kenny turns away from unfamiliar people who talk to him, but she was not sure if that really fit the item. When Dr. Winter asked her to describe Kenny's behavior in more detail, Ms. Randall said that Kenny would even run to his room sometimes when unfamiliar people visited their home. Dr. Winter and Ms. Randall then agreed that she had scored item 92 appropriately.

Mr. Randall added other examples of how Kenny reacted negatively to most people. He also said that filling out the CBCL/1½-5 had started him thinking about ways in which Kenny may be different from other children. Although Mr. Randall had not viewed Kenny as a problem child, some of the items on the CBCL/1½-5 made him realize that Kenny did not seem to care about other children or even adults who should be important to him, such as his grandparents and teachers. Ms. Randall had always thought of Kenny as being very shy like herself. However, the number of items on the CBCL that seemed to fit Kenny pretty well and the preschool staff's concerns about Kenny made her think that special help might be needed. The developmental history completed by the Randalls and their descriptions of Kenny's past behavior indicated normal developmental milestones but a long-term lack of interest in social interaction.

When Dr. Winter met with Kenny, he showed little interest in her and was difficult to engage. He repeatedly ran to the window to look at passing cars, seldom made eye contact, and was oblivious to Dr. Winter's attempts to converse with him. However, he responded correctly to directives and questions, such as identifying objects.

Kenny's vocabulary and use of multi-word phrases were consistent with the results of the LDS, which had indicated language in the normal range. However, many of his remarks were not addressed to anyone, and he repeated phrases in a mechanical way, such as saying "I'll be cold" six times during the session. Even when he seemed to want to communicate, he did so indirectly, saying, "It goes right here," as he looked to his parents for help when struggling with a piece of a puzzle.

Diagnostic Conclusions and Recommendations

Based on the behavioral deviance revealed by the CBCL/1½-5 and C-TRF profiles, the developmental history, and her own inability to engage Kenny, Dr. Winter concluded that Kenny met DSM criteria for Pervasive Developmental Disorder (PDD), including social deficits, restricted behavioral repertoire, resistance to change, and communicative abnormalities. In particular, Kenny fit the picture of Asperger's Disorder, which is characterized by well-developed language and normal nonverbal ability but social oddities.

Dr. Winter shared her impressions of Kenny with the Randalls and indicated that Kenny would qualify for early intervention services through the local school district. The Randalls agreed that Kenny probably did need such services. Dr. Winter offered to work with the Randalls, the preschool staff, and the school district to design interventions for increasing Kenny's ability to use language communicatively, play with other children, cope with change, and attend to instruction in school.

The CBCL/1½-5 and C-TRF profiles provided baseline documentation of Kenny's functioning against which changes and outcomes could be measured. As part of the intervention plan, Mr. and Ms. Randall would each complete a CBCL/1½-5 and Kenny's teachers would each complete a C-TRF every 4 months. Dr. Winter would then determine whether the profiles showed improvements in Kenny's functioning as seen by his parents and teachers. If improvements were not evident, Dr. Winter would work with the Randalls and the school staff to modify the interventions.

SUMMARY

ASEBA software scores the CBCL/1½-5, LDS, and C-TRF. It displays scores on profiles, narrative summaries, and comparisons of problem items and scale scores for up to eight forms per child.

The case of Kenny Randall illustrated the use of the computerized scoring and cross-informant comparisons in the evaluation of a 30-month-old boy. The cross-informant comparisons revealed that both of Kenny's parents scored him in the clinical range on the Withdrawn scale of the CBCL/1½-5 and that both teachers scored him in the clinical range on the Withdrawn scale of the C-TRF. A considerably lower level of social interaction than reported for a normative sample of peers was thus consistent across the home and school contexts. However, the cross-informant comparisons also revealed that Kenny's teachers reported more attention problems than his parents did. The finding that the Attention Problems syndrome scores from the C-TRFs completed by both teachers placed Kenny in the clinical range indicated that his adaptation outside the home was impaired in ways that were not evident to his parents.

Kenny's LDS scores indicated no delays in general language development that might either explain or result from his other problems. However, the open-ended comments on the CBCL/1½-5 from both parents and on the C-TRF from both teachers indicated concerns about Kenny's failure to use language for communicative purposes.

Completing the CBCL/1½-5 helped Kenny's parents realize that Kenny needed special help. On the basis of the CBCL/1½-5 and C-TRF profiles, the developmental history, and her own inability to engage Kenny, Dr. Winter concluded that Kenny fit the picture of Asperger's Disorder. The CBCL/1½-5 and C-TRF profiles provided baseline measures of Kenny's functioning that were used to design interventions for helping Kenny. By having Kenny's parents complete the CBCL/1½-5 and his teachers complete the C-TRF every 4 months, Dr. Winter planned to evaluate improvements and possible needs for changes in the interventions.

Chapter 4
DSM-Oriented Scales for Scoring ASEBA Preschool Forms

Chapters 2 and 3 presented profiles for scoring syndrome scales derived from statistical analyses that reflect patterns of co-occurring problems. Children's problems can also be viewed from the perspectives of formal diagnostic systems. The dominant system in the United States is embodied in the American Psychiatric Association's *Diagnostic and Statistical Manual of Mental Disorders* (Fourth Edition, 1994; "DSM-IV").

The DSM's diagnostic categories are intended to serve many purposes. Unlike the syndromes derived from the CBCL/1½-5 and C-TRF, DSM diagnostic categories for behavioral/emotional problems are not derived directly from problem scores obtained from standardized assessment of children. Nevertheless, assessment instruments such as the CBCL/1½-5 and C-TRF are often used to obtain data on which to base diagnoses.

Studies have shown significant associations between DSM diagnoses and ASEBA scale scores (e.g., Arend, Lavigne, Rosenbaum, Binns, & Christoffel, 1996; Edelbrock & Costello, 1988; Kasius, Ferdinand, van den Berg, & Verhulst, 1997; Kazdin & Heidish, 1984). However, the strength of such associations depends on many factors. Examples of factors that affect associations between diagnoses and scale scores include the following: The training and orientation of the diagnosticians; the age of the children being diagnosed; the kinds of problems manifested by the children; the data used by the diagnosticians; how the diagnosticians obtain and combine the data; and the particular empirically based scales that are analyzed in relation to the diagnoses.

CONSTRUCTING DSM-ORIENTED SCALES

To aid practitioners and researchers who work with preschoolers, we have constructed scales for scoring the CBCL/1½-5 and C-TRF in terms of items that experienced psychiatrists and psychologists judged to be very consistent with DSM-IV diagnostic categories. The procedures were as follows (details are provided by Achenbach, Dumenci, and Rescorla, 2000):

1. The descriptive criteria for the following nine DSM-IV diagnostic categories were reproduced: Asperger's and Autistic Disorders; Attention-Deficit/Hyperactivity Disorder (ADHD) Hyperactive-Impulsive and Inattentive types; Dysthymic Disorder; Major Depressive Disorder; Generalized Anxiety Disorder (GAD); Specific Phobia; Separation Anxiety Disorder (SAD); Oppositional Defiant Disorder (ODD).

2. We constructed forms for rating the consistency of each problem item of the CBCL/1½-5 and C-TRF with each of the nine diagnostic categories.

3. Experienced psychiatrists and psychologists were asked to rate items as *not consistent* with each diagnostic category; *somewhat consistent*; or *very consistent*. Raters were given the DSM criteria for guidance, but one-to-one matching of DSM criteria to CBCL/1½-5 and C-TRF items was not necessary to justify ratings of *very consistent*. Some CBCL/1½-5 and C-TRF items could thus be judged as very consistent with the raters' concepts of particular DSM categories even if the DSM did not include precise counterparts of the items.

4. The raters were sixteen highly experienced child psychiatrists and psychologists from nine cultures. All the raters had published research on children's behavioral/emotional problems.

5. Items that were rated as *very consistent* by at least 10 of the 16 raters (63%) were deemed to be sufficiently consistent with DSM categories to be included in the DSM-oriented scales.

6. Because of major overlaps in DSM diagnostic criteria, as well as in the obtained ratings of items, the Hyperactive-Impulsive and Inattentive types of ADHD were combined into a single *Attention Deficit/Hyperactivity Problems* scale; Major Depressive Disorder and Dysthymic Disorder were combined into a single *Affective Problems* scale; and GAD, SAD, and Specific Phobia were combined into a single *Anxiety Problems* scale.

7. The items that were rated as *very consistent* with the categories by at least 10 of the 16 raters were grouped into the following five scales that are displayed on profiles analogous to the profiles of empirically based syndrome scales shown in Chapters 2 and 3: *Affective Problems*; *Anxiety Problems*; *Pervasive Developmental Problems*; *Attention Deficit/ Hyperactivity Problems*; and *Oppositional Defiant Problems*.

PROFILES OF DSM-ORIENTED SCALES

Figure 4-1 illustrates a hand-scored profile displaying the five DSM-oriented scales scored from the CBCL/1½-5 completed for 30-month-old Kenny Randall by his mother. Like the empirically based ASEBA scales, the DSM-oriented scales are scored by summing the 0-1-2 ratings assigned to each item by the person who completed the form. After summing the item ratings to obtain the total score for a scale, you circle the corresponding number in the column of numbers above the scale. You can then draw a line to connect the circled numbers. The resulting profile pattern enables you to quickly see how high the child is on each DSM-oriented scale, compared to a national sample of children rated on the same items by their parents or parent surrogates. As Figure 4-1 shows, Kenny received scores in the clinical range on the Affective and Pervasive Developmental Problem scales.

C-TRF items are scored on a similar profile of DSM-oriented scales. The CBCL/1½-5 and C-TRF versions of the DSM-oriented scales differ with respect to a few items, because some items rated as very consistent with DSM categories do not have counterparts on both forms. For example, C-TRF item *51. Fidgets* is on the C-TRF version of the C-TRF Attention Deficit/Hyperactivity Problems scale. However, *Fidgets* is not on the CBCL/1½-5 version of this scale, because this item is not on the CBCL/1½-5. The C-TRF profile of DSM-oriented scales compares a child's scores with scores obtained by a national sample of children rated by their preschool teachers and daycare providers, rather than by parent figures.

Like the profiles shown in Chapters 2 and 3, the profiles of DSM-oriented scales display broken lines to demarcate a borderline clinical range from the 93rd to the 97th percentile. Percentiles for particular scale scores can be read from the left side of the graph, while *T* scores (explained in Chapter 6) can be read from the right side of the graph. The percentiles and *T* scores, plus broken lines demarcating the borderline clinical range, guide users in determining the degree to which a child's scores on the DSM-oriented scales deviate from those of peers.

Users should keep in mind that a particular score on a DSM-oriented scale is not directly equivalent to a DSM diagnosis, for the following reasons:

1. The items of the DSM-oriented scales do not correspond precisely to criteria for DSM diagnoses.

2. The item scores reflect the respondent's judgment of whether the child manifested particular problems over the preceding 2 months. However, the scores do not include criteria for age of onset or duration of problems, which are included in the criteria for some DSM diagnoses.

3. The 0-1-2 item scores are summed to obtain a total score for each scale. By contrast, each DSM criterial attribute must be judged as present-vs.-absent, and diagnoses are based on yes-vs.-no judgments of whether enough DSM criterial attributes are present.

4. The profile indicates how high a child is on each DSM-oriented scale, compared to a national sample of peers of the same age and gender, rated by the same kinds of respondents. By contrast, the criteria for the yes-vs.-no DSM diagnoses are the same for children of both genders, different ages, and all sources of data.

PROFILES AND CROSS-INFORMANT COMPARISONS OF DSM-ORIENTED SCALES

Figure 4-1 illustrates a hand-scored CBCL profile of DSM-oriented scales. The Windows® software for the ASEBA preschool instruments can display profiles for the DSM-oriented scales analogous to the profiles for the empirically based scales that were illustrated in Chapter 3. In addition, the software can also display side-by-side comparisons of DSM-oriented item and scale scores for any combination of up to eight CBCL/1½-5 and C-TRF forms completed for a child, like the comparisons displayed for the empirically based scales shown in Chapter 3.

Figure 4-2 shows the comparison of DSM-oriented scales for Kenny Randall. As you can see from Figure 4-2, ratings by both parents and both teachers placed Kenny in the clinical range on the Pervasive Developmental Problems scale. In addition, ratings by both teachers but not his parents placed Kenny in the clinical range on the Attention Deficit/Hyperactivity Problems scale.

GUIDELINES FOR USING DSM-ORIENTED SCALES

The DSM-oriented scales can help to relate standardized, quantified, normed assessment of behavioral/emotional problems to DSM categories in a variety of ways. For example, if the CBCL/1½-5 and C-TRF profiles obtained from multiple informants show that a child consistently scores in the borderline or clinical range on one DSM-oriented scale, such as the Pervasive Developmental Problems scale, this would suggest that you should consider a diagnosis corresponding to that scale, such as PDD. Of course, the requisite DSM criteria for symptoms, impairment, age of onset, and exclusion of other diagnoses would need to be judged on the basis of additional information.

To distinguish between DSM categories of PDD, such as Autistic Disorder vs. Asperger's Disorder, you would also need to consider factors such as communicative skills. Similarly, if profiles yield scores in the borderline or clinical range for the Oppositional Defiant Problems scale, this would suggest that you should consider a diagnosis of ODD. However, to determine whether formal DSM diagnostic criteria for ODD are met, you need to judge whether the pattern of problems has lasted at least 6 months, whether the requisite number of DSM-defined symptoms are present, whether the behavior problems impair functioning, and whether exclusionary criteria are met.

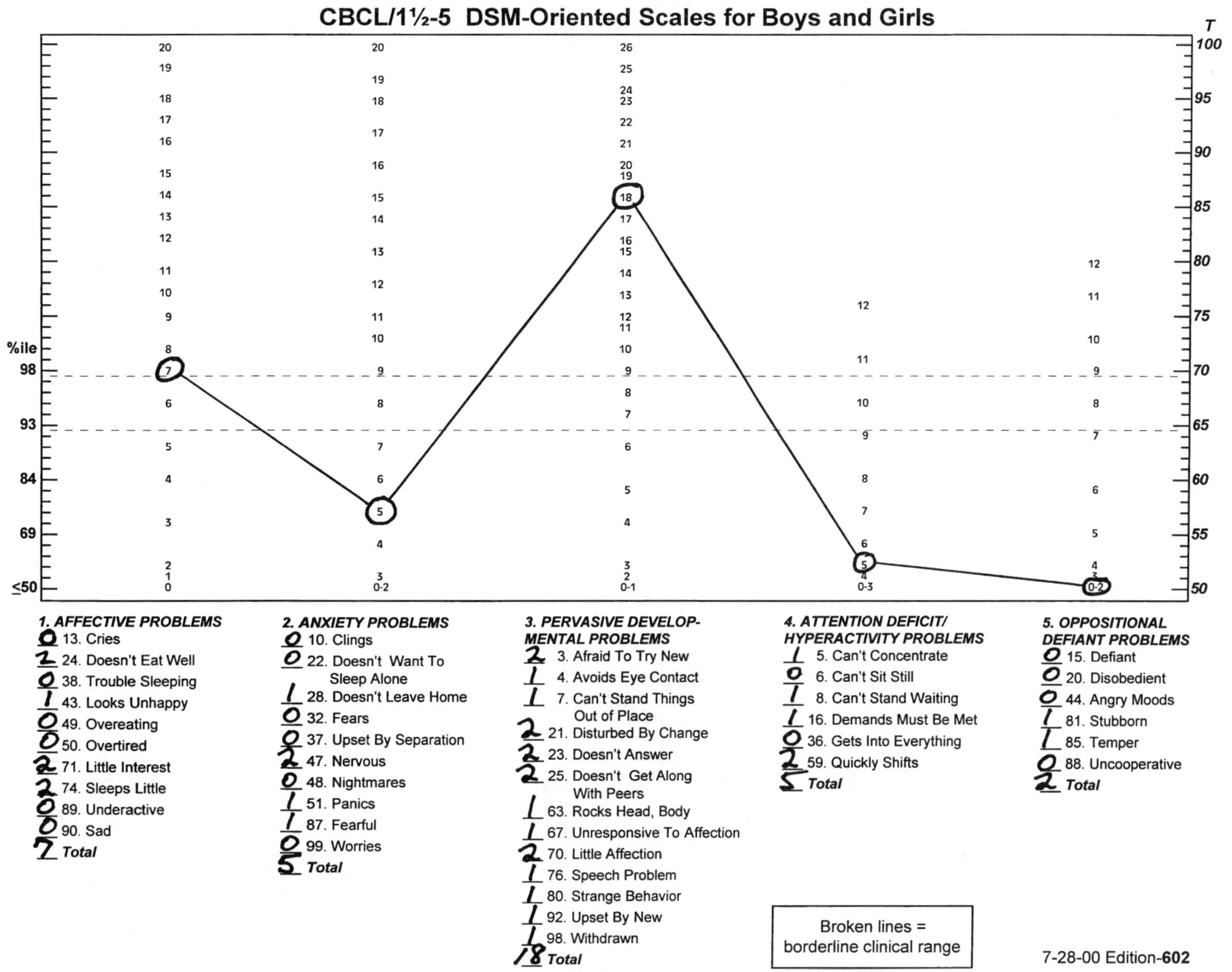

DSM-ORIENTED SCALES

Figure 4-1. Hand-scored CBCL/1½-5 DSM-oriented profile for Kenny Randall. (Instructions printed at right side of profile are not shown.)

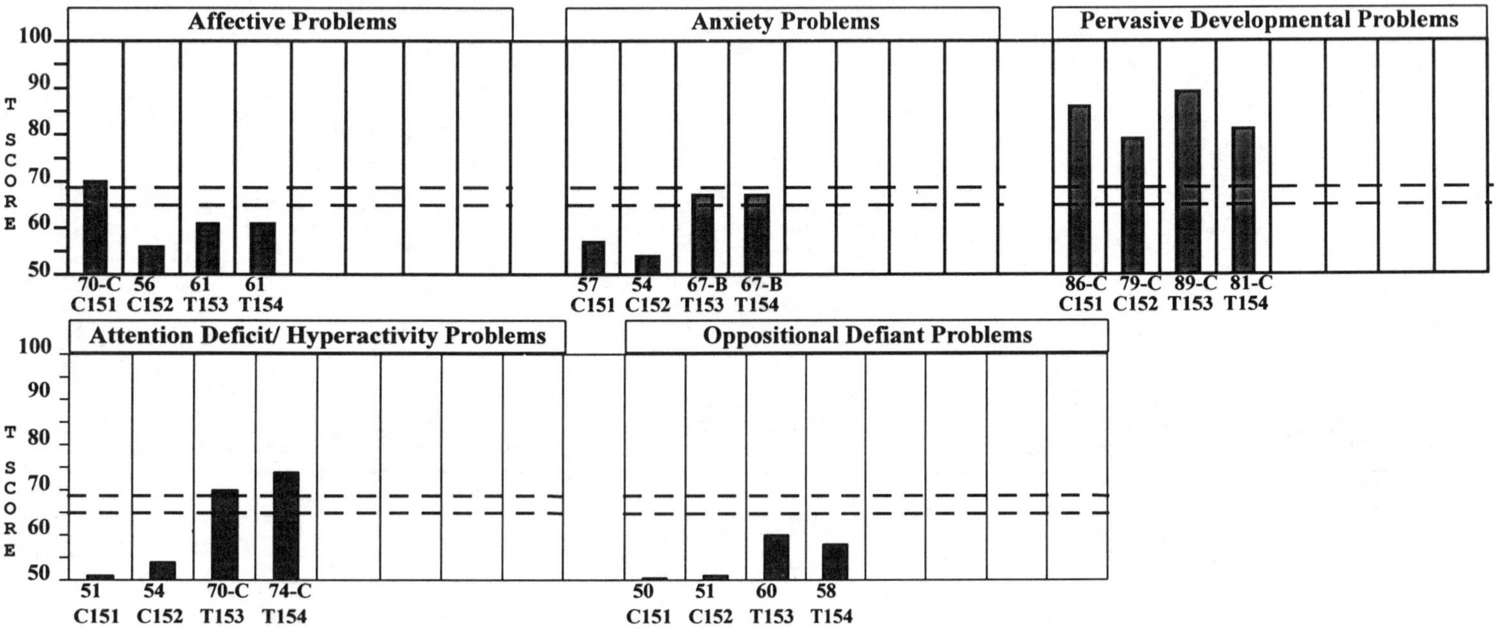

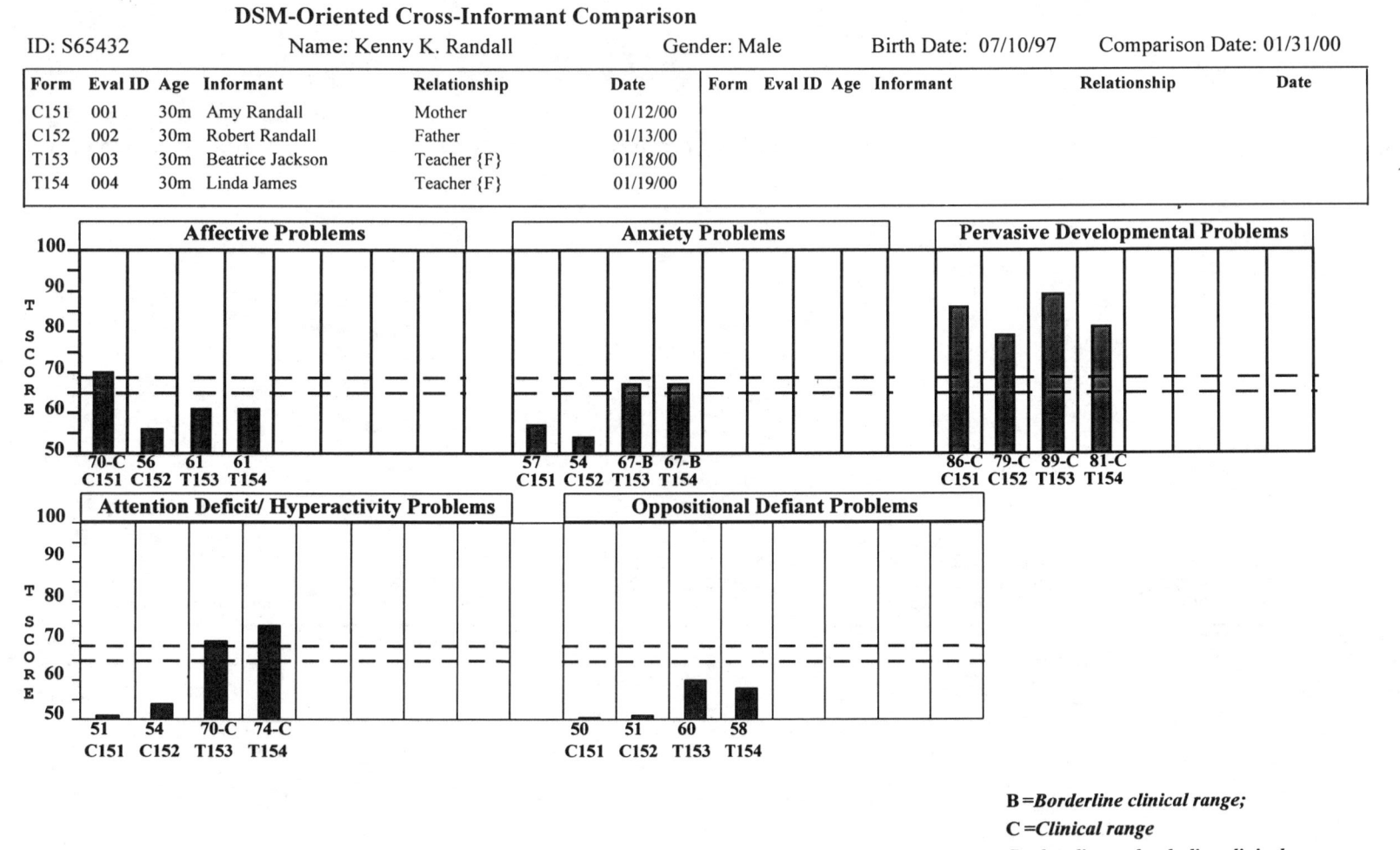

Figure 4-2. Cross-informant comparisons of DSM-oriented scale scores for Kenny Randall.

High Scores on Multiple Scales

A single DSM-oriented scale may be elevated for some children, whereas multiple DSM-oriented scales may be elevated for other children. When multiple scales are elevated, you should consider multiple diagnoses or "comorbidity," i.e., the co-occurrence of multiple disorders. Profiles of quantitatively scored DSM-oriented scales enable you to quickly see relations among the different kinds of problems represented by the five scales. Although you might routinely expect certain disorders to be comorbid, such as ADHD with ODD, the profiles may alert you to less expected comorbidities, such as a child who is high on the Oppositional Defiant Problems scale but is also high on the Affective Problems scale.

You can also compare the pattern of scores on the DSM-oriented profile with the pattern of scores on the empirically based CBCL/1½-5 and C-TRF syndrome profiles. For example, you may see that the CBCL/1½-5 completed by each parent yields scores in the clinical range on the DSM-oriented Oppositional Defiant Problems and Anxiety Problems scales, and also on the empirically based Sleep Problems and Somatic Problems syndromes. If you need to make DSM diagnoses, this pattern would suggest that you should determine whether the child met criteria for diagnoses that correspond to each of these problem areas. However, even if the child failed to meet criteria for one or more DSM diagnoses, the high scores on the two DSM-oriented scales and two empirically based syndromes indicate a need for help in these areas.

Cross-Informant Differences in Scale Scores

If marked differences are found among profiles from different informants, this would suggest situational variations in problems that may argue for interventions to modify the particular contingencies under which the problems occur. For example, the profile scored from Ms. Randall's ratings of 30-month-old Kenny Randall yielded scores in the clinical range on the DSM-oriented Affective and Pervasive Developmental Problems scales. However, profiles from both of Kenny's preschool teachers yielded scores in the clinical range on the DSM-oriented Attention-Deficit/Hyperactivity Problems scale, as well as on the Pervasive Developmental Problems scale. This would suggest that you should determine whether Kenny met DSM criteria for PDD and for either of the types of ADHD.

Whether or not Kenny met DSM criteria for one or both disorders, the scores in the clinical range on the different scales indicate that considerably more problems of both kinds were reported for Kenny than for 97% of the national normative sample. Interventions should therefore take account of both pervasive developmental and attention problems, although the focus of interventions may differ from home to school.

Severity of Problems on DSM-Oriented Scales

Because the DSM-oriented scales are quantitatively scored, they can be used to assess the severity of problems. In addition, by comparing the DSM-oriented scale scores obtained prior to and following interventions, you can determine whether improvements occur in problems related to DSM categories, even though children may continue to meet DSM criteria for particular disorders. The quantitative scoring of the DSM-oriented scales also facilitates research and statistical analyses, as discussed in Chapter 12.

SUMMARY

To aid practitioners and researchers who work with preschoolers, we have constructed scales for scoring the CBCL/1½-5 and C-TRF in terms of items that experienced mental health professionals judged to be very consistent with DSM-IV diagnostic categories. Reflecting overlap among DSM criteria and among item ratings for different DSM categories, we formed the following scales: *Affective Problems* (items rated as very consistent with Dysthymia and Major Depressive Disorder); *Anxiety Problems* (items rated as very consistent with Generalized Anxiety Disorder, Separation Anxiety Disorder, and Specific Phobia); *Pervasive Developmental Problems* (items rated as very consistent with Asperger's Disorder and Autistic Disorder); *Attention Deficit/ Hyperactivity Problems* (items rated as very consistent with Hyperactive-Impulsive and Inattentive types of ADHD); and *Oppositional Defiant Problems*.

The DSM-oriented scales can be scored on hand-scored and computer-scored profiles for the CBCL/1½-5 and C-TRF, analogous to the profiles shown in Chapters 2 and 3 for the empirically based syndromes. The profiles for the DSM-oriented scales display percentiles and *T* scores, plus normal, borderline, and clinical ranges based on the same national normative samples as for the empirically based scales. In addition, the ASEBA software can display side-by-side comparisons of DSM-oriented scale scores for any combination of up to eight CBCL/1½-5 and C-TRF forms completed for a child. Users should remember that a particular score on a DSM-oriented scale is not directly equivalent to a DSM diagnosis. Although high scores on DSM-oriented scales suggest diagnoses that should be considered, users should consult the DSM to determine whether specific diagnostic criteria are met.

Chapter 5
Practical Applications of ASEBA Preschool Forms

This chapter addresses applications of ASEBA forms to *practical decisions* about *particular* children, groups, programs, policies, and situations. Practical applications can be contrasted with *research applications*, discussed in Chapter 12, which aim to establish knowledge that is *generalizable* beyond the individual case or situation. Designed for both practical and research applications, ASEBA forms provide a common language for describing preschoolers' functioning under diverse conditions.

We believe that the meaning and utility of assessment data depend on the situations in which they are obtained and used. In evaluating children, the skilled practitioner applies knowledge and procedures derived from other cases to obtain a clear picture of the individual case. A primary reason for developing ASEBA forms was to provide more differentiated assessment of children's functioning. The problem items and scales provide the practitioner with a well-differentiated picture of the child's problems as seen by particular informants and compared with normative samples of peers. The profiles reveal areas in which the child's reported problems are in the normal, borderline, or clinical range. This helps the practitioner to identify distinguishing features of the child in terms of problems reported by each informant.

Responsible practice requires practitioners to continually test their judgments against various kinds of evidence. ASEBA profiles facilitate this process by enabling the practitioner to compare informants' descriptions with those obtained for normative samples of children, as well as with the practitioner's own impressions of a particular child. The profiles also make it easy to compare descriptions of a child at different points in time, such as at an initial evaluation, after an intervention, and at follow-up.

In this chapter, we present practical applications of ASEBA preschool forms in the following contexts: *(a) mental health and developmental service settings*, such as clinics, community mental health centers, and independent practices; *(b) educational settings*, such as Head Start, early childhood education, daycare, and intervention programs; *(c) medical settings*, such as pediatric and family practices; *(d) child and family service settings*, such as protective service, adoption, and foster care agencies; and *(e) forensic contexts* such as custody cases.

GUIDELINES FOR PRACTICAL APPLICATIONS

The following sections present guidelines for using ASEBA preschool instruments in a variety of settings. These guidelines should be helpful for people who use ASEBA forms in their settings, as well as for those who train others to work with young children.

Use ASEBA Forms Routinely

ASEBA forms are especially valuable when used routinely, such as being completed at intake in mental health settings, for screening in educational and medical settings, and for evaluations by child and family service workers. The ASEBA norms provide standardized benchmarks with which to compare what is reported for each child. In addition, by routinely obtaining ASEBA forms, users develop their own ASEBA guidelines for evaluating the children they serve.

Obtain Reports from Multiple Informants Whenever Feasible

Informants may differ in how they view a child. Children may also behave quite differently in different settings or with different interaction partners. It is therefore helpful to obtain multiple perspectives on children's functioning. ASEBA profiles make systematic comparisons between informants simple and straightforward. Agreements and disagreements between informants may be equally crucial for planning effective interventions.

To sharpen trainees' skills, they can be asked to complete ASEBA forms in the course of evaluating children. Their ratings can then be compared with ratings by parents, teachers, and experienced practitioners, and the reasons for discrepancies can be explored. This is especially helpful for training child care workers, foster parents, and special educators. If multiple trainees rate the same child, the profiles scored from their ratings can be compared to provide better perspectives on variations in the child's behavior.

Use ASEBA Data to Guide Interviews

Professionals who interview parents, teachers, and caregivers will find that ASEBA data provide excellent starting points for discussing informants' views. Rather than using precious interview time to obtain basic descriptive data, interviewers can use ASEBA results to focus on respondents' concerns, on the strengths of the child and family, and on building therapeutic alliances. When respondents' views differ, interviewers can use ASEBA profiles to document the nature and size of the differences.

Use ASEBA Data in the Diagnostic Process

ASEBA data can facilitate the diagnostic process, which consists of gathering, weighing, and integrating information to provide comprehensive understanding of cases. Practitioners often need to assign formal diagnoses for purposes of record keeping or third party payment. However, preschoolers' problems may not always fit into formal diagnostic categories. For example, a child may manifest features of several DSM categories without necessarily having several separate disorders. A child may also manifest serious problems that are not included in the DSM categories, but that nevertheless need attention. It is therefore important to document all relevant problems, needs, and strengths, rather than viewing children only in terms of diagnostic categories. By assessing a wide range of functioning in terms of specific problems, empirically based syndromes, DSM-oriented scales, broad groupings of problems, and respondents' own comments, ASEBA instruments provide a broad database for diagnostic formulations.

Use ASEBA Forms for Assessing Service Delivery and Outcomes

It is increasingly essential to document presenting problems in order to justify services, obtain third party payments, protect against liability, and qualify programs for accreditation. ASEBA forms are quick to administer and score, are widely used, and can be readministered periodically. They therefore provide ideal tools for assessing service delivery and for evaluating outcomes. The completed forms and scored profiles can be retained to provide standardized documentation of the presenting problems and to indicate the areas in which each child's problems are in the normal, borderline, or clinical range.

ASEBA forms can also be used to evaluate changes in reported problems. For example, by having parents complete the CBCL/1½-5 at 3-month intervals, you can determine which problems are improving, remaining the same, or getting worse. You can also determine whether scales that were in the clinical range have moved into the borderline or normal range.

Across a caseload, ASEBA forms can be used to document the prevalence and distribution of specific problems over particular periods, such as annually. For example, if our computer scoring program is used to score the forms, it is easy to tabulate the number of cases that were reported to have each of the problems, the number that were in the clinical range on each scale, and the association of the problem scores with the age, gender, SES, ethnicity and other characteristics of the children. These data can be used for annual reports, requests for funding, and planning for staff and services.

Users can also compare services to identify differences between the kinds and severity of problems seen in different services. Changes in the rates of particular problems or in deviance on particular scales from one period to another can be used to guide restructuring of services, if needed. Children who are followed beyond their sixth birthday can continue to be assessed in a similar fashion with the ASEBA school-age forms.

Reassessment at Uniform Intervals. Standardized reassessment of cases over uniform intervals, such as 3, 6, or 12 months, is especially valuable to determine the typical course and outcome for children having particular presenting problems. We recommend that users first select intervals that are appropriate for their setting and then reassess all cases at approximately the same intervals, such as every 3 months. It is usually easier for staff to request respondents to complete forms according to a schedule that is specified in advance on a calendar rather than trying to obtain completed forms at variable intervals. Furthermore, to compare the progress of different cases, it is important to reassess them at fairly uniform intervals. If the intervals are too variable, differences in intervals will be confounded with treatment effects as possible influences on changes in scores.

If certain initial ASEBA scale scores or profile patterns are consistently followed by especially poor outcomes, this would argue for finding better ways to help children with these problems. When new cases having these problems are identified from their profiles at intake, new ways of helping them can be evaluated by comparing the outcomes obtained with each approach.

MENTAL HEALTH AND DEVELOPMENTAL SERVICE SETTINGS

Many preschoolers manifest problems that distress their parents. As shown in Chapter 10, common problems include the following: *15. Defiant; 16. Demands must be met immediately; 20. Disobedient; 81. Stubborn, sullen, or irritable;* and *96. Wants a lot of attention.* Problems related to toilet training, eating, and sleeping are also common. When parents are sufficiently troubled by such problems, they often seek the help of their pediatrician or family doctor. In many cases, a specific problem can be alleviated by changes in environmental conditions.

When problems are more pervasive, persistent, or indicative of possible developmental delays, a developmental evaluation may be sought. Developmental evaluations often begin with screening procedures to compare a child's skills with those reported for normative groups of peers. Common developmental screening instruments include the Preschool Development Inventories (Ireton, 1984), the Vineland Adaptive Behavior Scales (Sparrow, Cicchetti, & Balla, 1984), and the Denver Developmental Screening Test (Frankenburg, Dodds, Archer, Shapiro, & Bresnick, 1992). Comprehensive developmental evaluations often include a standardized test of mental development, such as the Bayley Scales of Infant Development-II (Bayley, 1993). The main aim of such evaluations is to determine whether a child's developmental progress lags behind norms for the child's age.

ASEBA forms can be used in most contexts

where preschoolers are evaluated for developmental and/or behavioral/emotional problems. The CBCL can be especially useful if it is routinely completed at intake for all children seen in a particular setting. Routine use of the CBCL provides standardized documentation for each child's record, plus a baseline from which to assess changes in the child. Figure 5-1 illustrates a typical sequence for using ASEBA forms. The case of Kenny Randall in Chapter 3 illustrated applications of ASEBA forms in a mental health setting.

ASEBA forms are easy to include in evaluations for developmental and behavioral/emotional problems, because they typically require no professional time to administer. The CBCL/1½-5 can be completed by parents with fifth grade reading skills. For parents who have difficulty completing forms independently, it can be administered by an interviewer according to the instructions in Chapter 1.

Because most parents seeking help for their child expect to report on the child's behavior, they typically accept the CBCL as a natural part of an intake procedure. If intake materials are mailed to parents before their first appointment, the CBCL can be enclosed to be completed at home and returned by mail or brought to the first appointment.

If intake materials are not routinely mailed in advance, parents can be scheduled to come 20 minutes before their interview to fill out the CBCL in the waiting room. A receptionist or intake worker who is familiar with the CBCL should be available to help parents as needed.

Having Both Parents Fill Out CBCLs

Whenever feasible, it is helpful to have both parents independently fill out a separate copy of the CBCL. If both parents are not available, it is useful to have the CBCL filled out by whatever adults know the child well, such as a parent and grandparent, or by parent surrogates if no parent is available. The reason for having both parents (or surrogates) complete the CBCL can be explained as follows:

"We would like each of you to fill out a form to describe your child's behavior. Parents sometimes differ in the way they see their children, so don't worry if your spouse does not report exactly the same behavior as you do. Just fill out the form to describe the way you see your child."

The specific behaviors reported and the profiles scored from the CBCL completed by different informants can be compared to identify areas of agreement and disagreement. Small semantic disagreements are not uncommon. For example, one parent may score item *35. Gets in many fights* for approximately the same behavior as another parent scores item *40. Hits others*. However, most such semantic differences do not result in different scale scores on the profile, because the items are closely enough related to be scored on the same scales.

The profiles scored from the CBCL completed by different informants can be directly compared to identify areas of agreement and disagreement. Such comparisons are facilitated by the computer program for scoring the CBCL profile. If more than one CBCL has been obtained for a child, the program can display side-by-side comparisons of item scores from each CBCL. It is thus easy to compare the scores given each item by each informant. To provide a quantitative index of the overall level of agreement between pairs of informants, the program computes a Q correlation between the scores that were assigned to the problem items by one informant and the scores assigned to the problem items by the other informant, as explained in Chapter 3. For consistency across forms, the correlations are computed on the 82 items that have counterparts on the CBCL and

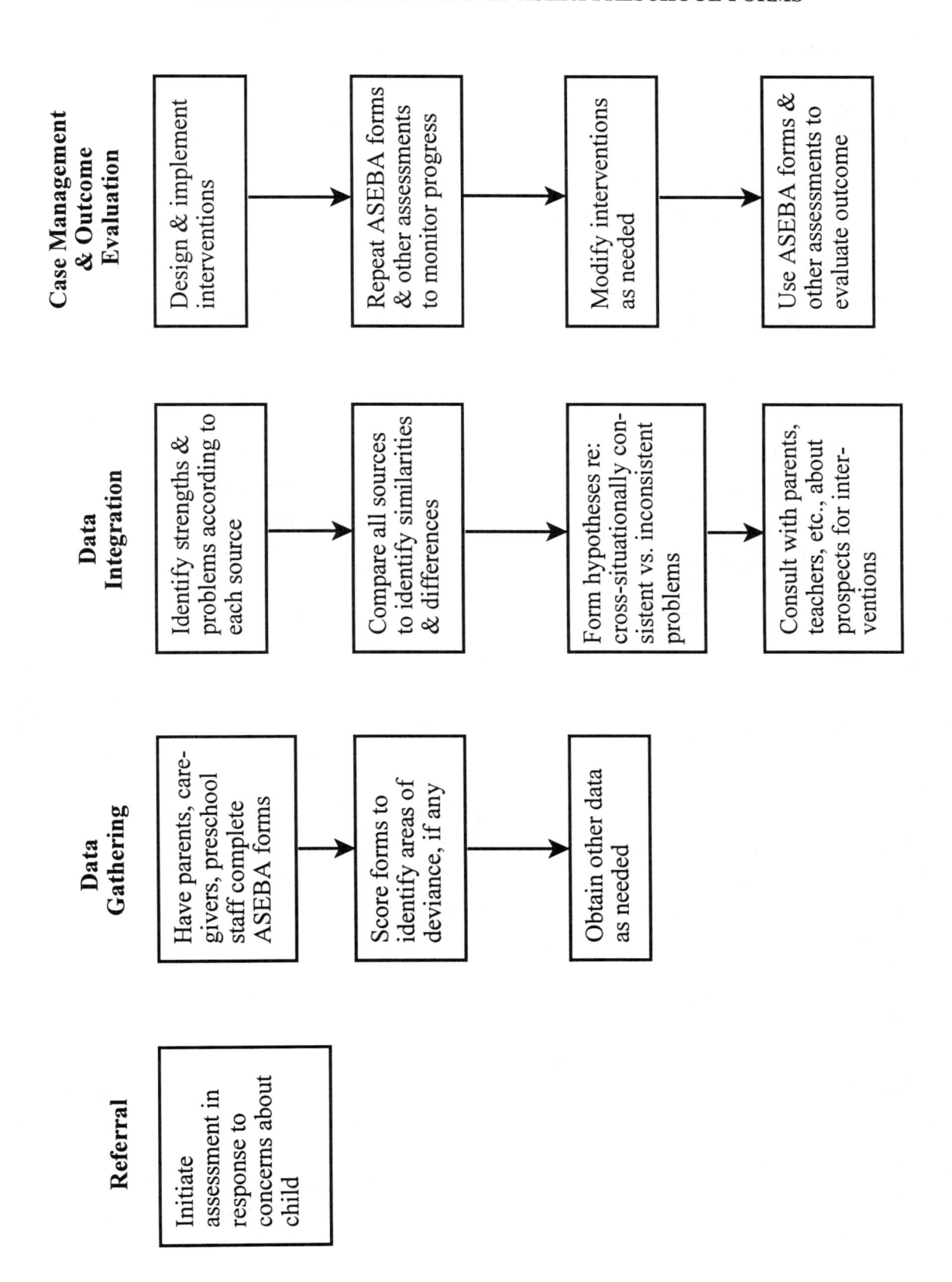

PRACTICAL APPLICATIONS OF ASEBA PRESCHOOL FORMS 41

Referral

Initiate assessment in response to concerns about child

Data Gathering

Have parents, caregivers, preschool staff complete ASEBA forms → Score forms to identify areas of deviance, if any → Obtain other data as needed

Data Integration

Identify strengths & problems according to each source → Compare all sources to identify similarities & differences → Form hypotheses re: cross-situationally consistent vs. inconsistent problems → Consult with parents, teachers, etc., about prospects for interventions

Case Management & Outcome Evaluation

Design & implement interventions → Repeat ASEBA forms & other assessments to monitor progress → Modify interventions as needed → Use ASEBA forms & other assessments to evaluate outcome

Figure 5-1. Illustrative sequence for employing ASEBA forms.

the C-TRF. Although small differences between mothers' and fathers' scale scores are common, large differences should be explored to answer questions such as the following:

1. Do a parent's own problems or biases toward the child make that parent a poor informant?

2. Does lack of contact with the child make one parent a poor informant?

3. Does one parent evoke particular problem behaviors from the child?

4. Is one parent absent when the problems occur?

5. Do differences in values cause one parent to judge particular behavior more harshly than the other parent?

6. Is one parent less tolerant of difficult behavior than the other parent?

7. Is one parent prone to deny problems for reasons of social desirability?

Disagreements between parents' CBCL responses can be explored in interviews with the parents. The reasons for the disagreements should be considered in formulating plans for interventions. In some cases, for example, a practitioner may choose to work on changing a parent's perceptions of the child or behavior toward the child, rather than trying to change the child's behavior. In such cases, reassessment with the CBCL after the intervention can show whether a parent's perceptions have indeed changed.

Interviewing Parents

When the practitioner first interviews parents, it is helpful to have the completed CBCLs (and, if possible the scored profiles) as a take-off point for interviewing. The practitioner can begin by asking the parents if they have any questions about the CBCL. This provides an opportunity to clarify items for the parents and to encourage them to spontaneously discuss their understanding of items and their responses. The practitioner may wish to ask parents to elaborate on items that they rated as *1* or *2*, especially items that request descriptions, such as *24. Doesn't eat well; 46. Nervous movements or twitching; 65. Resists toilet training; 76. Speech problem; 80. Strange behavior;* and *92. Upset by new people or situations.*

After obtaining clarification of the parents' responses, the practitioner can use the items of greatest concern and the profile scales showing the most deviance as foci for interviewing about the history and context of the problems. As other data become available, such as developmental, medical, and direct observational data, these can be compared with the picture presented by the CBCL and its profile. Disagreements with other types of data do not necessarily mean that the parents' CBCL reports are wrong. The parents' reports may accurately reflect what the parents see, but the child may behave differently in other contexts. On the other hand, if the practitioner concludes that parents' perceptions are distorted, the practitioner may elect to deal with the misperceptions revealed by their responses to the CBCL.

Diagnostic Issues

In many mental health settings, it is customary to make diagnoses. The term "diagnosis" is used in a variety of ways. In its narrow sense, diagnosis is "the medical term for classification" (Guze, 1978, p. 53). As applied to diagnosis of children's behavioral/emotional problems, this would refer to matching a child's pattern of problems to the criteria for disorders specified in a classification system such as the DSM. Diagnosis in this sense is called *formal diagnosis*.

In a broader sense, diagnosis is defined as: *(a)* "investigation or analysis of the cause or nature of a condition, situation or problem;" and *(b)* "a statement or conclusion concerning the nature or cause of some phenomenon" (Mish, 1988, p. 349). Diagnosis in this sense concerns *diagnostic formulations*.

Diagnosis is also used to refer to the *diagnostic process*, which is the process of gathering, weighing, and integrating information about a case. ASEBA instruments contribute to this information-processing aspect of diagnosis by providing standardized data from multiple informants that can be systematically compared and used to document variations in reported problems.

Practitioners often need to assign diagnoses for purposes of record keeping, providing feedback to others, and justifying services. However, preschoolers may have problems that do not match diagnostic criteria. Furthermore, a child may manifest characteristics of several diagnoses, without necessarily having several different disorders. It is therefore important to base diagnostic formulations on comprehensive assessment of the child's problems, needs, and strengths, rather than viewing the child only in terms of diagnostic categories.

ASEBA forms assess a wide range of problems that characterize preschoolers. Furthermore, because ASEBA profiles display children's standing across the empirically derived syndromes, plus the DSM-oriented scales, you can identify many combinations of problems. In using ASEBA forms to evaluate children, you are not forced to make choices among categories of problems. Instead, you can base diagnostic formulations and intervention plans on a child's entire pattern, whether or not it corresponds to a diagnostic category. Nevertheless, if a formal diagnosis is required, the syndromes and DSM-oriented scales can be used to aid in deciding among possible diagnoses, although other data are also needed to determine whether specific diagnostic criteria are met.

EDUCATIONAL SETTINGS

General procedures for using ASEBA forms in educational and other group settings are described in the next sections, followed by a case illustration in Head Start.

Identifying Problems

Increasing numbers of children attend daycare or preschool. These settings are therefore especially important arenas where behavior problems may arise. They are also key contexts in which to evaluate problems whose origins may lie elsewhere. In addition, such settings can foster adaptive functioning, regardless of the sources of the problems. If concerns about a child initially arise in daycare or preschool, the C-TRF can be completed by all staff members who know the child well in order to determine whether the perceived problems actually deviate from the relevant norms.

If a child's C-TRF scores are all found to be in the normal range according to ratings by multiple staff members in a particular setting, this would argue against a need for major changes in the child's behavior in that setting. Nevertheless, certain specific problems or problem areas might be targeted for change in order to enhance the child's functioning. For example, C-TRFs from several staff members may agree in reporting a particular problem, such as stomachaches without known medical cause. This finding would warrant a medical examination to determine whether the child was suffering from a previously undiagnosed medical condition. If no physical reason can be found, the circumstances surrounding the stomachaches should be carefully documented to identify specific dietary or emotional contingencies that may trigger the stomachaches.

If a child obtains C-TRF scale scores in the clinical range in ratings by at least one staff member or in the borderline clinical range in ratings by multiple staff members, this would usually warrant further evaluation. Both parents (or other adults who live with the child) could be asked to complete the CBCL. If the CBCLs also yielded scores in the clinical range, this would indicate that significant problems are evident to the child's parents as well as to the daycare or preschool staff.

Planning Interventions

Based on findings from all sources of data, specific hypotheses regarding the possible causes of the problems and ideas about possible interventions to alleviate the problems could be considered. After consultation with all parties concerned (e.g., parents, teachers, caregivers), interventions would then be designed to help the child. After interventions begin, ASEBA forms can be readministered to determine whether the intended improvements are occurring. The forms can be readministered again after completion of the intervention to determine whether the outcome is satisfactory. If feasible, follow-up assessments should be done by readministering forms at one or more intervals, such as 3 months and 6 months after the outcome assessment, to determine whether improvements are maintained.

If the child is in grade school by the time of the outcome or follow-up assessments, ASEBA school-age forms can be used. Although the instruments for preschool and school-age children differ somewhat in their items, scales, and normative samples, they all indicate whether the scores obtained by a child at a particular age are deviant from the scores obtained by normative samples of agemates. Thus, if a preschooler who obtained deviant scores on the C-TRF later obtained TRF scores in the normal range when in first grade, this would indicate a satisfactory outcome.

Head Start and similar preschool programs provide opportunities for helping children with behavioral and emotional problems, as well as for facilitating school readiness. Head Start staff are well positioned to identify children who may need special help and to initiate evaluations of children's functioning. Concerns about a child may arise in the group setting, or parents may approach teachers because they are worried about their child. If evaluations document needs for special help, Head Start staff can often collaborate with other professionals and with parents in helping children. The case of Tyrone Jenkins illustrates ways in which ASEBA forms can be used in programs like Head Start to assess problems, guide interventions, and evaluate outcomes.

Case Example in Head Start: Tyrone Jenkins, Age 5

Tyrone's Head Start teacher, Ruth Albert, had been concerned about Tyrone's behavior since he entered her class. When Tyrone showed no improvement over several months, Ms. Albert contacted the program's consultant psychologist, Dr. Maxwell. To obtain permission for an evaluation, Dr. Maxwell met with Tyrone's mother to discuss the teacher's concerns. Ms. Jenkins mentioned that Tyrone's daycare provider had also been concerned about his behavior. Because she had recently started a new job, Ms. Jenkins said that she had little time to spend with Tyrone, but she agreed to complete the CBCL/1½-5 and to permit Ms. Albert and the assistant teacher to complete C-TRFs.

Cross-Informant Comparisons. As shown in Figure 5-2, Ms. Albert's C-TRF yielded scores in the clinical range on the Aggressive Behavior, Attention Problems, and Anxious/Depressed syndromes. Her C-TRF also yielded

ID: 1357-008
Name: Tyrone T. Jenkins
Clinician: Dr. Maxwell

CTRF/1.5-5 Syndrome Scale Scores for Boys

Gender: Male
Age: 5 years
Verified: Yes

Date Filled: 01/05/00
Birth Date: 12/01/94
Agency: Head Start

Informant: Ruth Jackson Albert
Relationship: Teacher {F}

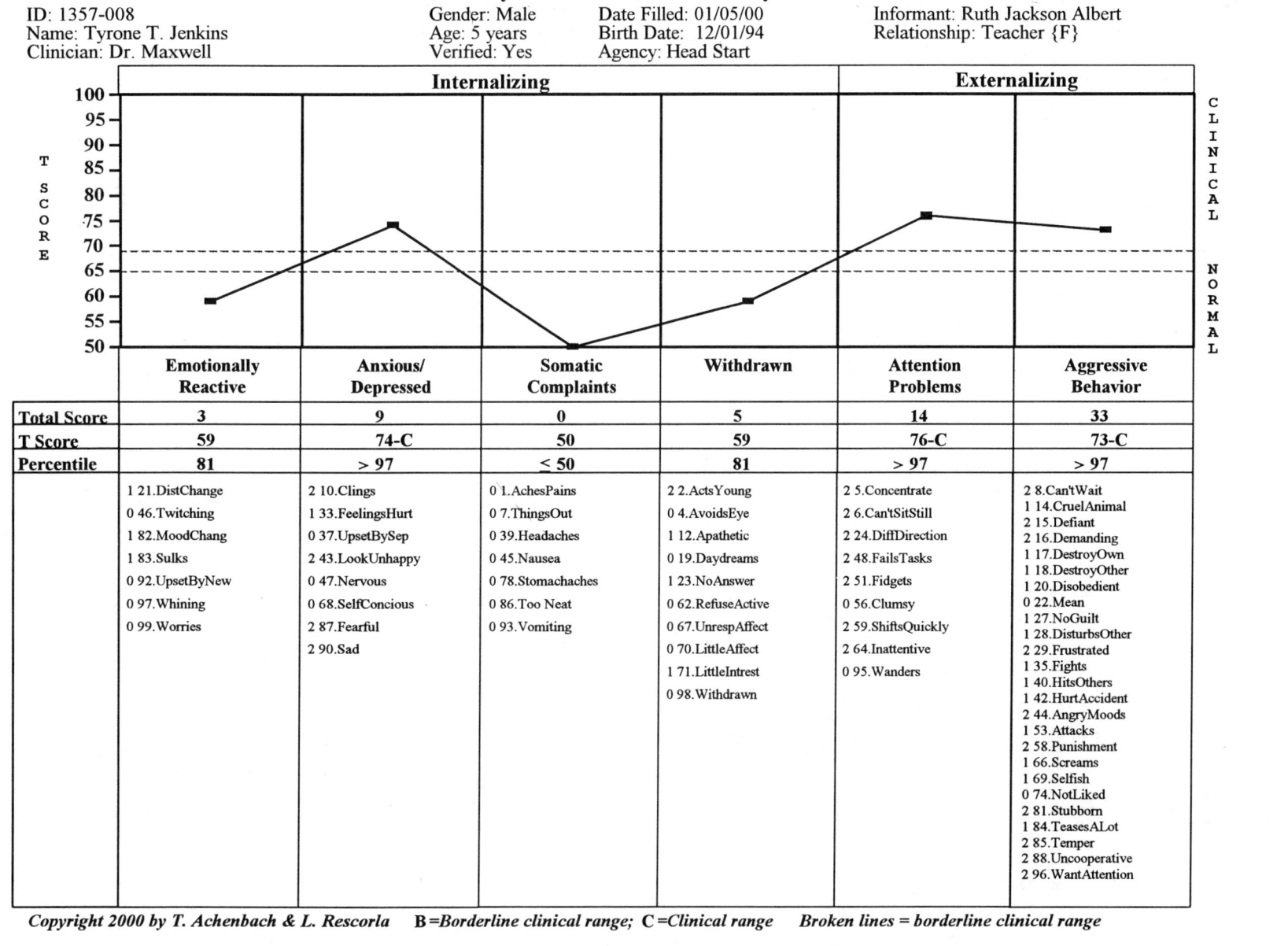

Page 1 of 3

	Emotionally Reactive	Anxious/ Depressed	Somatic Complaints	Withdrawn	Attention Problems	Aggressive Behavior
Total Score	3	9	0	5	14	33
T Score	59	74-C	50	59	76-C	73-C
Percentile	81	>97	<50	81	>97	>97

Internalizing — Externalizing

Items listed under each syndrome:

Emotionally Reactive: 1 21.DistChange, 0 46.Twitching, 1 82.MoodChang, 1 83.Sulks, 0 92.UpsetByNew, 0 97.Whining, 0 99.Worries

Anxious/Depressed: 2 10.Clings, 1 33.FeelingsHurt, 0 37.UpsetBySep, 2 43.LookUnhappy, 0 47.Nervous, 0 68.SelfConcious, 2 87.Fearful, 2 90.Sad

Somatic Complaints: 0 1.AchesPains, 0 7.ThingsOut, 0 39.Headaches, 0 45.Nausea, 0 78.Stomachaches, 0 86.TooNeat, 0 93.Vomiting

Withdrawn: 2 2.ActsYoung, 0 4.AvoidsEye, 1 12.Apathetic, 0 19.Daydreams, 1 23.NoAnswer, 0 62.RefuseActive, 0 67.UnrespAffect, 0 70.LittleAffect, 1 71.LittleIntrest, 0 98.Withdrawn

Attention Problems: 2 5.Concentrate, 2 6.CantSitStill, 2 24.DiffDirection, 2 48.FailsTasks, 2 51.Fidgets, 0 56.Clumsy, 2 59.ShiftsQuickly, 2 64.Inattentive, 0 95.Wanders

Aggressive Behavior: 2 8.CantWait, 1 14.CruelAnimal, 2 15.Defiant, 2 16.Demanding, 1 17.DestroyOwn, 1 18.DestroyOther, 1 20.Disobedient, 0 22.Mean, 1 27.NoGuilt, 1 28.DisturbsOther, 2 29.Frustrated, 1 35.Fights, 1 40.HitsOthers, 1 42.HurtAccident, 2 44.AngryMoods, 1 53.Attacks, 1 58.Punishment, 1 66.Screams, 1 69.Selfish, 0 74.NotLiked, 2 81.Stubborn, 1 84.TeasesALot, 2 85.Temper, 2 88.Uncooperative, 2 96.WantAttention

Copyright 2000 by T. Achenbach & L. Rescorla   B=Borderline clinical range;   C=Clinical range   Broken lines = borderline clinical range

Figure 5-2. Syndromes profile scored for Tyrone Jenkins from C-TRF completed by his teacher Ruth Albert.

scores in the clinical range on the DSM-oriented Oppositional Defiant Problems, Attention Deficit/Hyperactivity Problems, and Anxiety Problems scales. Ms. Albert's comments on the C-TRF indicated that Tyrone was preoccupied with fears of robbers, monsters, and especially bugs. She also reported that his play was unusually violent and gory. In the section for describing the best things about the child, she wrote that Tyrone could be very sweet and affectionate, especially when interacting one-to-one with a teacher.

The cross-informant correlation showed an average level of agreement between the C-TRF ratings by Ms. Albert and the assistant teacher, whose ratings yielded scores in the clinical range for the Aggressive Behavior and Attention Problems syndromes and for the Oppositional Defiant and Attention Deficit/Hyperactivity Problems DSM-oriented scales, but just below the borderline clinical range for the Anxious/Depressed syndrome and for the DSM-oriented Anxiety Problems scale.

The CBCL/1½-5 completed by Ms. Jenkins yielded a score in the clinical range for the Aggressive Behavior syndrome, in the borderline range for the Attention Problems syndrome, and somewhat below the borderline range for the Anxious/Depressed syndrome. None of the DSM-oriented scales reached the clinical or borderline range. The cross-informant correlations showed average levels of agreement with the two C-TRFs.

Direct Evaluation. The high problem scores on both C-TRFs and the CBCL/1½-5 indicated a need for direct evaluation by Dr. Maxwell. To obtain a first-hand picture of Tyrone's behavior in Head Start, Dr. Maxwell used the Direct Observation Form (DOF; Achenbach, 1991a) to record observations of Tyrone during three 10-minute periods over the course of a week.

Compared to two other boys observed by Dr. Maxwell, Tyrone obtained higher scores on the DOF Hyperactive and Aggressive syndromes and a lower score for on-task behavior. Dr. Maxwell's narrative descriptions on the DOF documented several examples of Tyrone being quite inattentive, resistant to teachers' instructions, and aggressive. However, the descriptions also documented Tyrone's close attachment to his teachers, especially evident when he looked radiant in response to praise from Ms. Albert and when he snuggled up to her as they read a book together.

When Dr. Maxwell met with Tyrone, he found him to be friendly and animated. Despite difficulties in sustaining attention, Tyrone scored in the average range on brief cognitive tests. Tyrone became engrossed in play with toy soldiers in Dr. Maxwell's office and needed clear directives when it was time to return to class, but he did cooperate. He beamed when Dr. Maxwell said he might be able to come back to play again.

Based on the ratings from the C-TRF, CBCL/1½-5, DOF, and his session with Tyrone, Dr. Maxwell concluded that Tyrone needed help with both his fears and his Externalizing behaviors. Tyrone's positive responses to attention from his teachers and from Dr. Maxwell indicated that adult attention could be a powerful reinforcer of more adaptive behavior.

Intervention. When he met with Ms. Jenkins and Ms. Albert, Dr. Maxwell emphasized Tyrone's sensitivity to adults' approval. They discussed how both Ms. Jenkins and the teachers could give Tyrone clear signals about acceptable behavior and about their availability to help him with his fears. Dr. Maxwell suggested that Ms. Albert involve Tyrone in short but frequent pre-academic readiness activities by letting him earn a special reading time with her in exchange for good concentration and effort during 5- to 10-minute structured tasks. He also encouraged Ms. Jenkins to talk with Tyrone about his fears of robbers, monsters, and bugs and to reassure him that she would protect him.

Dr. Maxwell, Ms. Albert, and Ms. Jenkins worked together to develop a classroom behavior modification plan focused on reducing aggression and improving compliance. This was to be done by providing clear, simple instructions, immediate feedback, and "happy face" stickers for acceptable behavior. On each day when Tyrone's behavior was acceptable, Ms. Albert would give him a card with a happy face sticker to take home to his mother. On weeks when Tyrone earned at least three stickers, his mother would let him choose a video to rent. Whenever Tyrone accumulated 10 stickers, he could have a special play time with Dr. Maxwell.

Follow-up Evaluation. Four months after the initial assessment, Dr. Maxwell asked Ms. Jenkins to complete the CBCL and Ms. Albert and the assistant teacher to complete C-TRFs. On the profile scored from his mother's CBCL, Tyrone was now in the borderline range on the Aggressive Behavior syndrome and in the normal range on the remaining syndromes. On the profiles scored from both C-TRFs, Tyrone was still in the clinical range on the Attention Problems syndrome, but in the borderline or normal range on all other scales.

The lower problem scores indicated important progress, which was also evident in Ms. Albert's favorable comments on the C-TRF, where she praised Tyrone's improved interactions with others and responsiveness to teachers' expectations. However, because both C-TRFs still yielded scores in the clinical range on the Attention Problems syndrome and because kindergarten readiness screening indicated slow development of pre-academic skills, Dr. Maxwell recommended a comprehensive evaluation of Tyrone's academic, language, and motor skills to determine whether he should be placed in a developmental kindergarten program.

MEDICAL SETTINGS

In this section, we first provide an overview of how ASEBA forms are used in medical settings such as HMOs, pediatric practices, and family practices. We then illustrate such applications with the case of Lily Chang, age 4.

When parents are concerned about their preschool child, they often turn to their pediatrician or family doctor. Even when parents do not raise questions about their child's functioning or development, medical practitioners are often in a position to identify problems that may need attention. The CBCL and LDS can be obtained routinely by pediatricians, family physicians, HMOs, pediatric psychologists, and nurse practitioners by having parents complete the forms while waiting for their appointments. A receptionist can score the CBCL and LDS by hand or computer and give the completed form and scored profile to the practitioner. If both parents are available, they can be asked to complete separate copies of the CBCL and LDS, thereby enabling the practitioner to compare their perceptions of the child's functioning.

A glance at the CBCL and LDS scores can alert the practitioner to areas of deviance that should be explored with the parent or child. The CBCL profile and LDS scoring form can also be used in answering parents' questions about whether certain problems are normal for a child's age. A standardized basis for assessing behavioral/emotional problems and language development is especially important for helping children who have physical disabilities or illnesses.

Without a standardized basis for comparing the problems and language reported for an ill child with those reported for normative samples of agemates, practitioners might infer that the child's illness is causing behavioral/emotional problems or a language delay, when in fact the child is actually functioning in the normal range. On the other hand, certain medical conditions may truly raise the risk of particular behavioral/emotional problems or of delayed language.

Practitioners who specialize in particular medical conditions can accumulate ASEBA forms for children having those conditions in order to determine what problems are most commonly associated with each condition. By readministering the ASEBA forms before and after treatment, practitioners can also determine whether particular behavioral/emotional problems tend to be associated with particular treatments.

In addition to their own findings, practitioners can access the many published findings on use of the ASEBA in relation to medical conditions. Chapter 12 lists some 90 medical conditions for which research has been published on the use of ASEBA. The *Bibliography of Published Studies Using ASEBA Instruments* (Bérubé & Achenbach, 2000) provides the bibliographic reference for each publication related to each medical condition. The *Medical Practitioners' Guide for the Achenbach System of Empirically Based Assessment* (Achenbach & Ruffle, 2000) provides detailed illustrations of applications in medical contexts.

Knowledge of the behavioral/emotional problems associated with particular medical conditions and treatments enables practitioners to anticipate problems and to help parents and children cope with them. Advice, therapy, and support programs can focus on the problems accompanying particular medical conditions. The outcomes of interventions can be evaluated by readministering ASEBA forms to assess changes in reported problems. Siblings of children with severe medical conditions may also show behavioral/emotional reactions that can be assessed with ASEBA forms.

Case Example in an HMO: Lily Chang, Age 4

When preschoolers come to the HMO where Dr. Rosen works, each parent is asked to complete the CBCL, which a clerical worker scores. Some providers prefer to examine each child's profile, but Dr. Rosen has a nurse practitioner flag profiles that raise concerns. If the nurse sees scores in the borderline or clinical range, scores of 2 on important items, parental concerns expressed in the open-ended items, or low scores on the LDS, she gives the completed CBCL and profile to Dr. Rosen.

Obtaining ASEBA Data. When Lily Chang was brought to the HMO for her 4-year check-up, her mother's CBCL yielded scores in the clinical range on the Sleep Problems and Anxious/Depressed syndromes, as shown in Figure 5-3. The CBCL also yielded a score in the clinical range on the DSM-oriented Anxiety Problems scale. Items scored 2 included *22. Doesn't want to sleep alone; 32. Fears certain animals, situations, or places; 37. Gets too upset when separated from parents;* and *64. Resists going to bed at night.* Ms. Chang's written comments revealed that Lily was terrified of shots, repeatedly came into her parents' room at night, was afraid to go on swings and slides, and cried daily when her mother took her to daycare.

Cross-Informant Comparisons. Alerted by the nurse, Dr. Rosen explored these concerns with Ms. Chang, who said that Lily had been showing signs of anxiety for the past 6 months. Ms. Chang had assumed that Lily would outgrow these problems, but they were now starting to interfere with more activities. Dr. Rosen asked Ms. Chang to have Mr. Chang and Lily's

CBCL/1.5-5 Syndrome Scale Scores for Girls

ID: 114988-005
Name: Lily L. Chang
Clinician: Dr. Rosen

Gender: Female Date Filled: 05/05/00
Age: 4 years Birth Date: 02/02/96
Verified: Yes Agency: HMO

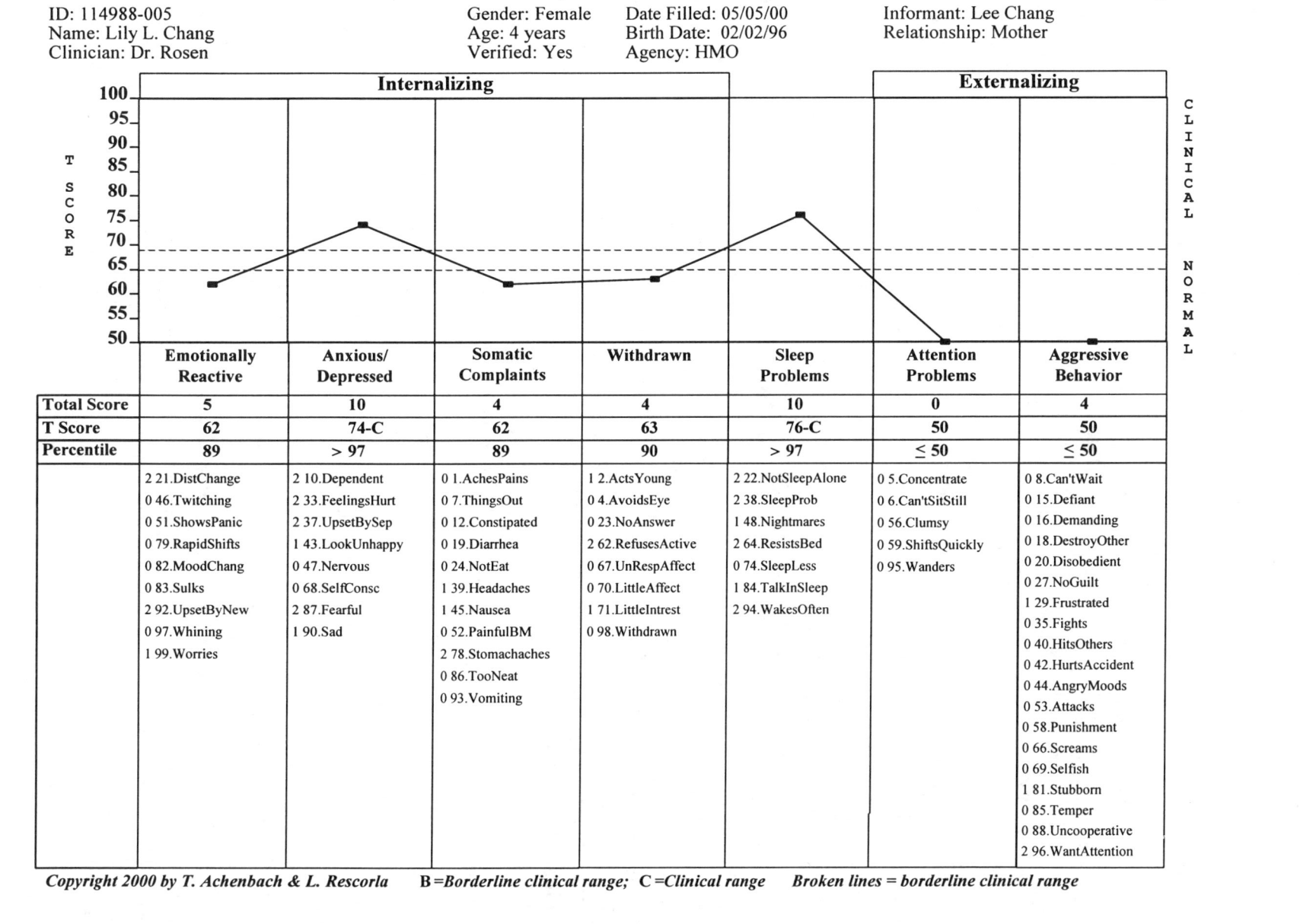

Informant: Lee Chang
Relationship: Mother

Page 1 of 3

Internalizing

	Emotionally Reactive	Anxious/ Depressed	Somatic Complaints	Withdrawn
Total Score	5	10	4	4
T Score	62	74-C	62	63
Percentile	89	>97	89	90

Emotionally Reactive:
2 21.DistChange
0 46.Twitching
0 51.ShowsPanic
0 79.RapidShifts
0 82.MoodChang
0 83.Sulks
2 92.UpsetByNew
0 97.Whining
1 99.Worries

Anxious/Depressed:
2 10.Dependent
2 33.FeelingsHurt
2 37.UpsetBySep
1 43.LookUnhappy
0 47.Nervous
0 68.SelfConsc
2 87.Fearful
1 90.Sad

Somatic Complaints:
0 1.AchesPains
0 7.ThingsOut
0 12.Constipated
0 19.Diarrhea
0 24.NotEat
1 39.Headaches
1 45.Nausea
0 52.PainfulBM
2 78.Stomachaches
0 86.TooNeat
0 93.Vomiting

Withdrawn:
1 2.ActsYoung
0 4.AvoidsEye
0 23.NoAnswer
2 62.RefusesActive
0 67.UnRespAffect
0 70.LittleAffect
1 71.LittleIntrest
0 98.Withdrawn

Externalizing

	Sleep Problems	Attention Problems	Aggressive Behavior
Total Score	10	0	4
T Score	76-C	50	50
Percentile	>97	≤50	≤50

Sleep Problems:
2 22.NotSleepAlone
2 38.SleepProb
1 48.Nightmares
2 64.ResistsBed
0 74.SleepLess
1 84.TalkInSleep
2 94.WakesOften

Attention Problems:
0 5.Concentrate
0 6.Can'tSitStill
0 56.Clumsy
0 59.ShiftsQuickly
0 95.Wanders

Aggressive Behavior:
0 8.Can'tWait
0 15.Defiant
0 16.Demanding
0 18.DestroyOther
0 20.Disobedient
0 27.NoGuilt
1 29.Frustrated
0 35.Fights
0 40.HitsOthers
0 42.HurtsAccident
0 44.AngryMoods
0 53.Attacks
0 58.Punishment
0 66.Screams
0 69.Selfish
1 81.Stubborn
0 85.Temper
0 88.Uncooperative
2 96.WantAttention

Copyright 2000 by T. Achenbach & L. Rescorla B =Borderline clinical range; C =Clinical range Broken lines = borderline clinical range

Figure 5-3. Syndromes profile scored for Lily Chang from CBCL completed by her mother.

grandmother, who lived with the Changs, each complete a CBCL. He also said that it would be helpful to have Lily's two daycare providers each complete a C-TRF. Ms. Chang agreed and made an appointment to meet with the nurse practitioner two weeks later, after the completed forms were to be mailed in and scored.

When the nurse reviewed the printouts for the three CBCLs and two C-TRFs, she saw that the grandmother's CBCL correlated .75 with Ms. Chang's, indicating above-average agreement. Mr. Chang's CBCL, on the other hand, showed correlations in the low average range with the CBCLs completed by his wife and by Lily's grandmother. The grandmother's ratings yielded scores in the clinical and borderline ranges on the same scales as Ms. Chang's ratings, but Mr. Chang's ratings yielded a high score only for the Sleep Problems syndrome, which was in the borderline range. Both C-TRFs yielded scores in the clinical range for the Anxious/Depressed syndrome and for the DSM-oriented Anxiety Problems scale. Although Mr. Chang tended to minimize Lily's problems, the consistencies among the other informants indicated a need for help with both sleep problems and anxiety.

Intervention. After consulting with Dr. Rosen, the nurse met with Ms. Chang to work on helping Lily overcome anxieties associated with sleep, implementing routines for moving Lily progressively toward bed at night, and reinforcing Lily for staying in bed. To help Lily overcome her anxiety about daycare, the nurse recommended that Ms. Chang provide Lily with a special stuffed animal and a picture of her family to keep in her cubby, that she remind Lily when she would be picked up, and that she make good-byes positive but brief. The nurse also recommended that Ms. Chang return in 3 months for a follow-up visit, but that she should call in the interim if she had questions or concerns.

Follow-up Evaluation. For the follow-up evaluation, the nurse requested that Ms. Chang, Lily's grandmother, and the daycare providers complete ASEBA forms again. Several problem items that had been scored 2 were now scored 1, and no problem scales were in the clinical range. Although Lily was still afraid of shots and reluctant to go on swings and slides, she had made significant progress with respect to sleep and daycare. Ms. Chang was especially pleased that Lily was getting excited about kindergarten, reporting that Lily liked to walk by the "big school" and talk about what it would be like to go there.

CHILD AND FAMILY SERVICE SETTINGS

In this section, we outline applications of ASEBA forms by child and family workers who deal with foster placement, adoption, abuse/neglect, and other challenges. We will use the case of Luisa Solano, age 2, to illustrate how ASEBA instruments can be applied by child and family service workers.

ASEBA forms can be routinely used for most children served by child and family service workers. When birth parents are unavailable or are poor informants, the forms can be completed by other relatives, foster parents, and child care workers. For informants who cannot complete forms independently, workers can administer them orally, as described in Chapter 1. Translations are also available in the 58 languages listed in Table 12-1.

Because ASEBA forms are completed by others or in brief interviews, they do not require much of the worker's time. They are also compatible with casework interviews. When completed before a casework interview, the forms can save valuable time. For example, the worker can ask the respondent to elaborate on problems that were scored as present and on comments written in the open-ended items.

The completed forms and their scored profiles provide standardized documentation that is clear to other professionals. Initial profiles can be used as baselines against which to assess changes and outcomes reflected in profiles scored from forms completed after placements or interventions.

Case Example in Foster Care: Luisa Solano, Age 2

Child and family worker Rosa Garcia arranged a temporary foster placement for 2-year-old Luisa Solano as part of an evaluation for a longer term placement. At the end of 4 months, Luisa's foster parents, Raymond and Maria Maldonado, were each asked to complete a CBCL and LDS. English was the dominant language in Luisa's previous home, as well as in the Maldonados' home. The Maldonados preferred to complete the English language version of the CBCL and LDS. (Correlations of .88 to .91 have been found between English and Spanish versions; Weiss, Goebel, Page, Wilson, & Warda, 1999).

The LDS completed by each foster parent indicated mean scores for word combinations below 2.0 and a vocabulary score below 20, which suggested delayed language development.

The cross-informant correlation between the problem scores obtained from the two foster parents indicated average agreement. Both foster parents' ratings yielded scores in the clinical range on the Emotionally Reactive and Withdrawn syndromes, the Total Problems scale, and the DSM-oriented Affective Problems scale. Maria Maldonado's ratings yielded scores in the borderline range on the Anxious/Depressed and Sleep Problems syndromes, while Raymond Maldonado's ratings yielded scores just below the borderline range on these syndromes, as shown in Figure 5-4.

Developmental Evaluation. Based on the evidence for delayed language and high levels of problems, the worker arranged for a comprehensive developmental evaluation. The examiner reported normal functioning on the Motor Scale of the Bayley Scales of Infant Development-II (Bayley, 1993), but a score of 75 on the Mental Scale, with delays in both expressive and receptive language. During the evaluation, Luisa appeared withdrawn, passive, and difficult to engage. She had temper tantrums when she was frustrated by tasks.

Based on the CBCLs and the developmental evaluation, the worker concluded that Luisa needed specialized foster care and a therapeutic preschool program for her behavior problems and developmental delays. With help from mental health consultants and collaboration with teachers in the therapeutic preschool program, the Maldonados were able to provide appropriately specialized foster care.

Follow-up Evaluation. At a 1-year follow-up, the worker had Raymond and Maria Maldonado each complete a CBCL and two preschool teachers each complete a C-TRF. Although Luisa was now above the age range for the LDS, the worker asked the Maldonados to complete it in order to evaluate Luisa's language progress.

On both CBCL profiles and one C-TRF profile, the Emotionally Reactive syndrome was in the clinical range, but all other scales were in the normal range. Both foster parents rated the following items as *2: 21. Disturbed by any change in routine; 51. Shows panic for no good reason; 79. Rapid shifts between sadness and excitement; 82. Sudden changes in mood or feelings;* and *92. Upset by new people or situations.* The preschool teachers also rated some of these items as 2, plus item *38. Explosive and unpredictable behavior.*

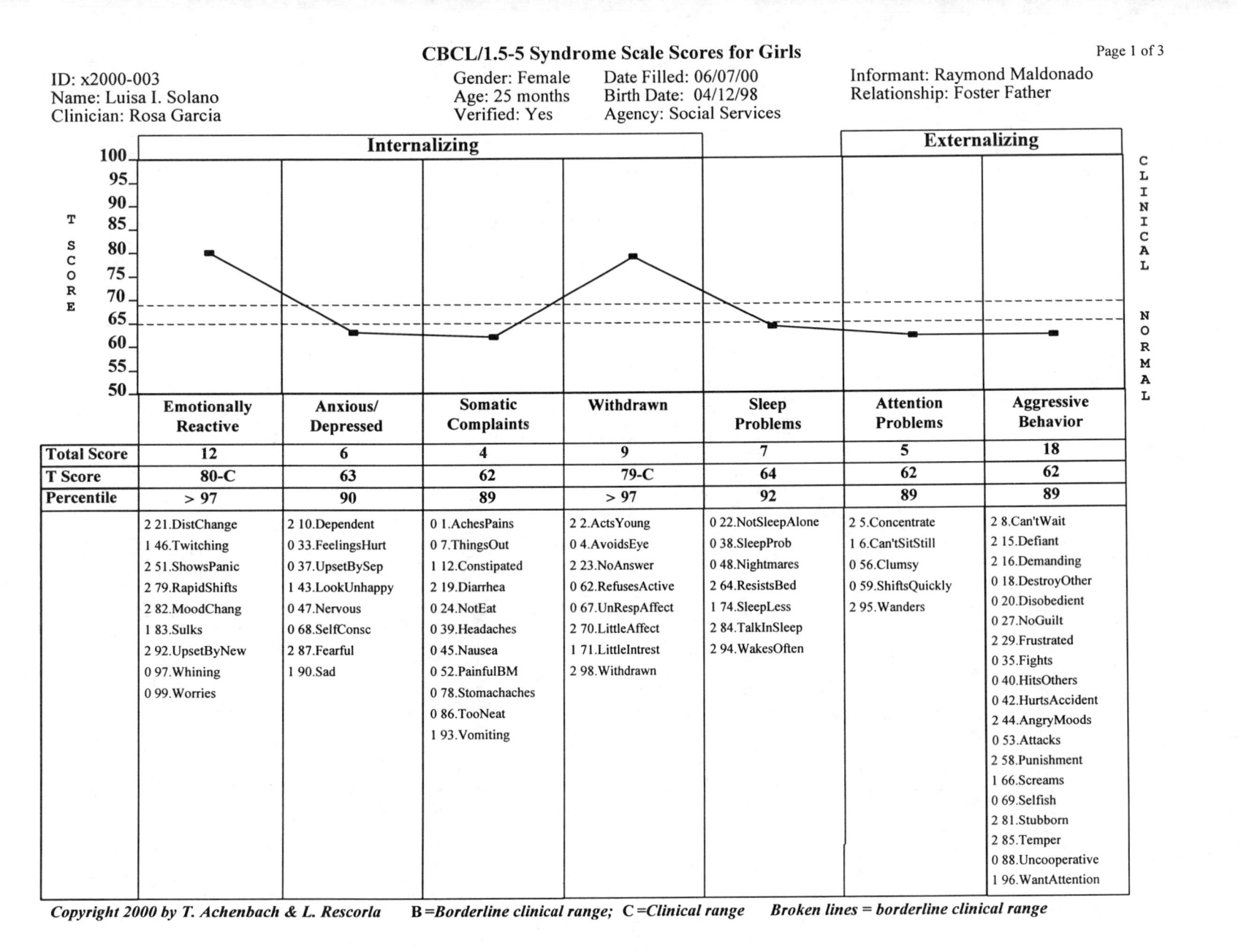

Figure 5-4. Syndromes profile scored for Luisa Solano from CBCL completed by her foster father.

According to the item and scale scores, which were amplified by comments written on the forms, it was apparent that Luisa had become happier and more sociable. However, she continued to be quite volatile, as indicated by her scores of 2 on the foregoing items and in the clinical range on the Emotionally Reactive syndrome. On the LDS, both foster parents reported examples of 4-word combinations and nearly 200 vocabulary words, indicating significant progress in language.

The worker concluded that the foster placement and the therapeutic preschool were working well, but that Luisa would continue to need special help for her intense emotional reactivity and mild to moderate developmental delays. If Luisa's emotional reactions continued to be so intense despite progress in other areas, an evaluation for a possible mood disorder and treatment with medication might be needed.

FORENSIC APPLICATIONS

Young children may become involved with the legal system when custody disputes arise, when concerns arise about children's living conditions, and when child abuse occurs or is suspected. In custody disputes, profiles scored from CBCLs completed by the contesting parents or other relevant adults can be compared to determine how each of them views the child. The C-TRF can also be used to determine how the child is viewed by daycare providers and teachers. If one respondent's report differs sharply from everything else that is known about the child, this could raise questions about the respondent's perceptions of the child.

Child Abuse

Forensic applications often involve questions of child abuse, but the implications of child abuse extend well beyond forensic applications. No single assessment procedure can infallibly detect all cases of either physical or sexual abuse. Furthermore, abuse may be only one of many factors affecting children's functioning. The possibility of abuse should be considered as one hypothesis for explaining problems reported on ASEBA forms. If abuse has occurred, the reported problems may be a function of the respondent's relationship to the child and involvement in or knowledge of abuse, as well as of the child's actual experience of abuse, preexisting characteristics of the child, and current strengths, stresses, and supports.

Comparisons of ASEBA forms from parents and other informants with data from other sources may reveal that a particular informant is minimizing or exaggerating a child's problems. If a suspected abuser reports many fewer problems than all other informants, for example, this might be evidence for the informant's involvement in abuse. On the other hand, if an informant reports far more problems than are indicated by other sources, this may suggest an effort to blame a suspected abuser.

Children receiving help to remedy the effects of abuse should be periodically reassessed to evaluate their progress. For example, ASEBA forms can be obtained at regular intervals, such as every 3 months, from parents, parent surrogates, and others who know the child well.

SUMMARY

In this chapter, we outlined applications of ASEBA forms to *practical decisions* about *particular* cases, groups, programs, policies, etc. The following guidelines were provided: *(a)* use ASEBA forms routinely; *(b)* obtain reports from multiple informants; *(c)* use ASEBA data to guide interviews; *(d)* use ASEBA data in the diagnostic process; and *(e)* readminister ASEBA forms at regular intervals to assess service delivery and outcomes. ASEBA forms can help in training people to work with preschoolers by having them complete ASEBA forms for comparison with data obtained from other sources and for evaluating changes in children who receive services.

We illustrated applications of ASEBA in mental health, educational, medical, child and family service, and forensic contexts. Issues arising from various aspects of diagnosis were discussed, including the need for broad approaches to diagnostic processes and diagnostic formulations. We also showed how ASEBA instruments can contribute to planning and accountability for services by providing standardized documentation of presenting problems and periodic reassessment of the course and outcome of problems. In addition, ASEBA instruments can be used to document the prevalence and distribution of each kind of problem in entire caseloads, to compare the caseloads of different services, to identify cases with good vs. poor outcomes for which alternative approaches may be needed, and as a basis for restructuring services.

Chapter 6
Construction of Syndrome and LDS Scales

Earlier chapters presented profiles of syndrome scales for scoring the preschool forms. In this chapter, we explain how the syndromes were derived and how the scales were constructed for scoring the syndromes on the profiles. Readers who are not interested in scale construction should feel free to skim or skip this chapter, as well as Chapter 7.

STATISTICAL DERIVATION OF THE SYNDROMES

Like other ASEBA forms, our preschool forms were developed both to document specific problems and to identify syndromes of co-occurring problems. We have used various statistical procedures to identify syndromes of co-occurring problems. The original Greek meaning of the word *syndrome* is *the act of running together*. Although "syndrome" is often equated with disease, its most general meaning is "a set of concurrent things" (Gove, 1971).

Some ASEBA syndromes may be shaped largely by genetic and other physical factors, whereas others may be shaped more by environmental stressors, learning, and other experiential factors. However, most syndromes are likely to be shaped by multiple factors. By identifying syndromes, we seek to help users evaluate children in terms of patterns of problems. We also seek to help users learn more about the causes, risk and protective factors, effective interventions, and outcomes for each pattern. In the following sections, we outline the statistical procedures used to derive the syndromes displayed on the current editions of our preschool profiles.

Factor Analysis of Item Scores

Factor analysis refers to a family of statistical methods for identifying patterns of co-occurring items. In factor analyzing the items of our preschool forms, we first computed correlations between the scores on each item and the scores on every other item. For example, in a large sample of children, we computed correlations between the 0-1-2 scores on item *1. Aches or pains* and the 0-1-2 scores on each of the other items of the CBCL/1½-5. Similarly, we computed correlations between the 0-1-2 scores on item *2. Acts too young for age* and the 0-1-2 scores on all the other items of the CBCL, and so on for each other item on the CBCL. This yielded a big matrix of correlations in which each correlation reflected the degree of association between 0-1-2 scores obtained by children on a pair of items.

As an example, if the correlation between item *1* and item *2* were +1.00, this would indicate that children who received high scores on item *1* always received high scores on item *2*. Likewise, children who received low scores on item *1* always received low scores on item *2*. On the other hand, if the correlation between item *1* and item *2* were .00, this would mean that there was no relation between scores on the two items. A correlation of .50 between item *1* and item *2* would indicate a moderate association between the items, meaning that children who received high scores on item *1* tended to receive relatively high scores on item *2*, but not uniformly so.

If you looked at each correlation, you could see the degree of association between every item and every other item. However, because there were 4,851 correlations among the 99 specific problem items of the CBCL/1½-5, you could not mentally identify patterns of co-occurrence among all the items. To identify patterns of co-occurring items, factor analytic methods apply mathematical algorithms to the matrix of correlations among the items. The output consists of "factors," which are sets of items whose scores tend to be mutually associated with each other. For example, factor analyses of the CBCL/1½-5 (and most other ASEBA forms) typically identify a set of co-occurring somatic complaints, such as aches, nausea, and vomiting. We designate such sets of co-occurring problems as "syndromes." Each syndrome consists of a set of problems that tend to occur together.

CBCL/1½-5 Samples

We factor analyzed CBCL/1½-5 scores for children from our 1999 National Survey (described later in this chapter), plus children assessed in mental health, special education, Head Start, preschool, and daycare settings. To maximize possibilities for identifying clinically important syndromes, we wished to exclude children for whom few problem items were endorsed. On the other hand, we wished to include children who had relatively high problem scores but who were not referred for mental health or special education services, as well as children who were referred for such services.

To accomplish these goals, we first identified the median Total Problems score in our 1999 National Survey sample to use as a criterion for relatively high problem scores. The median Total Problems score was 32 for boys and 30 for girls. From all our sources of completed CBCL/1½-5 forms, we then analyzed CBCL item scores for all children whose Total Problems scores were at or above the 1999 National Survey median (N = 922 boys and 806 girls). The sources of data included our 1999 National Survey, 5 other general population samples, and 19 clinical settings. The children resided in 40 U.S. states, 2 Canadian provinces, 3 Australian states, and Jamaica. Ethnicity was 59% white, 17% African descent, 9% Latino, and 15% mixed or other; mean socioeconomic status (SES) was 1.9, SD = 0.7, scored 1 = lower, 2 = middle, 3 = upper. The three SES categories were based on an updated version of Hollingshead's (1975) scale for occupations, where 1 = lowest and 9 = highest, scored for the parent having the higher status occupation. We grouped the Hollingshead scores into three categories as follows: 1.0-3.9 = lower, 4.0-6.9 = middle, 7.0-9.0 = upper. (We expanded the Hollingshead occupational codes to two digits by giving occupations that were not clearly scorable the mean of their most likely scores.) Mothers completed 88% of the forms, fathers completed 10%, and other adults completed 2%.

C-TRF Samples

To form C-TRF samples that included children from diverse sources who had relatively high Total Problems scores, we followed the same strategy as for the CBCL. That is, we selected from many sources C-TRFs that had Total Problems scores at or above the median of 14 found for C-TRFs in our 1999 National Survey sample. (Because there were only 219 C-TRFs in the National Survey sample, we based the median on both genders combined.) The resulting samples of 675 C-TRFs for boys and 438 for girls were drawn from our 1999 National Survey, 7 other general population samples, and 11 clinical settings. The children resided in 40 U.S. states, 1 Australian state, and 1 Dutch province. Ethnicity was 68% white, 20% African descent, 4% Latino, and 8% mixed or other; mean SES was 2.0, SD = 0.8; and 46% were completed by teachers, while 54% were completed by caregivers.

Items Analyzed

On the CBCL, all 99 specific items were reported for $\geq$5% of the factor analytic samples of each gender. On the C-TRF, five items were endorsed for < 5% of the factor analytic samples of each gender. With the percentage indicated in parentheses, the C-TRF items endorsed for < 5% of both genders were: *41. Holds his/her breath

(2.6% boys; 2.5% girls) and *57. Problems with eyes (without medical cause)* (1.2% boys; 2.1% girls). For boys only, the other low frequency items were: *39. Headaches (without known medical cause)* (4.4%); *45. Nausea, feels sick (without medical cause)* (4.1%); and *60. Rashes or other skin problems (without medical cause)* (2.8%). For girls only, the other low frequency items were: *14. Cruel to animals* (4.3%); *63. Repeatedly rocks head or body* (3.2%); and *93. Vomiting, throwing up (without medical cause)* (2.7%).

Because all the low frequency C-TRF items were endorsed for ≥5% of boys and girls on the CBCL and because our factor analyses tested similar syndrome structures for both forms, we retained these items for analysis. In our initial exploratory factor analyses, we used 0-1-2 scores for each item to compute Pearson correlations among all the items. However, to avoid the possible distorting effects of low frequency cells on correlations, our final analyses, which involved confirmatory methods, employed tetrachoric correlations. For these correlations, we dichotomized item scores to 0 vs. 1 + 2 and combined both genders, as specified later.

Factor-Analytic Methods

Because different factor-analytic approaches may produce different results, we used several approaches. These approaches included exploratory factor-analytic methodology (EFA), which seeks factors that will summarize the associations among problem items without testing specific models for the factor structure, and confirmatory factor-analytic methodology (CFA), which tests the fit between the data and particular measurement structures.

Separately for the CBCL and C-TRF, we performed exploratory Unweighted Least Squares (LS), Maximum Likelihood (ML), and Principal Components (PCA) analyses of Pearson correlations among items. We analyzed data for each gender separately and for both genders combined. The factor solutions were subjected to Varimax rotations to produce uncorrelated factors and to Oblimin rotations to allow correlations among factors. For each gender separately and for both genders combined, all methods identified 7 factors for the CBCL/1½-5, and 6 factors for the C-TRF.

We then applied Weighted Least Squares (WLS) analyses to the items comprising each of the 7 CBCL and 6 C-TRF factors to test the unidimensionality of candidate items identified in the previous analyses. To avoid statistical risks associated with low frequency cells, we applied the WLS analyses to tetrachoric correlations between item scores dichotomized as 0 vs. 1 and 2. To be retained as potential candidates for factors, items were required to meet the following criteria in the samples for both genders analyzed separately and together: *(a)* the item's factor loading had to be statistically significant at $p<.01$; *(b)* the loading had to exceed .20; and *(c)* the sign of the loading had to be positive.

Following the WLS analyses of each of the 7 CBCL and 6 C-TRF factors, we used WLS analyses of tetrachoric correlations of 0 vs. 1 and 2 item scores to obtain a correlated 7-factor solution for the CBCL and a correlated 6-factor solution for the C-TRF. We repeated these analyses until solutions with the following characteristics were achieved: *(a)* proper convergence; *(b)* no out-of-range parameter estimates; *(c)* reasonable model fit; *(d)* the same factor structure for each gender analyzed separately and together; *(e)* retention of items according to the three criteria stated earlier. The model restrictions included zero cross-loadings for all items and uncorrelated item residuals. In these analyses, we used CFA methodology in an exploratory manner, rather than seeking "confirmation" of factor structures.

Steps Specific to the C-TRF. In developing the syndrome structure for the C-TRF, we took the following additional steps:

1. For the C-TRF, factors that reflected oppositional-defiant and aggressive behavior were found to correlate >.90 in the correlated factor solutions for both genders separately and combined. We therefore combined the oppositional-defiant and aggressive items into a single factor.

2. A strong factor designated as Emotionally Reactive was found in all the CBCL analyses. CBCL items *51. Shows panic for no good reason* and *79. Rapid shifts between sadness and excitement*, which were not on the CBCL/2-3, both contributed to this factor with substantial loadings in analyses for boys, girls, and both genders combined (loadings = .62 to .81 for item *51*; .47 to .50 for item *79*). However, these items are not on the C-TRF. To determine whether a counterpart of the Emotionally Reactive syndrome could be found among the C-TRF counterparts of the CBCL items comprising this syndrome, we tested a 1-factor model for the C-TRF counterpart items. The resulting factor, plus the combined oppositional-defiant and aggressive behavior factor, were successfully integrated into the C-TRF factor structure. We then repeated the analyses until the previously listed characteristics *(a)—(e)* were achieved again.

Results of the Factor Analyses

The final steps of the factor analyses yielded models containing 7 correlated CBCL factors and 6 correlated C-TRF factors for each gender. Because there were no significant differences between factor structures for the boys vs. girls on either the CBCL or C-TRF, we based the final syndromes on the analyses of both genders combined (N = 1,728 CBCL and 1,113 C-TRF). The goodness-of-fit between the data and the models was evaluated with the Root Mean Square Error of Approximation (RMSEA; Browne & Cudek, 1993), which has been recommended as the best measure of fit (Loehlin, 1998). For both genders combined, the RMSEA was .06 for the CBCL and .07 for the C-TRF, which are both in the range of .03 to .07 generally considered to indicate good fit. The factor that was found for the CBCL but not the C-TRF comprised sleep-related problems that do not appear on the C-TRF. The items that loaded on the final versions of the factors were retained to define the syndromes for the CBCL and C-TRF. Table 6-1 displays the problem items of each syndrome common to both forms and the problem items of each syndrome that are specific to one of the two forms. The items of each syndrome common to both forms define the *cross-informant construct* of the syndrome.

CONSTRUCTION OF SYNDROME SCALES

The items shown in Table 6-1 comprise the syndrome scales displayed on the profiles that were illustrated in earlier chapters. A child's raw score on a syndrome scale is computed by summing the *1* and *2* scores circled on the CBCL or C-TRF items for that child. To help users evaluate a child's syndrome scale scores in relation to scores obtained by typical children, our profiles provide norms. We used data from the same samples to norm the syndrome scales, the Internalizing, Externalizing, and Total Problems scales, and the DSM-oriented scales. The normative samples are described in the following sections.

Normative Samples

To obtain normative data, we commissioned Temple University's Institute for Survey Research (ISR) to use its national sampling frame to have ASEBA child and adult forms completed for a national probability sample. Conducted from February, 1999, through January, 2000, our 1999 National Survey of Children, Youths, and Adults proceeded as follows:

Table 6-1
Items Defining the Preschool Cross-Informant Syndrome Constructs, plus Items Specific to the CBCL/1½-5 and C-TRF Syndrome Scales[a]

Emotionally Reactive
- 21. Disturbed by change
- 46. Twitches
- 82. Moody
- 83. Sulks
- 92. Upset by new
- 97. Whining
- 99. Worries

Specific to CBCL/1½-5
- 51. Panics[b]
- 79. Shifts between sadness and excitement[b]

Anxious/Depressed
- 10. Clings
- 33. Feelings hurt
- 37. Upset by separation
- 43. Looks unhappy
- 47. Nervous
- 68. Self-conscious
- 87. Fearful
- 90. Sad

Somatic Complaints
- 1. Aches
- 7. Can't stand things out of place
- 39. Headaches
- 45. Nausea
- 78. Stomach aches
- 86. Too concerned with neatness or cleanliness
- 93. Vomits

Specific to CBCL/1½-5
- 12. Constipated[b]
- 19. Diarrhea[b]
- 24. Doesn't eat well[b]
- 52. Painful b.m.[b]

Withdrawn
- 2. Acts too young
- 4. Avoids eye contact
- 23. Doesn't answer
- 62. Refuses active games
- 67. Unresponsive to affection
- 70. Little affection
- 71. Little interest
- 98. Withdrawn

Specific to C-TRF
- 12. Apathetic[c]
- 19. Daydreams[c]

Sleep Problems (CBCL/1½-5 only)
- 22. Doesn't want to sleep alone[b]
- 38. Trouble sleeping[b]
- 48. Nightmares[b]
- 64. Resists bed[b]
- 74. Sleeps little[b]
- 84. Talks, cries in sleep[b]
- 94. Wakes often[b]

Attention Problems
- 5. Can't concentrate
- 6. Can't sit still
- 56. Clumsy
- 59. Quickly shifts activity
- 95. Wanders away

Specific to C-TRF
- 24. Difficulty with directions[c]
- 48. Fails to carry out tasks[c]
- 51. Fidgets[c]
- 64. Inattentive[c]

Aggressive Behavior
- 8. Can't stand waiting
- 15. Defiant
- 16. Demands must be met
- 18. Destroys others' things
- 20. Disobedient
- 27. Lacks guilt
- 29. Easily frustrated
- 35. Fights
- 40. Hits others
- 42. Hurts accidentally
- 44. Angry moods
- 53. Attacks people
- 58. Punishment doesn't change behavior
- 66. Screams
- 69. Selfish
- 81. Stubborn
- 85. Temper
- 88. Uncooperative
- 96. Wants attention

Specific to C-TRF
- 14. Cruel to animals
- 17. Destroys own things
- 22. Mean[c]
- 28. Disturbs others[c]
- 74. Not liked[c]
- 84. Teases[c]

[a] Items are designated by the numbers they bear on the CBCL/1½-5 and C-TRF and summaries of their content.
[b] Not on C-TRF.
[c] Not on CBCL/1½-5.

1. ISR selected and trained interviewers who lived in 100 Primary Sampling Units (PSUs), which are areas chosen to be collectively representative of the 48 contiguous United States.

2. In each PSU, interviewers were initially assigned Listing Areas of approximately 150 households to visit in order to determine the age and gender of residents who were eligible for the Survey.

3. To be eligible, residents had to be at least 18 months old and to have no major physical or mental disabilities. For children to be eligible, a parent or guardian had to be available who spoke English.

4. After eligible residents were identified, candidate subjects were selected by stratified randomized procedures to produce the overall age distribution sought for the entire National Survey, with similar proportions of each gender at each age. No more than one candidate subject was selected in each household.

5. For children 18 through 71 months old, interviewers then contacted parents to arrange for interviews in which the CBCL was administered, followed by questions about the child's stressful experiences and referrals for mental health and special education services during the preceding 12 months. The parent was handed a copy of the CBCL to look at while the interviewer read each item and wrote the parent's answers on a second copy. Parents were also asked for permission to mail the C-TRF to their children's teachers or daycare providers. Each person who completed a CBCL or C-TRF received $10.

6. After completing interviews in their initial Listing Areas, interviewers were assigned additional Listing Areas.

7. Completed forms were sent to the ASEBA offices. ASEBA staff phoned respondents to verify that interviews had been conducted as reported by interviewers.

8. For the 781 eligible 18-71-month-olds identified in the initial household screening, the CBCL was completed for 738, yielding a completion rate of 94.4%. The 5.6% attrition was accounted for by parents who declined to participate, parents who agreed to participate but were unable to be interviewed at mutually convenient times, and interviews that were begun but not completed.

9. For the 277 18-71-month-olds who were currently attending daycare or preschool and whose parents granted permission to send the C-TRF, 219 completed C-TRFs were received, yielding a completion rate of 79.1%.

10. The final normative samples included children from 40 states.

Selection of Nonreferred Children for Norms

To provide a basis for evaluating individual children in relation to large samples of children who were not considered to have serious behavioral/emotional problems, we excluded from our National Survey sample all the children whose parents responded affirmatively to either of the following questions: *(a)* "In the past 12 months, has (child) received any mental health services from a mental health professional, such as a psychiatrist, psychologist, social worker, therapist, counselor, or any other mental health professional?" *(b)* "During the past 12 months, has (child) received any special educational services for learning, behavioral, emotional, or any other problems?"

CBCL/1½-5 Normative Sample. Based on the parents' reports of mental health and special education services, we excluded 38 (5.1%) of the 738 children whose parents completed the CBCL, leaving 700 nonreferred children whose data provided the norms for the CBCL scales. (In epidemiological terms, the nonreferred children would be considered a "healthy" sample.)

To determine whether we should construct separate norms for each gender or younger vs. older children, we performed gender x age (18-44 months vs. 45-71 months) analyses of variance (ANOVAs) on raw scores obtained by the 362 boys and 338 girls on all 15 CBCL scales (7 syndromes, Internalizing, Externalizing, Total Problems, 5 DSM-oriented scales). There was a significant gender effect only on the DSM-oriented Attention Deficit/Hyperactivity Problems scale, where the mean scores were 5.2 for boys vs. 4.7 for girls, $SD = 2.8, p \leq .01$. This one significant gender effect was less than the two effects expected to be significant at $p \leq .01$ by chance in 15 analyses, with a $p = .01$ protection level (Sakoda, Cohen, & Beall, 1954). (In the analyses for this *Manual*, we used $p \leq .01$ as our criterion for statistical significance, unless otherwise noted.)

Younger children obtained significantly higher scores on the empirically based Attention Problems and Aggressive Behavior syndrome, as well as on the DSM-oriented Attention Deficit/Hyperactivity Problems scale. These three age effects are more than the two expected by chance using a $p = .01$ protection level but equal to the three expected by chance using a .001 protection level.

Because the gender and age differences for nonreferred children were minimal, we constructed norms based on the combined sample of 700 boys and girls whose demographic characteristics are summarized in Table 6-2.

C-TRF Normative Sample. After excluding the 16 (7.3%) children whose parents responded affirmatively to the questions about mental health and special education services, completed C-TRFs remained for 95 boys and 108 girls in our National Survey. The difference between the 700 CBCL forms for nonreferred children and the 203 C-TRF forms reflected the fact that many children did not attend either daycare or preschool programs, parents of some did not consent to having the C-TRF completed, and some C-TRFs that were sent to daycare and preschool programs were not completed.

To augment the 1999 National Survey C-TRF sample, we combined it with the C-TRFs for American children in our 1997 C-TRF normative sample, yielding a total sample of 588 boys and 604 girls. The 1997 normative sample included 753 children from the National Institute of Child Health and Development (NICHD) Study of Early Child Care (NICHD Early Child Care Research Network, 1994). The children's mothers had been recruited for the NICHD study when they were giving birth in 31 hospitals located in 9 states. Mothers who agreed to participate were selected according to a sampling plan designed to reflect the economic, educational, and ethnic diversity of each catchment area. The mothers and their children were then reassessed periodically. The remaining C-TRFs from the 1997 normative sample were drawn from 14 daycare and preschool programs in 12 states. A gender x 1997 vs. 1999 sample ANOVA showed no significant difference between the 1997 vs. 1999 C-TRF Total Problems scores, $M = 21.7$ vs. 20.3, $p = .40$.

Gender x age ANOVAs of the 14 C-TRF scales (6 syndromes, Internalizing, Externalizing, Total Problems, 5 DSM-oriented scales) yielded significantly ($p \leq .01$) higher scores for younger children on the DSM-oriented Oppositional Defiant Problems scale and for boys on the Attention Problems and Aggressive Behavior syndromes, Externalizing, and DSM-oriented Pervasive Developmental Problems, Attention Deficit/Hyperactivity Problems, and Oppositional Defiant Problems scales. Because the six significant gender differences were considerably above the two expected by chance (Sakoda et al., 1954), we constructed separate C-TRF norms for each gender based on the 588 boys and 604 girls whose characteristics are summarized in Table 6-2.

ASSIGNING NORMALIZED T SCORES

The sums of *1* and *2* scores on the items of the syndrome scales provide continuous distributions of scores that indicate the degree to which problems are reported for a child on each scale. As detailed in Chapter 12, these raw scale scores are especially useful for statistical analyses because they directly reflect all variation that is possible on each scale. However, to help users see how a child's scores on each scale compare with the scores of the normative samples of peers, we assigned the normalized *T* scores that are displayed on the profiles shown in earlier chapters. The *T* scores provide users with standard scores for comparing a child's scale scores with the scores obtained by normative samples of peers. The *T* scores also help users compare a child's standing across all scales in order to quickly identify the scales where the child has relatively high vs. low scores, compared to peers.

The *T* score is a particular kind of standard score designed to provide a similar quantitative metric for scales that have different numbers of items and different distributions of scores. Normalized *T* scores are assigned to the raw scores of a scale according to the percentiles found for the raw scores in a relevant sample. For our preschool profiles, the scores obtained by children in our normative samples provided the basis for assigning *T* scores to particular raw scores on each scale. For example, on the CBCL Aggressive Behavior syndrome, we found that a raw score of 21 was at the 93rd percentile for the national normative sample. In other words, 93% of the children in the normative sample obtained a score of 21 or lower. According to the procedure for assigning *T* scores to raw scores (Abramowitz & Stegun, 1968), the 93rd percentile score should get a *T* score of 65. By looking at a CBCL hand-scored profile (e.g., in Figure 2-1), you can see that the raw score of 21 on the Aggressive Behavior syndrome is aligned with the *T* score of 65 on the right side of the profile. By looking at the left side of the profile, you can see that the 93rd percentile is also aligned with the raw score of 21 on the Aggressive Behavior syndrome, as well as with the *T* score of 65 on the right side of the profile.

For each syndrome scale, we computed the percentile for each raw score according to the procedure for "midpoint" percentiles specified by Crocker and Algina (1986, p. 439; illustrated for the CBCL/2-3 by Achenbach, 1992, p. 24). According to this procedure, a raw score that occupies a particular percentile of the cumulative frequency distribution is assumed to also occupy all the next lower percentiles down to the percentile occupied by the next lower raw score. To represent the range of percentiles occupied by a raw score, the raw score is assigned to the midpoint of the percentiles that it occupies. For example, if the raw score of 21 on the Aggressive Behavior syndrome scale occupied the 91st through 95th percentiles, it was assigned to the 93rd percentile, which is midway between the 91st and 95th percentiles. After computing the midpoint percentile for each raw score, we used the midpoint percentiles to assign normalized *T* scores from 51 to 70, based on Abramowitz and Stegun (1968).

Truncation of Lower *T* Scores at 50

On some syndromes, very few children obtained the lowest possible score of 0, which would indicate that no problems of the syndrome were reported for these children. For example, on the Aggressive Behavior syndrome, only 3.3% of children in the normative samples obtained a score of 0. On other syndromes, substantially more children obtained scores of 0,

Table 6-2
Demographic Characteristics of Normative Samples

	CBCL/1½-5	C-TRF
	N = 700	N = 1,192
SES[a]		
Upper	33%	47%
Middle	49%	43%
Lower	17%	10%
Mean Score	2.2	2.4
SD of Score	0.7	0.7
Ethnicity		
NonLatino White	56%	48%
African-American	21%	36%
Latino	13%	8%
Mixed or Other	10%	9%
Region		
Northeast	17%	29%
Midwest	22%	17%
South	40%	32%
West	21%	22%
Respondent		
Mother	76%	Caregiver 81%
Father	22%	Teacher 19%
Other	2%	

[a]SES was scored 1 = lower, 2 = middle, 3 = upper, based on an updated version of Hollingshead's (1975) 9-step scale for the occupation of the parent holding the higher status job: Hollingshead scores 1.0-3.9 = lower; 4.0-6.9 = middle; 7.0-9.0 = upper; we assigned 2-digit codes because occupations that were not clearly scorable were given the mean of their most likely scores.

such as 27.4% on the Somatic Complaints syndrome.

If we based *T* scores directly on midpoint percentiles, the lowest *T* score for the Aggressive Behavior syndrome scale would be 32, reflecting the fact that only 3.3% of the normative sample obtained a score of 0. By contrast, the lowest *T* score for the Somatic Complaints syndrome scale would be 44, reflecting the fact that 27.4% of the normative sample obtained a score of 0 on this syndrome. If these *T* scores were displayed on a profile for a child whose score was 0 on both syndromes, the *T* score of 44 might suggest that the child had considerably more problems on the Somatic Complaints syndrome than on the Aggressive Behavior syndrome, where the child's *T* score would be 32. This difference in *T* scores would mask the fact that the child really had no problems on either syndrome.

To avoid misleading impressions of this sort and to prevent users from over-interpreting small differences among scores that are all well within the normal range, we truncated the assignment of T scores for the syndrome scales, as suggested by Petersen, Kolen, and Hoover (1993) and as done for previous editions of the preschool forms (Achenbach, 1992, 1997). To equalize the starting points for all syndrome scales, we assigned a T score of 50 to raw scores that fell at midpoint percentiles ≤50. As an example, on the Somatic Complaints syndrome scale, scores of 0 and 1 for the normative sample were ≤50th percentile. We therefore assigned a T score of 50 to raw scores of 0 and 1. On the Aggressive Behavior syndrome scale, scores of 0 to 8 were all assigned a T score of 50, because they were all ≤50th percentile.

Assignment of a T score of 50 to several raw scores reduces differentiation among low scores. However, loss of this differentiation is of little clinical importance, because it involves differences that are all at the low end of the normal range. If users nevertheless wish to preserve differences at the low end of the normal range, they can focus on the raw scale scores. For statistical analyses, raw scores are usually preferable, because they directly reflect all differences among scores without the effects of truncation or other transformations.

Assigning T Scores Above 70 (98th Percentile)

Most children in the normative samples obtained scores that were well below the maximum possible on each syndrome scale. It was therefore impossible to base the highest T scores on percentiles, because the highest scores were spread over a tiny percentage of children in the normative samples. Because there were hardly any children in the normative samples on whom to base T scores above the 98th percentile, we assigned T scores from 71 to 100 in as many increments as there were remaining raw scores on the scale.

As an example, on the Aggressive Behavior syndrome scale, the raw score of 25 (occupying the 98th percentile) was assigned a T score of 70. Because there are 19 items on the scale, the maximum possible score is 38 (i.e., if a child received a score of 2 on all 19 items, the child's raw scale score would be 38.) There are 30 intervals from 71 to 100, but only 13 possible raw scores from 26 through 38. To assign T scores to the 13 raw scores, we divided 30 by 13. Because 30/13 = 2.3, T scores were assigned to raw scores in intervals of 2.3. Thus, a raw score of 26 was assigned a T score of 70 + 2.3 = 72.3, rounded off to 72. A raw score of 27 was assigned a T score of 72.3 + 2.3 = 74.6, rounded off to 75, and so on.

Because the Attention Problems syndrome had only three raw scores above the raw score of 7 that was assigned a T score of 70, assignment of T scores from 71 to 100 to only the three raw scores above 7 would have caused each increment of one raw score to produce an increment of 10 T scores. To avoid having such large increments in T scores, we truncated the Attention Problems syndrome scale at a T score of 80. Dividing the 10 T scores from 71 to 80 into three intervals resulted in assigning the T scores of 73, 77, and 80 to the raw scores of 8, 9, and 10 respectively.

Mean T Scores

Because of the skewed raw score distributions and truncation of low scores at $T = 50$, the mean T scores of the syndrome scales are above 50 and their standard deviations are below 10 in the normative samples, as shown in Appendix C. The T scores of the syndrome scales thus deviate from the mean of 50 and standard deviation of 10 expected when normal distributions are transformed directly into T scores.

Users should also keep in mind that the

means and standard deviations of the syndrome scales may vary from one sample of children to another. In particular, the means and standard deviations for samples of children referred for mental health services are typically higher than for nonreferred children. An example of this can be seen in Appendix D, which displays means and standard deviations for scale scores obtained by referred and nonreferred children.

Figure 6-1 summarizes the steps in constructing cross-informant syndromes for the preschool forms.

BORDERLINE AND CLINICAL RANGES

As can be seen on the profiles shown in previous chapters, broken lines are printed across the syndrome profiles at T scores of 65 and 69 (93rd and 97th percentiles). Scores from 65 to 69 are considered to be in the borderline clinical range, because they are high enough to be of concern but not so high as to be so clearly deviant as those in the clinical range (T scores ≥70). As reported in Chapter 9, scores in the borderline and clinical ranges significantly discriminate between children who are referred for mental health or special education services for behavioral/emotional problems and children who are not referred.

Because scores on our scales are quantitative measures of the number and degree of problems reported for a child, the scores do not imply that there are categorical differences on these scales between children who are "sick" vs. "well." Instead, the borderline and clinical ranges help users identify groups of scores that are of enough concern to warrant consideration of children for professional help. Users may choose to apply higher or lower cutpoints for their own clinical or research purposes. If users wish to dichotomously classify children's scores as being clearly in the normal range vs. high enough to warrant concern, we suggest using T scores below 65 to designate the normal range and T scores ≥ 65 to designate the clinical range.

Readers familiar with the 1992 edition of the CBCL/2-3 profile and the 1997 edition of the C-TRF profile may recall that the borderline range on those profiles spanned from T = 67 to T = 70. We have lowered the borderline range to T scores of 65 to 69, because clinicians and researchers have suggested that this will increase the proportion of impaired children identified.

NORMS FOR DSM-ORIENTED SCALES

The DSM-oriented scales described in Chapter 4 were normed using the same procedures and data described in the preceding sections for our syndrome scales. That is, we used the normative samples of nonreferred children to form distributions of raw scores for each DSM-oriented scale. Because the gender differences on the CBCL DSM-oriented scales were negligible, we constructed CBCL norms for both genders combined. However, we constructed gender-specific norms for the C-TRF, where more DSM-oriented scales showed significant gender differences. We then assigned T scores to each raw score of each DSM-oriented scale according to the same procedure as for the syndrome scales.

As on the syndrome scales, we also defined the borderline clinical range as T scores of 65 to 69 on each DSM scale, with the clinical range being defined by T scores ≥70. Because the Attention Deficit/Hyperactivity Problems and Oppositional Defiant Problems scales had very few possible scores above the 98th percentile, we truncated the T scores on these scales below the score of 100 that is the upper limit of most of the scales.

NORMS FOR THE LDS

The normative sample consisted of the 278 children for whom the LDS was completed in

CONSTRUCTION OF SYNDROME AND LDS SCALES

```
       CBCL/1½-5              C-TRF
      Boys   Girls          Boys   Girls
      [1½-5 | 1½-5]         [1½-5 | 1½-5]
```

1. From 1999 National Survey & multiple clinical & nonclinical sources, select children whose total problem scores were ≥ median of National Survey sample.

2. Via exploratory & confirmatory factor-analytic methods, identify syndromes for each gender on each form.

3. Compare syndromes from CBCL/1½-5 & C-TRF. Re-factor C-TRF to *(a)* combine highly correlated oppositional & aggressive factors, & *(b)* test for counterpart of CBCL/1½-5 Emotionally Reactive factor.

4. Define *cross-informant syndrome constructs* in terms of items of each syndrome that are common to both forms.

5. Construct instrument-specific syndrome scales for CBCL/1½-5 & C-TRF profiles.

6. Norm each syndrome scale from normative sample for CBCL/1½-5 & C-TRF.

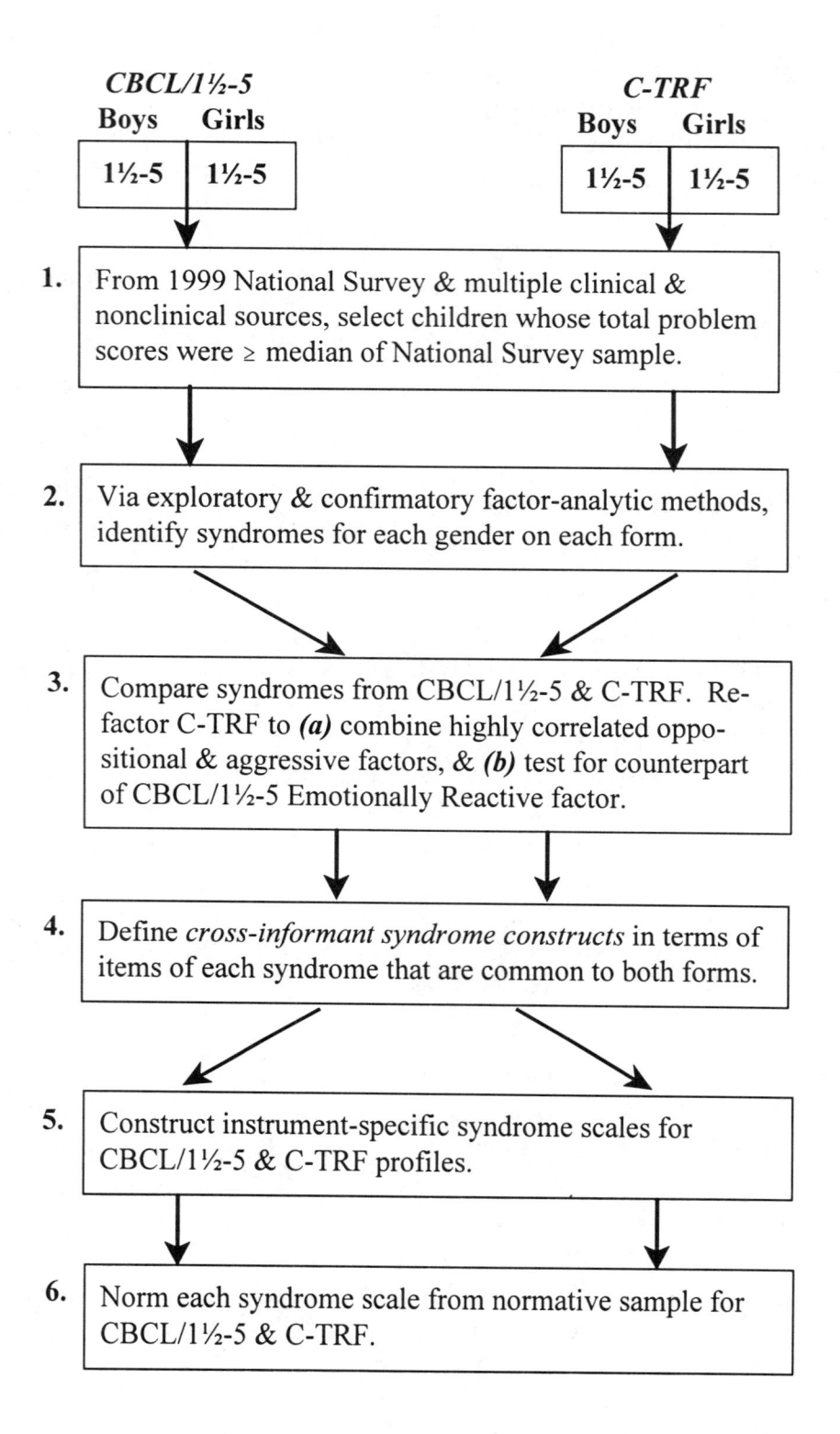

Figure 6-1. Summary of steps in constructing the cross-informant syndrome scales for the ASEBA preschool forms.

the 1999 National Survey. The sample was divided into three age brackets, with approximately equal numbers of subjects of each gender at ages 18-23 months (49 boys and 52 girls); 24-29 months (40 boys and 50 girls); and 30-35 months (46 boys and 41 girls).

Length of Phrases

Because few children below 24 months were reported to use 2-word phrases, we did not construct norms for average phrase length below 24 months. The average phrase length did not differ significantly for boys vs. girls. We therefore computed the cumulative frequency distributions in the 24-29 and 30-35-month brackets for both genders combined. Because the average length of phrases increased slowly and because the range within each age bracket was small, the LDS scoring form displays scores in 10-percentile increments within the 24-29 and 30-35-month age brackets.

For example, the 50th percentile phrase lengths are 3.01 to 3.20 words at ages 24-29 months. Phrase lengths ≤20th percentile suggest delayed phrase development.

Vocabulary Scores

As would be expected, vocabulary scores increased significantly across the three age brackets. Girls had significantly higher vocabulary scores in all three age groups. Consequently, we constructed gender-specific norms for vocabulary scores.

To construct norms, we computed cumulative frequency distributions of vocabulary scores for each gender in each age bracket. The hand-scoring form for the LDS (Figure 2-2) displays the vocabulary scores in 5-percentile increments for each gender within each age bracket. For example, at 18-23 months the 50th percentile vocabulary scores are 59-68 words for boys and 94-102 words for girls. At 24-29 months, the 50th percentile scores are 144-161 words for boys and 215-224 words for girls. Vocabulary scores ≤15th percentile suggest delayed vocabulary development.

SUMMARY

We constructed the preschool syndrome scales by applying exploratory and confirmatory factor-analytic methodology to the preschool forms for children whose Total Problems scores were at or above the median of scores obtained by our 1999 National Survey sample of preschoolers. Analyses were done for both genders separately and combined. Because there were no significant differences between factor structures for boys vs. girls, we retained factors derived from both genders combined. The following six syndrome scales were constructed for both preschool forms: *Aggressive Behavior, Anxious/Depressed, Attention Problems, Emotionally Reactive, Somatic Complaints*, and *Withdrawn*. A syndrome scale designated as *Sleep Problems* was constructed only for the CBCL/1½-5, because the C-TRF does not have sleep problems items.

Norms were constructed from the distributions of syndrome scores obtained by large representative samples of children. To provide a standard metric for similarly comparing children with peers across all syndromes and for comparing a child's standing on each syndrome with the child's standing on each other syndrome, we assigned normalized *T* scores to raw scores on each syndrome scale. To prevent over-interpretation of differences among low scores that are well within the normal range, we assigned a *T* score of 50 to all raw scores that were at or below approximately the 50th percentile of the normative sample. We assigned *T* scores from 51 to 70 according to the percentiles of the normative samples. We then assigned *T* scores from 71 to 100 in relation to equal intervals of the raw scores that were above the 98th percentile in the normative sample.

A borderline clinical range is demarcated by T scores of 65 (93rd percentile) to 69 (97th percentile). T scores ≥70 (≥98th percentile) are in the clinical range. Norms and T scores were constructed in the same way for the DSM-oriented scales. Because some syndrome and DSM-oriented scales had few raw scores above the 98th percentile, these scales terminate below the T score of 100 that is the upper limit for most of the scales.

LDS scores for the average length of phrases and vocabulary are displayed in terms of percentiles for children within particular age brackets. Phrase-length scores ≤20th percentile and vocabulary scores ≤15th percentile suggest delayed language development.

Chapter 7
Internalizing, Externalizing, and Total Problems Scales

In Figure 2-1 and other figures that display the profiles of syndromes, you can see that four syndromes on the left side of the profile are grouped under the heading *Internalizing*, whereas two syndromes on the right side of the profile are grouped under the heading *Externalizing*. These groupings of syndromes reflect a distinction that has been found for decades in numerous multivariate analyses of children's behavioral/emotional problems. The two groupings of problems were designated as "Personality Problems vs. Conduct Problems" by Peterson (1961); "Internalizing vs. Externalizing" by Achenbach (1965, 1966); "Inhibition vs. Aggression" by Miller (1967); and "Overcontrolled vs. Undercontrolled" by Achenbach and Edelbrock (1978).

The distinction that we call "Internalizing vs. Externalizing" represents more global groupings of problems than do the individual syndromes. The Internalizing grouping mainly reflects problems within the self, such as emotional reactivity, anxiety, depression, somatic complaints without known medical cause, and withdrawal from social contacts. The Externalizing grouping, by contrast, represents conflicts with other people and with their expectations for children's behavior. These global groupings may be useful for planning management of children who have problems mainly from one grouping or the other, although many children have both kinds of problems.

The Internalizing vs. Externalizing distinction represents a level in a hierarchy of the scores that are obtained from the preschool forms. The lowest level in the hierarchy comprises the specific problem items on the ASEBA forms. Each problem is scored 0-1-2 to reflect quite specific aspects of behavioral/emotional functioning. The next level comprises the syndrome scales, each of which represents a pattern of co-occurring behavioral/emotional problems, as identified by the factor analyses described in Chapter 6. The next level comprises the Internalizing and Externalizing Scales. The highest level in the hierarchy comprises the Total Problems scale, which is the sum of scores on all the problem items of a form. In this chapter, we describe how the Internalizing and Externalizing groupings were derived and how T scores were assigned to the Internalizing, Externalizing, and Total Problems scales.

DERIVATION OF INTERNALIZING AND EXTERNALIZING GROUPINGS OF SYNDROMES

To identify patterns of associations among the syndromes, we performed Unweighted Least Squares (ULS) factor analyses of correlations between syndrome scores obtained by the children whose item scores were used to derive the syndromes. As described in Chapter 6, these children came from many clinical and nonclinical sources, and obtained Total Problems scores that were at or above the median of our 1999 National Survey sample.

Factor analyses of items to derive scales, such as our syndrome scales, are known as *first-order factor analyses*. When the correlations among such factorially derived scales are in turn factor analyzed, this is known as *second-order factor analysis*. The ULS second-order factor analyses were applied to Pearson correlations among raw scale scores for the seven CBCL/1½-5 syndromes, separately for the factor-analytic samples of 922 boys and 806 girls described in Chapter 6. The 2-factor ULS solutions were then subjected to oblimin rotations with Kaiser normalization. We performed similar analyses on the six C-TRF syndromes, separately for the factor-analytic samples of 675 boys and 438 girls described in Chapter 6.

For both genders on both forms, the Aggressive Behavior and Attention Problems syndromes had their highest loadings on one factor, which we designated as *Externalizing*. The Emotionally Reactive, Anxious/Depressed, Somatic Complaints, and Withdrawn syndromes had their highest loadings on the other factor, which we designated as *Internalizing*. The Sleep Problems syndrome, which is scored only for the CBCL/1½-5, had low loadings on both factors.

Arrangement of Internalizing and Externalizing Syndromes on Profiles

Following the procedure used for previous editions of ASEBA profiles (e.g., Achenbach, 1997), we arranged syndromes across the profiles according to their mean loadings on the Internalizing and Externalizing factors, starting on the left with the syndrome that loaded highest on the Internalizing factor and ending on the right with the syndrome that loaded highest on the Externalizing factor.

From the four second-order analyses (each gender on each form), we averaged the loadings obtained by each syndrome on the factor on which it loaded highest. Across the four second-order analyses, the mean loadings on the Internalizing factor were: Emotionally Reactive = .81; Anxious/Depressed = .61; Somatic Complaints = .60; and Withdrawn = .54. The mean loadings on the Externalizing factor were: Attention Problems = .67; and Aggressive Behavior = .75. On the CBCL/1½-5 profile, the Sleep Problems syndrome, which did not load highly on either the Internalizing or Externalizing factor, is placed between the Withdrawn and Attention Problems syndromes.

ASSIGNMENT OF INTERNALIZING, EXTERNALIZING, AND TOTAL PROBLEMS *T* SCORES

The Total Problems scale for each form consists of the sum of the *1* and *2* scores on the 99 specific problem items of the form, plus the highest score (*1* or *2*) for any problems written by the respondent in the spaces for the open-ended item *100*. Item *100* provides three spaces for adding problems that are not listed elsewhere. However, only the highest score for added items is included in order to limit the effects of idiosyncratic problems on the Total Problems score.

To provide norm-referenced scores for the Internalizing, Externalizing, and Total Problems scales, we summed the scores obtained on the items of each scale by the normative samples described in Chapter 6. We then computed midpoint percentiles according to the procedure specified by Crocker and Algina (1986, p. 439). Next, we used the procedure provided by Abramowitz and Stegun (1968) to assign normalized *T* scores, as described in Chapter 6 for the syndrome scales but with the following differences:

1. There are more problem items on the Internalizing, Externalizing, and Total Problems scales than on any syndrome scale, and at least some of the problems are reported for most children. Consequently, relatively few children in our normative samples obtained extremely low scores. It was therefore unnecessary to truncate the *T* scores at 50, as we did for the syndrome scales. Instead, we based normalized *T* scores directly on midpoint percentiles of the Internalizing, Externalizing, and Total Problems scores obtained by our normative samples, up to the 98th percentile (*T* = 70).

2. No children in either our normative or clinical samples obtained Internalizing, Externalizing, or Total Problems scores close to the maximum scores possible on these scales. If we followed the same procedure as for the syndrome scales (described in Chapter 6), we would have compressed the scores actually obtained into a narrow range of T scores. We would also have assigned a relatively broad range of T scores to raw scores obtained by few or no children. To enable the upper T scores to reflect differences among the raw scores that are most likely to occur, we did the following: *(a)* separately for Internalizing, Externalizing, and Total Problems, we identified the five highest scores obtained by children in all our samples; *(b)* we computed the mean of the five highest scores on each scale (because we used gender-specific T scores for the C-TRF, we computed the mean of the five highest C-TRF scores separately for each gender); *(c)* we assigned a T score of 89 to the mean of the five highest raw scores on each scale; *(d)* we assigned T scores in equal intervals to the raw scores between those that had been assigned T scores of 70 and 89; *(e)* we then assigned T scores in equal intervals to the raw scores that were above those that had been assigned $T = 89$, up to $T = 100$.

The T score assigned to each Internalizing, Externalizing, and Total Problems raw score is displayed in a box to the right of the hand-scored profile and is printed out by the computer-scoring program. On hand-scored profiles, you can identify the mean of the five highest scores found on each scale by looking at the raw score that was assigned a T score of 89. As shown in Appendix B, the mean T scores for the Internalizing, Externalizing, and Total Problems scales are close to 50, and their standard deviations are close to 10 in our normative samples.

NORMAL, BORDERLINE, AND CLINICAL RANGES

To test the discriminative efficiency of various cutpoints on the Internalizing, Externalizing, and Total Problems scales, we used Receiver Operating Characteristics (ROC) analyses (Swets & Pickett, 1982). We did this by comparing the distributions of scale scores obtained by the demographically similar referred and nonreferred children described in Chapter 8. We identified a range of scores where the differences between the cumulative percents of referred and nonreferred children were greatest. That is, we computed the difference between the cumulative percent of referred children who obtained all scores up to a particular score and the cumulative percent of nonreferred children who obtained all scores above that same score. We thus sought the score that minimized the percent of referred children below it and nonreferred children above it. This score was the most efficient cutpoint, in terms of minimizing *false negatives* (referred children scoring in the normal range), plus *false positives* (nonreferred children scoring in the clinical range).

Our analyses of the Internalizing, Externalizing, and Total Problems scales on most ASEBA forms have shown that the most accurate cutpoints for discriminating between referred and nonreferred children are at about the 80th to the 84th percentiles of the normative samples. For consistency with the Internalizing, Externalizing, and Total Problems cutpoints on other ASEBA forms, we set the borderline clinical range at T scores of 60 through 63 (approximately the 83rd through the 90th percentiles), and the clinical range at $T \geq 64$.

The reason for selecting lower (less conservative) cutpoints on these scales than the borderline T scores of 65 through 69 and clinical range ≥ 70 on the syndrome scales is that the Internalizing, Externalizing, and Total Problems scales encompass more numerous and diverse problems than any of the syndrome scales. Because the syndrome scales comprise smaller, more homogeneous sets of problems, we believe that higher syndrome scores relative to the norms should be required to conclude that professional help is needed. However, because all our scales reflect quantitative variations in reported problems, users can choose their own cutpoints for all scales. For dichotomous discrimination between deviant and nondeviant scores, the borderline clinical range can be combined with the clinical range by classifying T scores ≥ 60 as deviant on the Internalizing, Externalizing, and Total Problems scales.

RELATIONS BETWEEN INTERNALIZING AND EXTERNALIZING SCORES

The Internalizing and Externalizing groupings each reflect empirical associations among a subset of syndromes. The Internalizing vs. Externalizing problems are not mutually exclusive, however, because some children may have both kinds of problems. In many samples, positive correlations are found between Internalizing and Externalizing scores. As shown in Appendix E, the mean correlation between Internalizing and Externalizing scores for referred and nonreferred children on the CBCL/1½-5 and C-TRF was .50 (computed by Fisher's z transformation). This reflects the fact that children who have very high problem scores in one of the two areas also tend to have at least above-average scores in the other area as well. Conversely, children who have very low scores in one area also tend to have relatively low scores in the other area.

Despite the positive associations between Internalizing and Externalizing scores found in broad samples, some children's problems are primarily Internalizing, whereas other children's problems are primarily Externalizing. This is analogous to the relation between Verbal IQ and Performance IQ on the Wechsler intelligence tests: In most samples of children, there is a positive correlation between the Wechsler Verbal IQ and Performance IQ (e.g., Wechsler, 1989). Nevertheless, some children have much higher Verbal than Performance IQs or vice versa. Children who have much higher Verbal than Performance IQs may differ in other important ways from those who show the opposite pattern.

Like large differences between Verbal vs. Performance IQs, large differences between Internalizing vs. Externalizing scores may be associated with other important differences, as has been found in numerous studies (e.g., Achenbach, 1966; Compas, Phares, Banez, & Howell, 1991; Ferdinand, Verhulst, & Wiznitzer, 1995; Keenan, Shaw, Delliquadri, Giovannelli, & Walsh, 1998; McConaughy, Achenbach, & Gent, 1988; Mesman & Koot, 2000; Zahn-Waxler, Schmitz, Fulker, Robinson, & Emde, 1996).

Distinguishing Between Internalizing and Externalizing Patterns

Users may wish to distinguish between children whose reported problems are primarily from the Internalizing vs. Externalizing groupings. Such distinctions may be clinically useful for choosing approaches to interventions and for identifying groups of children with similar problems for assignment to a particular intervention. Such distinctions may also be useful for testing hypotheses about differences in etiology, responsiveness to particular treatments, reasons for relations among syndromes, and long-term outcomes.

The specific criteria for distinguishing between children having primarily Internalizing vs. Externalizing problems should be based on the user's aims and the size and nature of the available sample. The criteria chosen for distinguishing between Internalizing and Externalizing patterns will affect the proportion of a sample that can be classified, the homogeneity of the resulting groups, and the associations that may be found between the Internalizing vs. Externalizing classification and other variables. Very stringent criteria, for example, will result in few children being classified as having primarily Internalizing vs. Externalizing problems. But stringent criteria will also yield relatively pure groups who are likely to differ more on other variables than would less pure Internalizing and Externalizing groups.

The trade-offs between stringency of criteria, number of children classified, and degree of association with other variables must be weighed by users when they choose criteria for their own purposes. However, as a general guideline, we suggest that children be classified as having primarily Internalizing vs. Externalizing problems only if *(a)* their Total Problems T score is ≥ 60, and *(b)* the difference between their Internalizing and Externalizing T score is at least 10 points on at least one preschool form or at least 5 points on both the CBCL/1½-5 and C-TRF. The larger the difference between T scores and the more consistent the difference in ratings by multiple informants, the more distinctive the Internalizing and Externalizing groups will be.

SUMMARY

On the preschool profiles, the Emotionally Reactive, Anxious/Depressed, Somatic Complaints, and Withdrawn syndromes are displayed under the heading *Internalizing* on the left. The Attention Problems and Aggressive Behavior syndromes are displayed under the heading *Externalizing* on the right side of the profile. The Internalizing and Externalizing groupings of syndromes were identified by performing second-order factor analyses of the syndrome scales, separately for children of each gender scored on each form. Averaged across all four analyses, the four syndromes identified as Internalizing had mean loadings of .54 to .81 on one second-order factor, while the two syndromes identified as Externalizing had mean loadings of .67 and .75 on the other second-order factor. Because the CBCL/1½-5 Sleep Problems syndrome had low loadings on both second-order factors, we did not assign it to either grouping.

Children's Internalizing raw scores are computed by summing their raw scores on the four Internalizing syndromes, while their Externalizing raw scores are computed by summing their raw scores on the two Externalizing syndromes. The Total Problems scale on each form consists of the sum of all 99 specific items on the form, plus the highest score (1 or 2) given to any additional problems entered on the open-ended item *100*.

Normalized T scores were assigned to the Internalizing, Externalizing, and Total Problems scales according to the procedure described in Chapter 6 for the syndromes, with two differences: *(a)* The lower scores were not truncated at $T = 50$; and *(b)* on each scale, the mean of the five highest scores in the clinical samples was assigned a T score of 89, with raw scores above this point being assigned T scores of 90 to 100 in equal intervals.

The relations between Internalizing and Externalizing scales are analogous to the relations between Verbal and Performance IQs. That is, although the Internalizing and Externalizing scales comprise different kinds of problems, they are not mutually exclusive. In typical samples of children, Internalizing scores tend to correlate positively with Externalizing scores, because children who have very high scores on one scale tend to have at least above average scores on the other scale as well. Nevertheless, children who have much higher Internalizing than Externalizing scores may differ in important ways from children who show the opposite pattern. Guidelines were provided for distinguishing between children who show relatively large differences between their Internalizing vs. Externalizing scores.

Chapter 8
Reliability, Cross-Informant Agreement, and Stability

Reliability refers to agreement between repeated assessments of phenomena when the phenomena themselves remain constant. When rating instruments such as the ASEBA forms are self-administered, it is important to know the degree to which the same informants provide the same scores over periods when the children's behavior is not expected to change, i.e., the degree of *test-retest reliability*. In this chapter, we first present the test-retest reliability obtained when ASEBA preschool forms were completed twice over intervals of about a week.

Beside reliability, it is also helpful to know the degree of *cross-informant agreement* between scores from different informants and the degree of *stability* in scores over periods long enough that the children's behavior may change significantly. Cross-informant agreement and long-term stability are not expected to be as high as test-retest reliability, because reliability involves agreement between assessments of the *same* phenomena. Ratings by different informants, on the other hand, are based on somewhat different samples of children's behavior. Analogously, the same informants re-rating children's behavior at long intervals are likely to see different behavior during different periods. Findings for cross-informant agreement and long-term stability are therefore presented separately from findings for reliability.

An additional property of scales is their *internal consistency*. This refers to the correlation between half of a scale's items and the other half of its items. Although internal consistency is sometimes referred to as "split-half reliability," it cannot tell us the degree to which a scale will produce the same results over different occasions when the target phenomena are expected to remain constant. Furthermore, some scales with relatively low internal consistency may be more *valid* than some scales with very high internal consistency.

As an example, if a scale consists of 20 versions of the same question, it should produce very high internal consistency, because respondents should give similar answers to the 20 versions of the question. However, such a scale would usually be less valid than a scale that uses 20 different questions to assess the same phenomenon. Because each of the 20 different questions is likely to tap different aspects of the target phenomenon and to be subject to different errors of measurement, the 20 different questions are likely to provide better measurement despite lower internal consistency than a scale that uses 20 versions of a single question.

Our syndrome scales were derived from factor analyses of the correlations among items. The composition of the scales is therefore based on internal consistency among certain subsets of items. Nevertheless, because some users may wish to know the degree of internal consistency of our scales, Cronbach's *alpha* (1951) is displayed for each scale in Appendix D. *Alpha* represents the mean of the correlations between all possible sets of half the items comprising a scale. *Alpha* tends to be directly related to the length of the scale, because half the items of a short scale provide a less stable measure than half the items of a long scale.

TEST-RETEST RELIABILITY OF SCALE SCORES

CBCL and C-TRF

To assess reliability in both the rank ordering and magnitude of scale scores, we computed test-retest Pearson correlations (*r*s) and *t* tests of differences between mothers' CBCL ratings of 68 nonreferred children on two occasions at a mean interval of 8 days. Forty-one of the children were from a Massachusetts general population sample, 20 were from a longitudinal study of children living in Vermont and northern New York, and 7 were from a preschool in Pennsylvania. Similar analyses were performed on caregiver and teacher C-TRF ratings of 59 children at a mean interval of 8 days. Twenty of the children attended a preschool in Vermont, while 39 attended pre-schools in The Netherlands.

As Table 8-1 shows, reliability was high for most scales, with most test-retest rs being in the .80s and .90s. The Total Problems r was .90 on the CBCL and .88 on the C-TRF. Across all scales, the mean r was .85 on the CBCL and .81 on the C-TRF. (All mean rs were computed by Fisher's z transformation.)

Test-Retest Attenuation. There were significant ($p < .01$) declines in scores on the problem scales that are marked with superscript a in Table 8-1. Two of the significant declines would be expected by chance in the number of comparisons that were made, using a $p < .01$ protection level (Sakoda, Cohen, & Beall, 1954). Superscript b indicates the differences that were most likely to be significant by chance, because they yielded the smallest t values.

The tendency for problem scores to decline over brief test-retest intervals is called a "practice effect" (Milich, Roberts, Loney, & Caputo, 1980) and a "test-retest attenuation effect." It has been found in many rating scales (e.g., Evans, 1975; Miller, Hampe, Barrett, & Noble, 1972). It has also been found in structured psychiatric interviews of children (Edelbrock, Costello, Dulcan, Kalas, & Conover, 1985) and adults (Robins, 1985). The declines in ASEBA problem scores were small, accounting for a mean of 0.9% of the variance on the CBCL and 1% on the C-TRF. These are very small effects according to Cohen (1988), who defined small effect sizes in t tests as ranging from 1% to 5.9% of the variance.

As reported later in the chapter, problem scores do not typically decline significantly for nonreferred children over longer periods, such as 3 to 12 months. Because assessment decisions are unlikely to be based on readministrations of rating forms over very brief periods, the small short-term declines in problem scores are unlikely to be of much practical importance. To evaluate a child's score relative to the ASEBA norms, the child's initial ASEBA ratings should be used, as was done in obtaining the normative data. If later reassessments are done to evaluate the effects of interventions on ASEBA scores or other measures, it is always advisable to have control groups that did not receive the intervention being evaluated.

If individual children are reassessed, it is advisable to allow at least 1 month between assessments, both to minimize possible "test-retest attenuation effects" and to allow time for behavioral changes to occur and become apparent to raters. If reassessment intervals shorter than 2 months are used, raters should be instructed to use the same rating period at each interval, rather than the standard 2-month period specified on the ASEBA preschool forms. For example, if children are to be reassessed over a 1-month interval, users should instruct raters to base their ratings on a 1-month period for both their initial and reassessment ratings in order to avoid allowing differences in lengths of the rating periods to be confounded with differences between the initial and reassessment scores. Differences in rating periods such as 1 versus 2 months are not likely to produce large differences in scale scores. Nevertheless, the standard 2-month rating period may pick up a few more reports of low frequency behaviors than shorter periods would.

Table 8-1
Test-Retest Reliabilities of Scale Scores

Scale	CBCL 8-Day r	C-TRF 8-Day r
	$N = 68$	$N = 59$
Syndromes		
Emotionally Reactive	.87	.72
Anxious/Depressed	.68	.68
Somatic Complaints	.84[a,b]	.91
Withdrawn	.80	.77[a]
Sleep Problems	.92	NA
Attention Problems	.78	.84[a]
Aggressive Behavior	.87[a]	.89[a]
Internalizing	.90[a]	.77
Externalizing	.87[a]	.89[a]
Total Problems	.90[a]	.88[a]
DSM-Oriented Scales		
Affective Problems	.79	.76
Anxiety Problems	.85[a,b]	.57
Pervasive Developmental Problems	.86	.83[a,b]
Attention Deficit/Hyperactivity Problems	.74[a]	.79[a,b]
Oppositional Defiant Problems	.87	.87
Mean r	.85	.81

Note: All Pearson *r*s were significant at $p < .01$. Mean *r*s were computed by *z* transformation.

[a] Time 1 > Time 2, $p < .01$ by *t* test.

[b] When corrected for the number of comparisons, Time 1 vs. Time 2 difference was not significant (Sakoda et al., 1954).

LDS

LDS test-retest reliability was assessed in 30 middle-to-upper middle class toddlers (age range 24-34 months) recruited for a longitudinal study of language delay (Rescorla, 1989). About half the children had delayed language development. The 1-week test-retest r for the vocabulary score was .99 ($p<.01$). Computed separately for each of the 14 categories of words on the LDS (e.g., animals, foods, people, vehicles), rs ranged from .86 to .99 ($p<.01$). Phi coefficients for the reliability of each word showed that 31% of the words were above .90 while 52% were between .70 and .89, and only 2% were below .40.

In a study by Rescorla and Alley (2000), 422 2-year-olds were assessed in their homes using the LDS and a brief expressive language test. Thirty-three children identified as delayed on the LDS (i.e., fewer than 50 words or no word combinations) and 33 nondelayed children were re-assessed with the LDS 1 month later. The Pearson r between the screening and follow-up vocabulary scores was .97 ($p<.01$). The number of words children acquired between the screening and follow-up testing assessments was significantly related to the number of days between the two sessions ($r = .46, p<.01$), indicating that increases in LDS scores reflected lexical growth during the 1-month interval.

In a study of 102 mostly low SES Spanish-English bilingual children, mothers completed a version of the LDS that had Spanish as well as English versions of each word (Patterson, 1998). The test-retest $r = .99$ indicated that mothers with little education can be reliable informants about their children's vocabularies in two languages.

CROSS-INFORMANT AGREEMENT

Cross-Informant Correlations

Table 8-2 displays Pearson rs between raw scale scores for the following cross-informant comparisons: CBCLs completed by mothers and fathers of Vermont and New York children participating in a longitudinal study, children referred to several clinical services, and children attending a preschool in Pennsylvania; C-TRFs completed by caregivers and teachers of 102 children in the NICHD (1994) Study of Early Child Care and children attending preschools in Vermont and The Netherlands; and CBCLs completed by parents vs. C-TRFs completed by caregivers and teachers for 226 children in our 1999 National Survey and in five clinical settings.

As Table 8-2 shows, all rs were significant at $p<.01$, except C-TRF Somatic Complaints, which was significant at $p<.05$. The rs between Total Problems scores were .65 for mothers vs. fathers completing CBCLs; .72 between pairs of caregivers and teachers completing C-TRFs; and .50 for parents completing CBCLs vs. caregivers or teachers completing C-TRFs. Across all scales, the mean rs were .61 for CBCL x CBCL ratings, .65 for C-TRF x C-TRF ratings, and .40 for CBCL x C-TRF ratings.

To provide a basis for comparison, the mean cross-informant rs found in meta-analyses of many instruments used in many studies were as follows (Achenbach, McConaughy, & Howell, 1987): Between pairs of parents, the mean r was .59; between pairs of teachers, the mean r was .64; and between parents and teachers, the mean r was .27. The cross-informant correlations for the ASEBA preschool instruments were thus as good or better than found in the meta-analyses of correlations from many other instruments.

Table 8-2
Cross-Informant Agreement on Scale Scores

Scale	CBCL r	CBCL OR[a]	C-TRF r	C-TRF OR[a]	CBCL x C-TRF r	CBCL x C-TRF OR[a]
	N = 72		N = 102		N = 226	
Syndromes						
Emotionally Reactive	.64	22**	.52	9	.28	4*
Anxious/Depressed	.48	22**	.60	[b]	.28	9**
Somatic Complaints	.66	78**	.21	24*	.30	3
Withdrawn	.57	33**	.62	32*	.29	5**
Sleep Problems	.67	38**	NA	NA	NA	NA
Attention Problems	.52	14*	.70	99**	.51	15**
Aggressive Behavior	.66	30**	.78	97**	.55	18**
Internalizing	.59	7**	.64	20**	.30	3**
Externalizing	.67	19**	.79	18**	.58	7**
Total Problems	.65	16**	.72	12**	.50	5**
DSM-Oriented Scales						
Affective Problems	.51	31**	.55	97**	.21	4*
Anxiety Problems	.66	99**	.66	71**	.26	1
Pervasive Developmental Problems	.67	20**	.66	11	.42	4**
Attention Deficit/Hyperactivity Problems	.51	[b]	.71	[b]	.52	13**
Oppositional Defiant Problems	.65	15**	.68	49*	.42	15**
Mean r	.61		.65		.40	

Note: All Pearson rs were significant at $p < .01$ except C-TRF Somatic Complaints, which was $p < .05$. The differences between mothers' and fathers' mean CBCL scale scores did not exceed chance expectations. Mean rs were computed by z transformation.

[a]OR = odds ratios that indicate the odds that Rater 2 scored the child in the clinical range if Rater 1 also scored the child in the clinical range, relative to the odds for children who were scored in the normal range by Rater 1. (Clinical range included borderline range.)

[b]OR could not be computed because some cells had no entries.

*OR $p < .05$ based on confidence intervals.

**OR $p < .01$ based on confidence intervals.

Relative Risk Odds Ratios (ORs)

The ORs in Table 8-2 indicate the odds that Rater 1 and Rater 2 agreed in scoring children in the normal vs. clinical range (including the borderline clinical range) relative to the odds that they disagreed. According to confidence intervals computed for the ORs in Table 8-2, most ORs were significant at $p<.01$, while a few were significant at $p<.05$, and four were not significant. Odds ratios could not be computed for three comparisons, because one cell was empty in each of the 2 x 2 tables on which the OR was to be computed. In all three comparisons, the empty cells resulted from the fact that all children who were scored in the normal range by Rater 1 were also scored in the normal range by Rater 2. That is, there were no children in the cell which would have contained cases of disagreement between the two raters for these children. The rs of .51 to .71 for these comparisons indicated good cross-informant agreement.

Mothers' vs. Fathers' Mean Scale Scores

Comparisons of mothers' vs. fathers' ratings via t tests showed no significant differences in mean scale scores after correcting for chance expectations (Sakoda et al., 1954). There was thus no consistent tendency for parents of one gender to report more problems than parents of the other gender.

There was no basis for testing the significance of differences between pairs of caregivers or teachers, because there was no way to consistently categorize one member of each pair of C-TRF raters vs. the other member, as was done for mothers vs. fathers who completed CBCLs. It would also not make sense to compute the significance of differences between parents who completed CBCLs and caregivers or teachers who completed C-TRFs for the same children, because the numbers of items and their prevalence rates differ between CBCL and C-TRF scales.

STABILITIES OF SCALE SCORES

Table 8-3 displays Pearson rs between scale scores for CBCLs completed over a 12-month interval by mothers of Vermont and New York children participating in a longitudinal study. Table 8-3 shows that all stability rs were significant at $p<.01$ over the 12-month period. The r for Total Problems was .76, while the mean r across all scales was .61. One scale showed a significant decline in scores, while five scales showed significant increases in scores over the 12-month period.

Table 8-3 also displays Pearson rs between scale scores for C-TRFs completed over a 3-month interval by teachers and caregivers in a Vermont preschool program. Eleven of the stability rs were significant at $p<.01$, while two were significant at $p<.05$, but the r for Somatic Complaints was not significant. The r for Total Problems was .56, while the mean r across all scales was .59. None of the scale scores changed significantly from Time 1 to Time 2.

SUMMARY

The test-retest reliability of ASEBA problem scale scores was supported by a mean test-retest $r = .85$ for the CBCL scales and .81 for the C-TRF scales over periods averaging 8 days. The commonly found tendency for problem scores to decline over brief rating intervals was evident in the scale scores, but it accounted for a mean of only 0.9% of the variance in the CBCL scores and 1% in the C-TRF scores. Test-retest reliability of the LDS vocabulary score has been $\geq .90$ in several studies.

For interparent agreement on the CBCL, the mean r was .61. The differences between mothers' and fathers' mean scales scores did not exceed chance expectations, indicating that there was no significant tendency for parents of one gender to report more problems than parents of the other gender. For agreement between pairs

Table 8-3
Stabilities of Scale Scores

Scale	CBCL 12-Month r	C-TRF 3-Month r
	N = 80	N = 32
Syndromes		
Emotionally Reactive	.55	.71
Anxious/Depressed	.64[b, c]	.65
Somatic Complaints	.56	.22
Withdrawn	.53	.61
Sleep Problems	.60[b]	NA
Attention Problems	.58	.64
Aggressive Behavior	.62	.37
Internalizing	.76[b]	.65
Externalizing	.66	.40
Total Problems	.76	.56
DSM-Oriented Scales		
Affective Problems	.55[b]	.85
Anxiety Problems	.60[b, c]	.53
Pervasive Developmental Problems	.52	.70
Attention Deficit/Hyperactivity Problems	.52[a]	.46
Oppositional Defiant Problems	.56	.60
Mean r	.61	.59

Note: All Pearson *r*s were significant at *p* < .01 except *C*-TRF Somatic Complaints (NS), Aggressive Behavior (*p* < .05), and Externalizing (*p* < .05). Mean *r*s were computed by *z* transformation.

[a]Time 1 > Time 2, *p* < .01 by *t* test.

[b]Time 1 < Time 2, *p* < .01 by *t* test.

[c]When corrected for the number of comparisons, Time 1 vs. Time 2 difference was not significant.

of caregivers and teachers completing the C-TRF, the mean r was .65. For agreement between CBCLs completed by parents, on the one hand, and C-TRFs completed by caregivers or teachers, on the other, the mean r was .40.

Odds ratios showed that large proportions of children classified as deviant on the basis of mothers' ratings were also classified as deviant on the basis of fathers' ratings. The same was also true for C-TRFs completed by different raters, and for CBCLs and C-TRFs completed for the same children by parents vs. caregivers and teachers.

CBCL stability correlations averaged .61 over a 12-month period, while C-TRF correlations averaged .59 over a 3-month period. Scores on 1 CBCL scale showed a significant decline, while scores on 5 scales showed significant increases over the 12 months. No C-TRF scores changed significantly over 3 months.

Chapter 9
Validity of the ASEBA Preschool Scales

A basic way to evaluate validity is to answer the following question: How well does a procedure measure what it is supposed to measure? Because assessment of preschoolers' functioning is at an early stage of development, there is no single gold standard for what is supposed to be measured. Instead, the validity of preschool assessment instruments must be viewed from multiple perspectives. We will present findings related to content validity, criterion-related validity, and construct validity. However, validation of assessment instruments involves a continual interplay of data and theory (Messick, 1993). The ASEBA instruments are designed to facilitate new research and applications that will advance both the collection of data and the formulation of theory.

CONTENT VALIDITY OF THE PROBLEM ITEMS

The most basic kind of validity is content validity—i.e., the degree to which an instrument's content includes what it is intended to measure.

Selection of CBCL Items

Since the 1960's, ASEBA problem items have been selected and revised on the basis of research and practical experience (Achenbach, 1965, 1966; Achenbach & Lewis, 1971). The initial ASEBA preschool form–the CBCL/2-3– was developed in 1982 on the basis of epidemiological findings for 4- and 5-year-olds (Achenbach & Edelbrock, 1981), consultation with practitioners, researchers, and parents of preschoolers, and reviews of previous research (Behar & Stringfield, 1974; Crowther, Bond, & Rolf, 1981; Heinstein, 1969; Kohn & Rosman, 1972; Richman, Stevenson, & Graham, 1982). After several pilot editions were tested and revised, the first version of the CBCL/2-3 was published, as reported by Achenbach, Edelbrock, and Howell (1987). A full-length *Manual* was then published that provided extensive reliability, validity, and epidemiological data (Achenbach, 1992).

As reported in the 1992 *Manual*, the following two items were excluded from the problem scales, because they were not scored higher for referred than nonreferred children and did not load on any of the empirically based syndromes: *51. Overweight* and *79. Stores up things he/she doesn't need.* On the CBCL/1½-5, these items have been replaced by: *51. Shows panic for no good reason* and *79. Rapid shifts between sadness and excitement.*

Selection of C-TRF Items

Because comprehensive assessment requires data from multiple sources, and because increasing numbers of children attend daycare and preschool, we developed the C-TRF to broaden the basis for assessing preschoolers. In developing the C-TRF, we selected 82 CBCL/2-3 items that were likely to be ratable by caregivers and teachers. We then developed an additional 17 items on the basis of literature reviews, consultations with researchers, caregivers, and teachers, and epidemiological findings with the Teacher's Report Form (TRF; Achenbach, 1991b).

After pilot editions were tested and revised, the C-TRF was published (Achenbach, 1997). Except for minor refinements, the current C-TRF is the same as the one published in 1997. The content validity of the C-TRF items is supported by the extensive process of selection and refinement on which the items rest, plus the ability of the items to discriminate significantly between children who were referred for mental health or special education services and demographically similar children who were not referred. The findings for each item are detailed in Chapter 10.

Associations of CBCL and C-TRF Items with Referral Status

All but two items discriminated significantly ($p \leq .01$) between referred and nonreferred children on either the CBCL/1½-5 or the C-TRF, and/or loaded on an empirically based syndrome, and/or were judged by experienced mental health professionals to be very consistent with a DSM-IV diagnostic category (Achenbach et al., 2000). The items were: *61. Refuses to eat* on both forms and *94. Unclean personal appearance* on the C-TRF only. Although these items were scored higher for referred than nonreferred children, the *p* values were only .07 for item *61* on the CBCL, .42 for item *61* on the C-TRF, and .06 for item *94* on the C-TRF. Because both items were scored significantly higher for referred than nonreferred children in our previous samples (Achenbach, 1992, 1997) and because they were scored (nonsignificantly) higher in our current samples, we have retained them for the Total Problems scale.

It is possible that items 61 and 94 would discriminate significantly between nonreferred children and children having particular kinds of disorders. (Our item analyses reported in Chapter 10 compared nonreferred children and children referred to many different services for many different problems). However, users should decide for themselves whether these items are useful as possible indicators of needs for professional help when assessed in the context of all the other items of the CBCL/1½-5 and C-TRF. The significant associations of the remaining items with referral status and/or their inclusion on empirically based or DSM-oriented scales support their value as indicators of need for professional help.

CONTENT VALIDITY OF THE LDS

The initial pool of LDS vocabulary words was constructed from diary studies of the commonest early words (Benedict, 1979; Dromi, 1987; Leopold, 1949; Nelson, 1973; Rescorla, 1980). Rescorla (1989) summarized the process of testing and revising successive versions of the vocabulary list. As was shown in Figure 1-2, the words are grouped into 14 semantic categories, such as foods, toys, body parts, and vehicles. Comparisons of four samples of children yielded very high consistency in the percentage of children in each sample who used each word, as indicated by Q correlations $> .90$ between word frequencies computed for each pair of samples (Rescorla, Alley, & Book, 2000). (The Q correlations reflected the degree of similarity between the rank ordering of word frequencies reported for each pair of samples.)

For all children 18-35 months old for whom the LDS was completed in our national sample and in our other samples, the internal consistency among the reported vocabulary words was very high, as indicated by Cronbach's (1951) alpha = 1.00, N = 274. This provides additional evidence for the consistency with which children's total LDS scores represent a statistically meaningful dimension of vocabulary development.

CRITERION-RELATED VALIDITY OF PROBLEM SCORES

Criterion-related validity refers to the association between a particular measure, such as a scale scored from an ASEBA form, and an external criterion for characteristics that the scale is intended to measure. In the section on the content validity of the ASEBA instruments, we mentioned that nearly all the ASEBA preschool items discriminated significantly ($p \leq .01$) between referred and nonreferred children and/or were assigned to empirically based or DSM-oriented scales. Here we focus on associations between *scales* comprising particular sets of ASEBA items and external criterion variables. We will first present new validity evidence based on analyses done for this *Manual*. Thereafter, we will summarize validity evidence from other sources.

CBCL and C-TRF Samples Analyzed

An important criterion for the validity of the ASEBA problem scales is their ability to discriminate between children who, independently of their ASEBA scores, have been judged to need referral for mental health or special education services. To test the ability of problem scale scores to distinguish between referred and nonreferred children, we performed a variety of statistical analyses comparing referred and nonreferred children who were matched for age, gender, SES, and ethnicity. We matched the referred and nonreferred children as closely as possible for these demographic characteristics to prevent possible demographic differences in problem scores from affecting our tests of the ability of ASEBA scales to distinguish between referred and nonreferred children. In addition, we used statistics that explicitly tested for differences in scale scores associated with age, gender, SES, and ethnicity.

Matched Nonreferred and Referred CBCL Samples. To form demographically matched samples for the CBCL, we drew 563 children from our national normative sample of nonreferred children (described in Chapter 6) who could be precisely matched to referred children for age and gender and closely matched for SES (lower, middle, upper, as described in Chapter 6) and ethnicity (nonLatino white vs. other ethnic groups). The demographic characteristics were as follows—Gender: both samples = 59% boys; SES: nonreferred mean = 2.1, *SD* = 0.7, referred mean = 2.2, *SD* = 0.7; ethnicity: nonreferred = 47% white, referred = 83% white. The referred children came from 14 mental health and special education facilities.

Matched Nonreferred and Referred C-TRF Samples. To form demographically matched samples for the C-TRF, we drew 303 children from our normative sample (described in Chapter 6) who could be precisely matched to referred children for age and gender and closely matched for SES (lower, middle, upper) and ethnicity (nonLatino white vs. other ethnic groups). The demographic characteristics were as follows—Gender: both samples 70% boys; SES: nonreferred mean = 2.4, *SD* = 0.6, referred mean = 1.8, *SD* = 0.8; ethnicity: nonreferred = 53% white, referred = 69% white. The referred children came from 11 mental health and special education settings.

Multiple Regression Analyses of Problem Scale Scores

To test the associations of referral status and demographic characteristics with problem scale scores, we regressed the raw scores for each scale (the dependent variable) on the independent variables of referral status, gender, age, SES, and ethnicity. For each independent variable that was significantly ($p \leq .01$) associated with scale scores, Table 9-1 displays the effect size in terms of the incremental percentage of variance that was accounted for by the variable after variables accounting for more variance were included in the regression (i.e., incremental R^2). According to Cohen's (1988) criteria for effect sizes in multiple regressions, effects accounting for 2 to 13% of variance in the dependent variable are small; effects accounting for 13 to 26% are medium; and effects accounting for >26% are large. Superscript *e* in Table 9-1 indicates effects that could be regarded as significant by chance when corrected for the number of analyses (Sakoda et al., 1954).

Table 9-1
Percent of Variance Accounted for by Significant ($p \leq .01$) Effects of Referral Status and Demographic Variables on Scale Scores in Multiple Regressions

Scale	Ref Stat[a] CBCL	Ref Stat[a] C-TRF	Gender[b] C-TRF	Age[c] CBCL	SES[d] CBCL
Syndromes					
Emotionally Reactive	14	16			
Anxious/Depressed	4	8			3
Somatic Complaints	17	2		4°	
Withdrawn	14	9	3	1^O	
Sleep Problems	9	NA	NA		<1[e]
Attention Problems	8	16	3		2
Aggressive Behavior	7	22	2	2^Y	3
Internalizing	20	14		2^O	
Externalizing	8	23	3	2^Y	3
Total Problems	22	24	2		2
DSM-Oriented Scales					
Affective Problems	20	5			<1[e]
Anxiety Problems	3	7			1
Pervasive Developmental Problems	25	17	2[e]	1[e]	
Attention Deficit/Hyperactivity Problems	5	19	3	2^Y	2
Oppositional Defiant Problems	6	20	2[e]	1$^{Y[e]}$	2

Note: $N = 1,126$ CBCL and 606 C-TRF equally divided between referred and nonreferred children. Analyses were multiple regressions of raw scale scores on referral status, gender, age, SES, and nonLatino white vs. other ethnicity. The percent of variance is the increment in R^2 attributable to the addition of an independent variable that was significant at $p \leq .01$. Effects of ethnicity did not exceed chance expectations.

[a]All scale scores were significantly ($p \leq .01$) higher for referred than nonreferred children.

[b]There were no significant gender effects on CBCL scales. All significant C-TRF gender effects reflected higher scores for boys.

[c]There were no significant age effects on C-TRF scales. On CBCL scales, O = older scored higher; Y = younger scored higher.

[d]There were no significant SES effects on C-TRF scales. All significant CBCL SES effects reflected higher scores for lower SES.

[e]Not significant when corrected for number of analyses. Because all effects of referral status were $p = .000$, none of them were likely to be significant by chance in the 15 CBCL or 14 C-TRF analyses.

Referral Status Differences in Problem Scale Scores

As indicated in Table 9-1, referred children obtained significantly higher scores than nonreferred children on all problem scales of the CBCL and C-TRF, with 16 of the 29 effects meeting Cohen's (1988) criteria for medium effects. Effects ≥20% of variance were found for the following scales: CBCL Internalizing, Total Problems, Affective Problems, and Pervasive Developmental Problems; C-TRF Aggressive Behavior, Externalizing, Total Problems, and Oppositional Defiant Problems. Figure 9-1 displays the mean CBCL and C-TRF scale scores for children grouped by age, gender, and referral status.

Demographic Differences in Problem Scale Scores

As Table 9-1 shows, all significant demographic effects were quite small, according to Cohen's (1988) criteria. The largest was the 4% age effect on the CBCL Somatic Complaints scale, where older children tended to score higher. There were also 3% effects of SES on the CBCL Anxious/Depressed, Aggressive Behavior, and Externalizing scales, where lower SES children tended to score higher. On the C-TRF, there were 3% effects of gender on the Withdrawn, Attention Problems, Externalizing, and Attention Deficit/Hyperactivity scales, reflecting higher scores for boys. The gender-specific norms for the C-TRF scales take account of these gender differences. Because age, SES, and ethnicity effects on the C-TRF scales did not exceed chance expectations, they are not shown in Table 9-1.

CLASSIFICATION OF CHILDREN ACCORDING TO CLINICAL CUTPOINTS

The regression analyses reported in the previous section showed that all quantitative scale scores significantly discriminated between referred and nonreferred children. Beside the quantitative scores, each scale has cutpoints for distinguishing categorically between the normal and clinical range. The choice of cutpoints for the different scales was discussed in Chapters 6 and 7.

For some clinical and research purposes, users may wish to distinguish between children who are in the normal vs. clinical range according to the cutpoints. Because categorical distinctions are usually least reliable for individuals who score close to the border of a category, we have identified a borderline clinical range for each scale. The addition of a borderline category improves the basis for decisions about children's need for help.

As an example, a scale score in the borderline range tells us that enough problems have been reported to be of concern but not so many that a child clearly needs professional help. If a child obtains one or more scale scores in the borderline range but none in the clinical range, we should consider options such as the following: Obtain ratings from more informants to determine whether they view the child as being in the normal, borderline, or clinical range; have the initial informants rate the child again after 2 to 3 months to see whether the child's borderline scores move into the normal or clinical range; use additional assessment procedures and/or direct observations to evaluate the specific kinds of problems on which the borderline scores were based. In other words, borderline scores can help users make more differentiated decisions than if all scores must be categorized as normal vs. clinical.

Despite the augmentation of statistical power afforded by continuous quantitative scores and by inclusion of a borderline range, users may wish to distinguish dichotomously between nondeviant and deviant scale scores. In the follow-

CBCL PROBLEM SCALES

□ = Nonreferred Girls   ○ = Nonreferred Boys   ■ = Referred Girls   ● = Referred Boys

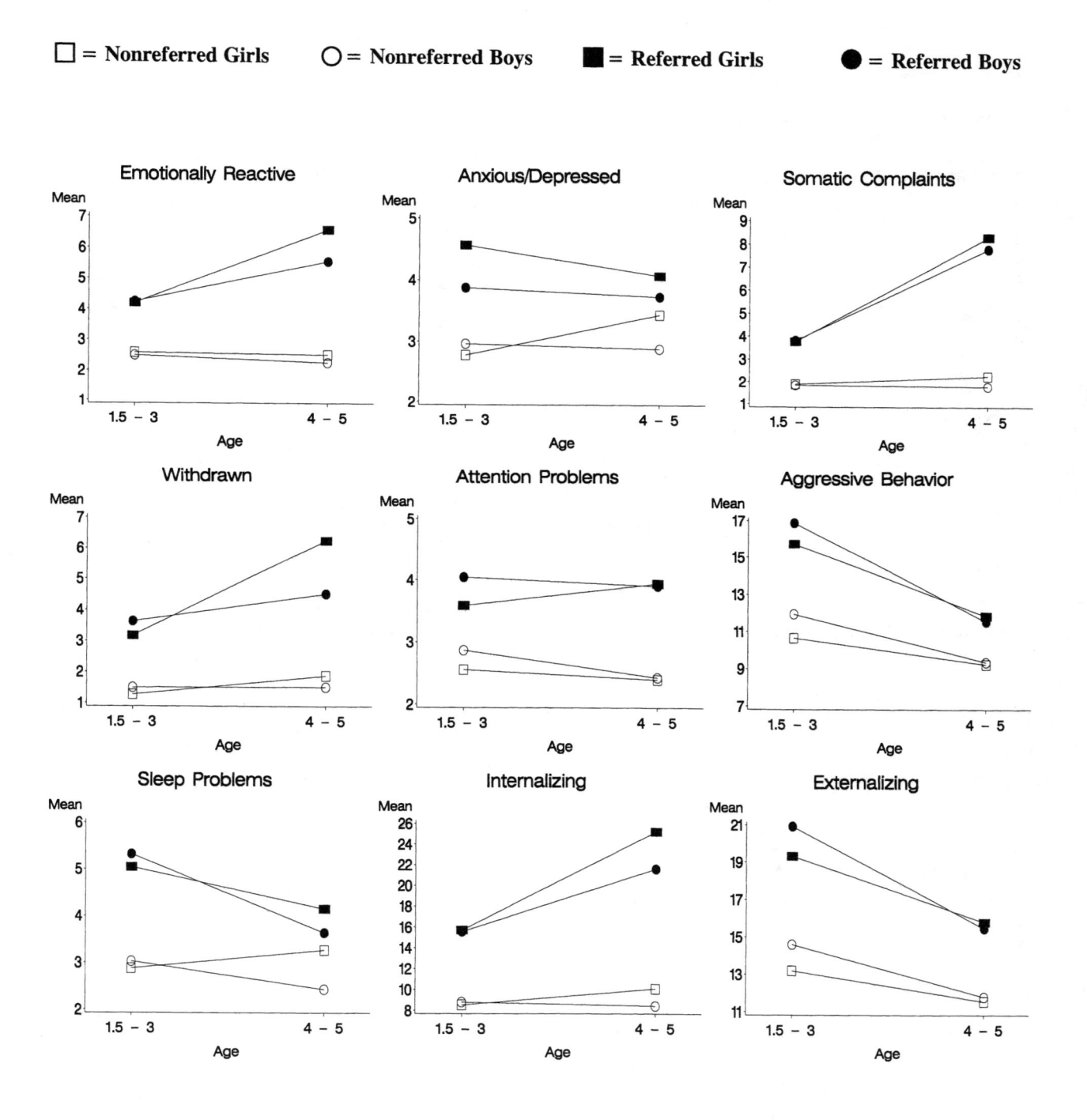

Figure 9-1. Mean scores for problem scales.

VALIDITY OF ASEBA PRESCHOOL SCALES

CBCL PROBLEM SCALES (cont.)

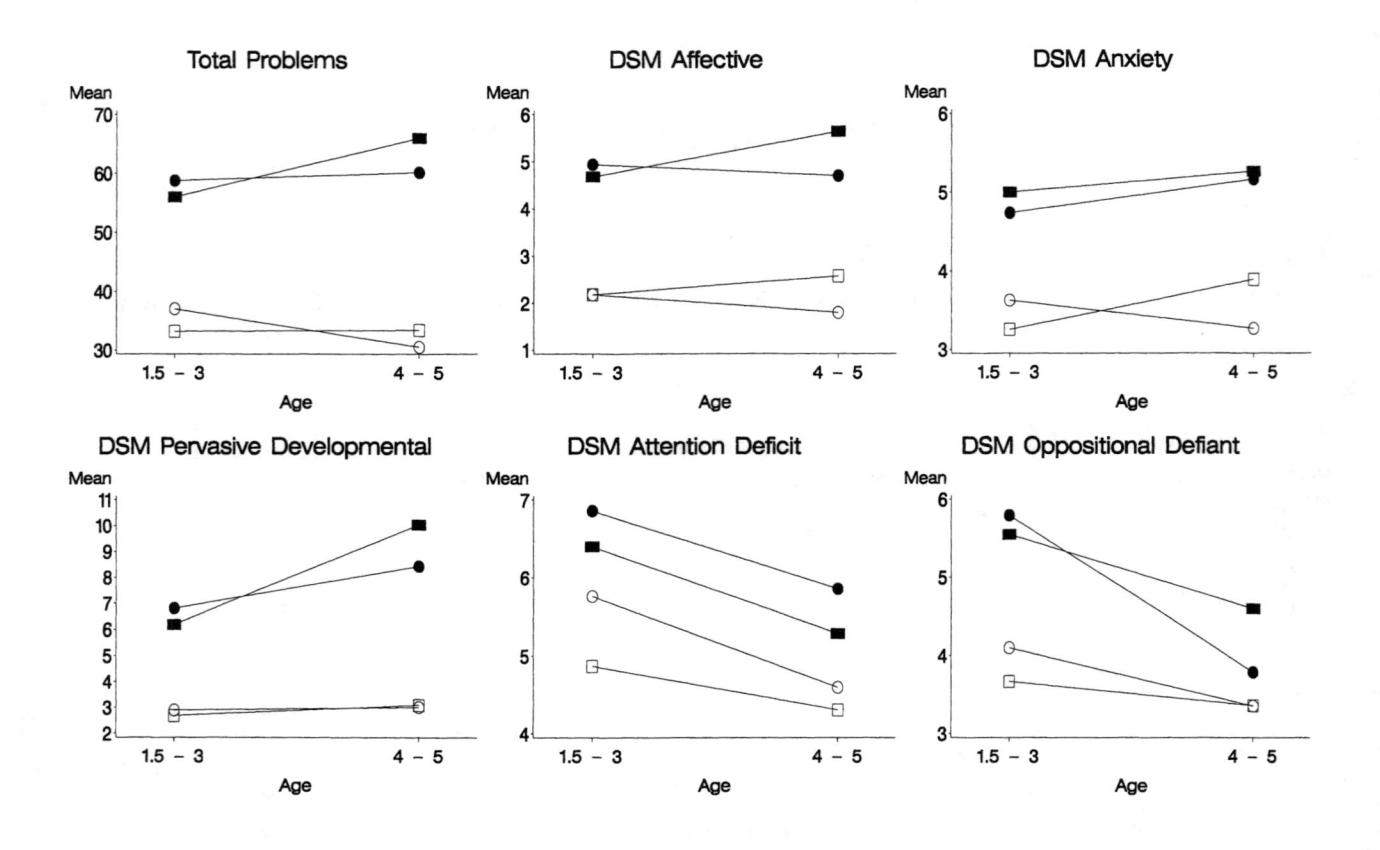

C-TRF PROBLEM SCALES

□ = Nonreferred Girls   ○ = Nonreferred Boys   ■ = Referred Girls   ● = Referred Boys

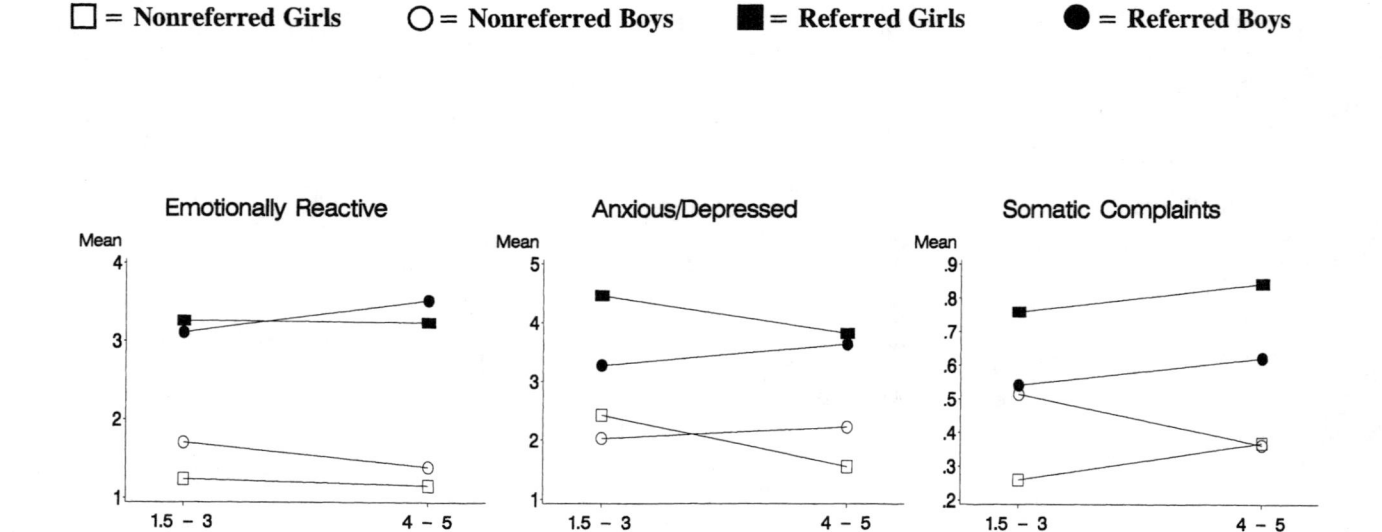

Figure 9-1 (cont.). Mean scores for problem scales.

VALIDITY OF ASEBA PRESCHOOL SCALES

C-TRF PROBLEM SCALES (cont.)

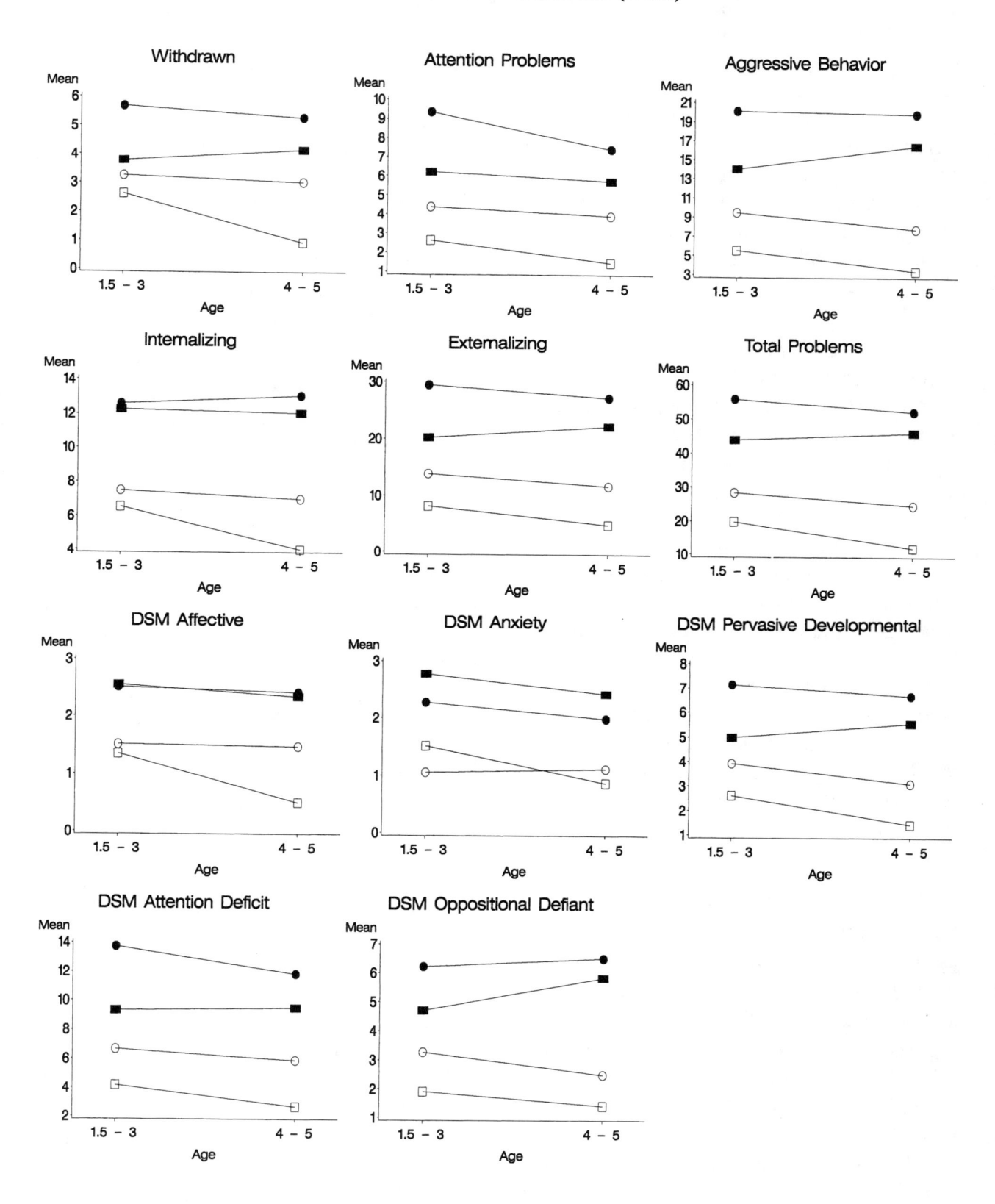

Figure 9-1 (cont.). Mean scores for problem scales.

ing sections, we report findings that indicate the degree to which dichotomous classification of ASEBA scale scores according to the normal range vs. combined borderline and clinical ranges distinguishes between demographically similar nonreferred vs. referred children. Because the borderline range encompasses scores that are high enough to be of concern, we have included it with the clinical range for our dichotomous comparisons with the normal range.

Odd Ratios (ORs)

One approach to analyzing associations between categorical classifications is by computing *relative risk odds ratios* (Fleiss, 1981), which are used in epidemiological research. The OR indicates the odds of having a particular condition (usually a disorder) among people who have a particular risk factor, relative to the odds of having the condition among people who lack that risk factor. The comparison between outcome rates for those who do and do not have the risk factor is expressed as the ratio of the odds of having the outcome if the risk factor is present, to the odds of having the outcome if the risk factor is absent. For example, a study of relations between smoking and lung cancer may yield a relative risk OR of 6. This means that people who smoke have 6 times greater odds of developing lung cancer than people who do not smoke.

We applied OR analyses to the relations between ASEBA scale scores and referral status as follows: For each ASEBA scale, we first classified children from our matched referred and nonreferred samples according to whether they scored in the normal range or in the clinical range (including the borderline clinical range). Being in the clinical range was thus equivalent to a "risk factor" in epidemiological research. We then computed the odds that children who were in the clinical range on a particular scale were from the referred sample, relative to the odds for children who were not in the clinical range. (Because referred children were already referred at the time they were rated on the ASEBA forms, we could also have made referral status the "risk factor" and ASEBA scores the "outcome variable." Because we used OR to indicate the strength of the contemporaneous association between ASEBA scores and referral status, rather than a predictive relation between a risk factor and a later outcome, the choice of the risk factor was not important and did not affect the obtained ORs.)

The relative risk OR is a nonparametric statistic computed from a 2 x 2 table. We therefore included both genders in each analysis to provide a summary OR across both genders. The statistical significance of the OR is evaluated by computing confidence intervals.

Table 9-2 summarizes the ORs for relations between scale scores in the clinical range and referral status. Table 9-2 also shows the percent of referred and nonreferred children who scored in the clinical range according to the cutpoints on the scales. Confidence intervals showed that all the ORs were significantly ($p < .01$) greater than 1.0, while chi squares showed that all the differences between referred and nonreferred children scoring in the clinical range were significant ($p < .01$), except for the C-TRF Somatic Complaints scale.

The largest ORs were for the CBCL Pervasive Developmental Problems scale (OR = 11), having ≥1 CBCL syndrome in the clinical range (OR = 9), and the CBCL Somatic Complaints, CBCL Withdrawn, CBCL Affective Problems, and C-TRF Total Problems scales (OR = 8). As Table 9-2 shows, the biggest difference between referred and nonreferred children was for the percentage who had ≥1 CBCL syndrome in the clinical range: 77% vs. 26%, a difference of 51%. The next biggest differences were 45% differences for the percentage who had CBCL

Table 9-2
Odds Ratios and Percent of Referred and
Nonreferred Children Scoring in the Clinical Range

Scale	Odds Ratio CBCL	Odds Ratio C-TRF	Referred CBCL	Referred C-TRF	Nonreferred CBCL	Nonreferred C-TRF
Syndromes						
Emotionally Reactive	5	6	36	32	10	8
Anxious/Depressed	3	3	19	21	8	10
Somatic Complaints	8	2	44	8	9	5
Withdrawn	8	3	36	19	7	8
Sleep Problems	6	NA	25	NA	5	NA
Attention Problems	5	5	27	29	7	8
Aggressive Behavior	6	7	31	38	7	8
Internalizing	6	4	60	43	21	17
Externalizing	4	6	42	62	17	21
Total Problems	6	8	57	63	18	18
≥1 Syndrome in Clinical Range	9	6	77	65	26	25
Int and/or Ext in Clinical Range	7	6	73	70	27	27
DSM-Oriented Scales						
Affective Problems	8	3	38	18	7	8
Anxiety Problems	3	3	20	16	8	6
Pervasive Developmental Problems	11	5	50	30	9	8
Attention Deficit/Hyperactivity Problems	4	5	21	35	7	10
Oppositional Defiant Problems	6	7	29	39	7	9
≥1 DSM Scale in Clinical Range	7	4	61	43	18	18

Note: $N = 1,126$ CBCL and 606 C-TRF equally divided between referred and nonreferred children. Clinical range included borderline range. The proportion of referred scoring in the clinical range was significantly ($p < .01$) greater than the proportion of nonreferred according to confidence intervals for odds ratios and chi squares for 2 x 2 tables for all scales except C-TRF Somatic Complaints.

Internalizing and/or Externalizing scores in the clinical range (73% vs. 27%) and for the percentage who had C-TRF Total Problems scores in the clinical range (63% vs. 18%).

Discriminant Analyses Using Problem Scores

The foregoing sections dealt with the use of unweighted problem scores to discriminate between children who were referred for help with behavioral/emotional problems vs. children who were not referred. It is possible that weighted combinations of scales or items might produce better discrimination. To test this possibility, we performed discriminant analyses using the demographically matched referred and non-referred children as the criterion groups.

The following four sets of discriminant analyses were performed for each gender on the CBCL and C-TRF: *(a)* the 99 problem items were tested as candidate predictors; *(b)* the syndrome scales were tested as candidate predictors; *(c)* the DSM-oriented scales were tested as candidate predictors; *(d)* the Internalizing and Externalizing scores were tested as candidate predictors.

Discriminant analyses selectively weight predictors to maximize their collective associations with the particular criterion groups being analyzed. The weighting process makes use of characteristics of the sample that may differ from other samples. To avoid overestimating the accuracy of the classification obtained by discriminant analyses, it is therefore necessary to correct for the "shrinkage" in associations that would occur when discriminant weights derived in one sample are applied in a new sample.

To correct for shrinkage, we employed a "jackknife" (cross-validation) procedure whereby discriminant functions are computed for every combination of $N-1$ subjects with a different subject excluded ("held out") of the sample each time (SAS Institute, 1999). Each discriminant function is then cross-validated by testing the accuracy of its prediction for the subject who was held out when the discriminant function was computed. Finally, the percentage of correct predictions is averaged across all the held-out subjects. It is these cross-validated predictions that we will present.

The discriminant analyses done for each gender separately and both genders combined yielded fairly similar rates of correct classifications, although the specific predictors differed somewhat for boys vs. girls. The most accurate cross-validated classification rate was achieved by using all 99 items on a form as candidate predictors.

Results for CBCL Problem Items as Predictors. With both genders combined, the discriminant analysis based on CBCL items correctly classified 84.2% of the children. Based on the total sample, the misclassifications were as follows: 7.3% of all children were non-re-ferred children incorrectly classified as referred (i.e., false positives) and 8.6% of all children were referred children incorrectly classified as nonreferred (i.e., false negatives). The items that contributed most to the discriminant analysis of both genders combined were: *82. Sudden changes in mood or feelings*; *1. Aches or pains (without medical cause)*; and *76. Speech problems.*

Results for C-TRF Items as Predictors. With both genders combined, the discriminant analysis based on C-TRF items correctly classified 74.3% of the children. Based on the total sample, misclassifications were equally divided between false positives and false negatives at 12.9% of all children in the sample. The items that contributed most to the discriminant function were: *15. Defiant*; *96. Wants a lot of attention*; and *2. Acts too young for age.*

Results for CBCL Problem Scales as Predictors. Because 99 items are available as candidate predictors, the order in which the items enter as predictors can vary considerably among samples. However, because each scale includes numerous items and there are many fewer scales than items, the order in which scales enter discriminant analyses is likely to be more stable from one sample to another. Our discriminant analyses of the CBCL showed that the Withdrawn syndrome, DSM-oriented Pervasive Developmental Problems scale, and Internalizing scale were the first to enter their respective discriminant analyses for each gender separately and for both genders combined. Classification accuracy ranged from 74% for the combination of Internalizing and Externalizing scales to 78% for syndromes.

Results for C-TRF Problem Scales as Predictors. The C-TRF Aggressive Behavior syndrome, DSM-oriented Oppositional Defiant Problems scale, and Externalizing scale were the first to enter their respective discriminant analyses. This indicates that caregivers' and teachers' reports of Externalizing kinds of problems were more strongly related to referral than were their reports of Internalizing kinds of problems. By contrast, parents' reports of Internalizing and developmental kinds of problems were more strongly related to referral than were their reports of Externalizing kinds of problems. Using C-TRF scale scores as predictors, classification accuracy was 71% both for the combination of Internalizing and Externalizing scales and for syndromes, and was 72% for DSM-oriented scales.

PROBABILITY OF PARTICULAR TOTAL PROBLEMS SCORES BEING FROM THE REFERRED VS. NONREFERRED SAMPLES

To provide a further picture of relations between particular problem scores and referral status, Table 9-3 displays the probability of particular Total Problems T scores being from our referred sample. The probabilities were determined by tabulating the percentage of children having T scores in each interval who were from our matched referred and nonreferred samples. Because T scores for the Total Problems scales were not truncated, they are highly correlated with the raw scores.

As can be seen from Table 9-3, the probability that a Total Problems score was from the referred sample increased steadily with the magnitude of the scores. Once a probability of .50 was reached, all the succeeding scores had probabilities $>.50$. Users can refer to Table 9-3 to estimate the likelihood that particular problem scores represent deviance severe enough to warrant concern.

CRITERION-RELATED VALIDITY OF LDS SCORES

Whereas the CBCL and C-TRF scales are designed to identify children who may need professional help for various kinds of behavioral and emotional problems, the LDS is designed to identify children whose speech development is significantly delayed. Because parents and parent-surrogates have the best opportunities for observing children's actual speech under everyday conditions, their reports are usually essential for identifying delayed speech development.

When developmental delays are suspected, children are often evaluated via formal tests. Such tests provide standardized stimulus situations, scoring rules, norms for performance, and evidence for reliability and validity from research samples. Test scores therefore provide important validity criteria for measures of language development based on parents' reports.

Correlations with Test Scores

Table 9-4 summarizes correlations found in

Table 9-3
**Probability of Total Problems *T* Score
Being from Referred Sample**

Total Problems T Score	CBCL	C-TRF
	N = 1,126	N = 606
28 - 39	.16	.06
40 - 43	.21	.05
44 - 47	.22	.28
48 - 51	.36	.29
52 - 55	.34	.42
56 - 59	.56	.52
60 - 63[a]	.63	.77
64 - 67	.67	.73
68 - 71	.82	.75
72 - 75	.86	.88
76 - 100	1.00	.89

Note. Samples were equally divided between referred and nonreferred children.
[a]*T* scores of 60-63 are in the borderline clinical range and >63 are in the clinical range.

11 samples between children's vocabulary scores on the LDS completed by parents and scores on other measures, most of which were standardized tests administered to the children by trained examiners. As Table 9-4 shows, LDS vocabulary scores correlated from .56 to .87 with a variety of other measures of early expressive language development. In addition, LDS scores for the average length of children's phrases had the following correlations with other expressive language scores in the Rescorla and Alley (2000) study: .64 with Bayley (1969) Mental Development Index; .63 with Reynell Expressive Language (Reynell & Gruber, 1985); .66 with Vineland Adaptive Behavior Scale (Sparrow et al., 1984); and .81 with LDS vocabulary score.

Classification of Children as Delayed vs. Not Delayed

The criterion-related validity of the LDS has also been tested using dichotomous classification analyses. In such analyses, children were classified as either delayed (<50 words or no word combinations) or as not delayed (≥50 words or some combinations) on the LDS and were then classified as being delayed or not delayed on a criterion measure, such as a standardized test or a speech sample.

In an early study (Rescorla, 1989), 81 toddlers were tested with the Reynell Expressive Language Scale (Reynell & Gruber, 1985). The LDS identified as delayed 87% of the toddlers who scored at least 6 months below age level on the Reynell, and it identified as not delayed 86% of toddlers who scored as not delayed on the Reynell.

Table 9-4
Correlations Between LDS Vocabulary Scores and Other Scores

Sample	N	Age in months	Criterion[a]	r[b]	Source
Middle-to-upper SES, half late talkers, suburban PA	81	24	Sum of Bayley objects + Reynell pictures named	.87	Rescorla, 1989
Low SES, African-American, inner-city PA	58	25	Sum of Bayley objects + Preschool Language Scale pictures named	.79	Rescorla, 1989
Middle-to-upper SES, PA, Washington, DC	108	18-30	Sum of Bayley objects + Binet pictures named	.78	Rescorla et al., 1993
Middle-to-upper SES suburban PA	92	24-26		.82	
Mexico City, half private & half public school	240	15-31	MacArthur CDI. WS Spanish	.84	Stelzer, 1995
Wyoming parents who completed LDS by mail	306	24-26	Mullen Scales & mean length of utterance from speech sample	.67-.77	Klee et al., 1998
Middle-to-upper SES suburban PA (4 samples)	145 104 65 108	24-28 23-27 24-27 23-29	Bayley objects named Binet pictures named	.66-.74 .67-.82	Rescorla & Alley, 2000
Middle-to-upper SES suburban PA, half "at-risk" on LDS screening	66	24-28	Reynell Expressive Reynell Receptive Bayley MDI Vineland	.78 .56 .79 .71	Rescorla & Alley, 2000

[a]See the following in Reference List: Bayley, 1969; Reynell & Gruber, 1985; for Binet, see Thorndike et al., 1986; for Preschool Language Scale, see Zimmerman et al., 1969; for MacArthur, see Fenson et al., 1993; Mullen (1993); for Vineland, see Sparrow et al., 1984.

[b]Pearson correlations

In a two-stage screening study conducted in Wyoming by Klee, Carson, Gavin, Hall, Kent, and Reece (1998), 64 children received follow-up testing after being identified as delayed or not delayed on the LDS in the screening-by-mail first stage. Multiple language measures were used to make a clinical diagnosis of delayed language. Klee et al. found that 91% of children diagnosed as delayed were also delayed on the LDS, whereas 87% of those diagnosed as normal showed no delay on the LDS.

In a community study of 422 children, 33 toddlers who were delayed on the LDS during a home screening and 33 comparison children with normal LDS scores were seen for follow-up assessments an average of 23 days later (Rescorla & Alley, 2000). Using a Reynell Expressive Language score $\leq 10^{th}$ percentile as the criterion for expressive language delay, 94% of the toddlers who were delayed on the Reynell had been delayed on the screening LDS, whereas 67% of those not delayed on the Reynell had not been delayed on the LDS. The 33 children who were initially delayed on the LDS had scores on the Bayley (1969) Mental Development Index 2 SDs below those of the comparison children, and their scores on the Reynell Expressive Language Scale were 1.25 SDs lower. An odds ratio (OR) of 34 ($p < .05$) was obtained for the prediction of Reynell scores $\leq 10^{th}$ percentile from LDS scores indicative of delays.

CONSTRUCT VALIDITY OF ASEBA PROBLEM SCALES

Construct validity is perhaps the most discussed but also the most elusive form of validity. For variables that lack a gold standard criterion measure, construct validity involves a "nomological network" of interrelated procedures intended to reflect the hypothesized variables in different ways (Cronbach & Meehl, 1955). It was the lack of satisfactory constructs and operational definitions for childhood disorders that prompted us to develop our assessment procedures and to derive syndromes empirically.

The Total Problems score can be viewed as representing a general dimension of problems analogous to the construct of general ability represented by total scores on intelligence tests. Similarly, the syndrome scales can be viewed as subgroupings of problems somewhat analogous to the subtests included in many general ability tests, such as the Wechsler (1989) tests. However, most ability subtests consist of items chosen to redundantly measure the hypothetical construct of a specific ability. Our syndromes, by contrast, were derived from statistical analyses of covariation among items selected to be nonredundant.

A key aim of the empirically based syndromes is to provide common foci for practical applications, research, and training based on sets of problems that have been found to co-occur. In addition, the syndromes can guide inferences about relations between childhood disorders and other variables and can be used to group children in order to test differences in etiology, prognosis, response to treatment, and outcomes.

Diverse practical and research applications are discussed in Chapters 5 and 12, respectively. The *Bibliography of Published Studies Using ASEBA Instruments* (Bérubé & Achenbach, 2000) lists numerous studies that report findings on relations between ASEBA syndrome scales and other variables. The correlates of the syndromes identified through research contribute to construct validity in the sense of advancing the nomological network of which the syndromes are a part.

Correlations with Other Measures of Problems

Several studies have reported significant correlations between CBCL/2-3 Total Problems scores and other general measures of problems among preschoolers. Because only two problem items have been changed from the CBCL/2-3 to the CBCL/1½-5, the correlations would be very similar for the CBCL/1½-5 Total Problems scale.

Correlations with the Richman BCL. Correlations ranging from .56 to .77 have been found between CBCL/2-3 Total Problems and total problems on the Behavior Checklist (BCL) developed in England by Naomi Richman (1977; Richman, Stevenson, & Graham, 1982). Although the structure of the BCL differs considerably from that of the CBCL and some BCL words are unfamiliar to American parents (e.g., "faddy"), we found a Pearson $r = .58$ ($N = 65$, $p < .01$) between the BCL and CBCL Total Problems scores for children rated by their parents.

In a study of predominantly low SES 3-year-old low-birthweight children, a Spearman correlation = .56 ($N = 272$, $p < .01$) was obtained between mothers' ratings on the CBCL and BCL, and a Spearman correlation = .77 between nursery school teachers' ratings on the two instruments ($N = 281$, $p < .01$) (Spiker, Kraemer, Constantine, & Bryant, 1992). A Dutch study obtained a Pearson $r = .65$ ($N = 207$, $p < .01$) between parents' ratings on Dutch translations of the two instruments (Koot, van den Oord, Verhulst, & Boomsma, 1997).

Correlations with New Measures of Problems. Articles describing the initial development work on two rating scales for toddlers have reported correlations with the CBCL. In developing the Toddler Behavior Screening Inventory (TBSI), Mouton-Simien, McCain, and Kelley (1997) obtained ratings on both instruments from parents of toddlers 12 to 41 months of age. The sum of frequency ratings for TBSI problem items correlated .70 with the CBCL Total Problems score, while the number of items on which parents circled *yes* in response to the question *Is this a problem for you?* correlated .54 with the CBCL Total Problems score ($N = 581$, $p < .01$).

In developing the Infant-Toddler Social and Emotional Assessment (ITSEA), Briggs-Gowan and Carter (1998) reported correlations of .46 to .72 between the ITSEA's four externalizing scales and the CBCL Externalizing scale. They also reported correlations of .48 and .62 between the ITSEA's two Internalizing scales and the CBCL Internalizing scale ($N = 97$, $p < .01$).

Correlations with DSM Criteria. In one of the few studies of DSM diagnoses among preschoolers, Keenan and Wakschlag (2000) reported that CBCL Externalizing scores correlated .49 with the sum of DSM Oppositional Defiant Disorder (ODD) and Conduct Disorder (CD) symptoms assessed via diagnostic interviews with mothers. Most children who qualified for ODD or CD diagnoses obtained T scores > 70. In another study, DSM diagnoses of disruptive disorders made from multiple sources of data correlated .47 with scores on the CBCL/2-3 Aggressive Behavior scale (Arend, Lavigne, Rosenbaum, Binns, & Christoffel, 1996).

Prediction of Later Problem Scores. Table 9-5 displays correlations between CBCL preschool scales at ages 2 and 3 and the counterpart CBCL/4-18 scales at ages 4 through 9. The children were low birthweight and normal birthweight residents of New York and Vermont participating in a longitudinal study of outcomes for an experimental intervention administered to some of the low birthweight children during their first 3 months (Achenbach, Howell, Aoki, & Rauh, 1993). At ages 2 and 3, parents rated their children on the CBCL/2-3. We rescored their ratings on the new CBCL/1½-5 scales. At ages 4 to 9, parents rated the same children on the CBCL/4-18 (Achenbach, 1991a).

Table 9-5
Longitudinal Correlations Between CBCL/1½-5 Scales and CBCL/4-18 Scales

Anxious/Depressed

Ages	4	5	6	7	8	9
2	.45	.24	(.20)	.33	.31	.30
3	.51	.39	.24	.36	.46	.40

Attention Problems

Ages	4	5	6	7	8	9
2	.51	.28	(.21)	(.05)	(.12)	.37
3	.56	.49	.43	.40	.30	.48

Somatic Problems

Ages	4	5	6	7	8	9
2	(.23)	(.21)	.33	.41	.36	(.09)
3	(.10)	(.17)	.42	.42	(.20)	(.12)

Aggressive Behavior

Ages	4	5	6	7	8	9
2	.65	.56	.47	.51	.50	.50
3	.71	.64	.50	.51	.59	.44

Withdrawn

Ages	4	5	6	7	8	9
2	(.14)	(.14)	(.22)	.26	.31	.34
3	.31	.24	.32	.32	.36	.43

Externalizing

Ages	4	5	6	7	8	9
2	.69	.59	.48	.54	.46	.49
3	.71	.64	.51	.53	.58	.48

Internalizing

Ages	4	5	6	7	8	9
2	.52	.39	.47	.53	.59	.46
3	.56	.45	.54	.61	.60	.50

Total Problems

Ages	4	5	6	7	8	9
2	.63	.61	.55	.56	.59	.56
3	.75	.68	.68	.66	.67	.64

Note: Data are from a longitudinal study of low birthweight and normal birthweight children (Achenbach et al., 1993). *N*s ranged from 54 for age 3 with age 9, to 74 for age 2 with ages 6 and 7. All *r*s were *p* < .05, except those in parentheses.

As you can see from Table 9-5, all correlations for the Total Problems scale were ≥ .55 through age 9, with the highest being .75 between ages 3 and 4. Even at age 9, the correlations were .56 with age 2 ratings and .64 with age 3 ratings. The Aggressive Behavior, Internalizing, and Externalizing scales also yielded high correlations between age 2 and 3 scores and scores through age 9.

For some scales, the age 2 and 3 scores yielded higher correlations with scores at older than younger ages, despite the longer time span between them. For example, the correlations for age 2 and 3 scores on the Withdrawn syndrome generally increased with age, reaching their largest size at age 9, despite the fact that they spanned 6 and 7 years by then. After being largest over the shortest intervals, the correlations for age 2 and 3 scores on the Attention Problems syndrome declined and then rose again at age 9. This suggests that the Withdrawn and Attention Problems syndromes reflect long-term patterns of functioning that may not be measured equally effectively at all ages. Thus, the relatively high correlations of age 9 scores with scores at ages 2 and 3 may indicate that age 9 ratings are better measures of the underlying constructs than are ratings at somewhat younger ages.

Age 2 scores were found to significantly predict teachers' ratings on the Aggressive Behavior, Externalizing, and Total Problems scales of the Teacher's Report Form (Achenbach, 1991b) through age 9. Similarly, a British study found that CBCL/2-3 Total Problems scores significantly predicted teachers' ratings for total difficulties on the Strengths and Difficulties Questionnaire (Goodman, 1997) at age 11 (Hay, Sharp, Pawlby, Schmucker, Mills, Allen, & Kumar, 1999).

Independence from Developmental Measures. The foregoing correlations indicated *convergent validity* between the CBCL and other measures of the general construct of maladaptive behavior. Concerns about young children's behavior often raise questions about developmental lags. The ASEBA problem items are designed to measure the behavioral/emotional problems of preschoolers rather than their developmental level. If ASEBA problem scale scores were merely a function of developmental level, they may not add much information beyond that provided by developmental measures.

To assess the *discriminant validity* of the CBCL/2-3 in terms of its independence of developmental measures, we computed correlations between CBCL scores and scores obtained from the Bayley (1969) Mental Scale at age 2, the McCarthy (1972) General Cognitive Index obtained at age 3, and the Minnesota Child Development Inventory (MCDI; Ireton & Thwing, 1974) obtained at ages 2 and 3. The subjects were 86 children participating in our longitudinal study of low birthweight and normal birthweight children (Achenbach et al., 1987). The Bayley and McCarthy tests were administered to the children in their homes while their parents completed the MCDI. No concurrent rs between the CBCL/2-3 total problem scores and the Bayley, McCarthy, or MCDI scores were significant at either age. In the previously cited Dutch study by Koot et al. (1997), correlations between the MCDI and CBCL/2-3 scales ranged from -.05 to -.16 (N = 391), also indicating negligible associations. Thus, the CBCL/2-3 scores showed discriminant validity in terms of their independence from both individually administered developmental tests and parents' ratings on a developmental inventory.

Correlations between CBCL/1½-5 problem scales and the LDS average phrase length and vocabulary score did not exceed chance expectations in our National Survey sample. However, correlations may be found in samples of children who have significant language delays.

Genetic Evidence. Research on genetic aspects of psychopathology is expanding rapidly. To be effective, genetic research requires good measures of phenotypic characteristics whose genetic underpinnings can then be studied. A constant interplay is needed between development of good measures of phenotypic characteristics and test of models for genetic influences on those characteristics.

Several genetic studies have used ASEBA scales to measure phenotypic characteristics. Twin studies have yielded substantial heritabilities for several CBCL/2-3 syndromes, which are highly correlated with the revised versions scored from the CBCL/1½-5, as documented in Chapter 11. For example, in a study of Colorado twins, heritability estimates were significant for most CBCL/2-3 scales, with the highest being .58 for Sleep Problems and .52 for Aggressive Behavior (Schmitz, Fulker, & Mrazek, 1995).

In two studies of Dutch twins, most scales scored from the CBCL/2-3 were found to have large proportions of genetic variance (van den Oord, Verhulst, & Boomsma, 1996; van der Valk, van den Oord, Verhulst, & Boomsma, 2000). In addition, van der Valk et al. analyzed the contributions of mothers' vs. fathers' ratings of 3,501 twin pairs to the assessment of genotypes represented by the problem scales. They concluded that disagreements between parents' ratings reflected unique information provided by each parent, rather than unreliability or rater bias. Genetic studies of ASEBA scales can thus illuminate discrepancies between scores obtained from different respondents, as well as testing the degree to which scales reflect underlying genetic factors.

A finding that low serotonin levels in newborns predicted high CBCL/2-3 Externalizing scores at 30 months suggests that genetically influenced serotonergic functioning may be one route by which genes affect syndromes assessed by ASEBA instruments (Clarke, Murphy, & Constantino, 1999).

CONSTRUCT VALIDITY OF THE LDS

Earlier sections documented the validity of the LDS for assessing children's vocabulary development and delays on the basis of parents' reports. However, long-term longitudinal findings indicate that the LDS also measures a persistent weakness in language related abilities. In an 11-year longitudinal study, Rescorla (2000) compared 30 children identified as language-delayed on the LDS at 24 to 31 months and 25 nondelayed children who were matched to the delayed children on age, gender, SES, and nonverbal ability. Initial LDS vocabulary scores significantly predicted age 13 scores for grammatical, vocabulary, and verbal memory skills, with correlations of .55, .43, and .38, respectively, all $p < .01$. This indicates that low scores on the LDS may reflect a trait-like weakness in verbal functioning, rather than only temporary delays in the acquisition of language.

SUMMARY

This chapter presented several kinds of evidence for the validity of ASEBA preschool scores. The *content validity* of the problem scales was supported by findings that nearly all items discriminated between referred and nonreferred children, as well as by the extensive process by which items were selected and refined. The content validity of the LDS was supported by the high Q correlations among the endorsement frequencies for the vocabulary words in different samples, as well as by the diverse sources from which the words were selected.

The *criterion-related* validity of the problem scales was supported by significant discrimination between referred and nonreferred children. The criterion-related validity of the LDS was supported by its correlations with other measures of language delay and language development in 11 samples. The criterion-related validity of the LDS was also supported by its accuracy in identifying children who were then diagnosed as language-delayed according to other criteria.

The *construct validity* of the problem scales was supported by concurrent and predictive associations with a variety of other measures, plus evidence for substantial genetic components of the patterns of problems assessed by the scales. The construct validity of the LDS was supported by its ability to predict a variety of weak verbal skills in 13-year-olds whom it identified as language-delayed at age 2.

Chapter 10
Problem Item Scores

In addition to being the basis for the profile scales, each ASEBA problem item may be important in its own right. To determine which items discriminated significantly between children referred for mental health or special education services and nonreferred children, we performed analyses of covariance (ANCOVA) on the item scores obtained by the demographically matched samples described in Chapter 9. The ANCOVA design was 2 (referral status) x 2 (gender), with age in years, lower-middle-upper SES, and nonLatino white vs. other ethnicity as covariates. The total N was 1,126 CBCL and 606 C-TRF, equally divided between referred and nonreferred children, as described in Chapter 9.

Table 10-1 summarizes the ANCOVA results for each item and the Total Problems score in terms of the percent of variance accounted for by each effect that was significant at $p \leq .01$. To flag the effects that might be significant by chance, superscript f indicates the 5 out of 101 tests of each variable that were most likely to be significant at $p \leq .01$ by chance (using a .01 protection level), because they had the smallest F values (Sakoda et al., 1954). The following effects are omitted from Table 10-1 because they did not exceed the number expected to be significant by chance: Interactions between referral status and gender on both forms; SES and ethnicity on the C-TRF.

REFERRAL STATUS DIFFERENCES IN PROBLEM ITEM SCORES

Of the problem items that appear on both forms, Table 10-1 shows that referred children were scored significantly higher ($p \leq .01$) on all items on at least one form, except items *33, 61,* and *100*. Item *33. Feelings are easily hurt* was scored slightly higher for nonreferred than referred children on the CBCL, but this difference would be considered nonsignificant when corrected for the number of analyses. Because this item loaded significantly on the CBCL and C-TRF Anxious/Depressed syndrome, it may contribute to the identification of children who are vulnerable to problems of negative affect. In our present samples, item *61. Refuses to eat* was scored higher for referred than nonreferred children at $p = .07$ on the CBCL and $p = .42$ on the C-TRF. In our CBCL/2-3 sample, it was scored significantly higher for referred than nonreferred children at $p < .05$ (Achenbach, 1992).

Being completely open-ended, item *100* includes whatever the respondent chooses to report. Although the specific responses are clinically useful, they do not form a clearcut class of problems that discriminated significantly between referred and nonreferred children.

Of the problem items that appear on only one form, the following C-TRF items were not scored significantly higher for referred than nonreferred children: *12. Apathetic or unmotivated; 19. Daydreams or gets lost in his/her thoughts; 49. Fears daycare or school;* and *94. Unclean personal appearance.* All of these except item *94* are on C-TRF empirically based syndromes or DSM-oriented scales. Item *94* was scored higher for referred than nonreferred children at $p = .06$ in our present sample and at $p < .01$ in our previous C-TRF sample (Achenbach, 1997).

Effect Sizes

According to Cohen's (1988) criteria for effect sizes, ANCOVA effects accounting for 1 to 5.9% of variance are small; effects accounting for 5.9 to 13.8% are medium; and effects accounting for $\geq 13.8\%$ are large. As Table 10-1 shows, the largest effect of referral status was

Table 10-1
Percent of Variance Accounted for by Significant ($p \leq .01$) Effects of Referral Status and Demographic Variables on Item Scores in ANCOVAs

Item	Ref Stat[a] CBCL	Ref Stat[a] C-TRF	Gender[b] CBCL	Gender[b] C-TRF	Age[c] CBCL	Age[c] C-TRF	SES[d] CBCL	Ethnicity[e] CBCL
1. Aches, pains	16				6[O]		1[U]	<1[Nf]
2. Acts too young	5	6		1[Bf]	2[O]			
3. Afraid to try new	1				1[O]			
4. Avoids eye contact	4	4		2[B]	1[O]			
5. Can't concentrate	4	7		4[B]			<1	
6. Can't sit still	6	8		3[B]			2	
7. Can't stand things out of place	3	5			1[O]			
8. Can't stand waiting		11			2[Y]		<1[f]	
9. Chews nonfood	10	3				3[Y]		1[N]
10. Too dependent	<1	2	1[Bf]	2[G]	2[Y]			
11. Seeks help	6	2						
12. Constipated-CBCL	4							
Apathetic-C-TRF				1[Bf]				
13. Cries a lot	4	2	2[G]		1[Y]			
14. Cruel to animals	13	3						
15. Defiant	1	13	<1[Gf]		1[Y]			
16. Demands must be met	9	13						
17. Destroys own things	12	5						<1[Nf]
18. Destroys others' things	9	6	1[Gf]	2[B]			2	
19. Diarrhea-CBCL	8							
Daydreams-C-TRF								
20. Disobedient	2	10		1[B]	2[Y]		<1[f]	
21. Disturbed by change	11	5						
22. Not sleep alone-CBCL	1							
Mean to others-C-TRF		7		2[B]				
23. Doesn't answer	7	6		2[B]				
24. Doesn't eat well-CBCL	6							
Difficulty with directions-C-TRF		7		4[B]				
25. Doesn't get along	11	8		1[Bf]				
26. No fun	4	1[f]			1[O]		<1	
27. Lacks guilt	4	9		3[B]	1[Y]			
28. Doesn't leave home-CBCL	8				4[O]			
Disturbs others-C-TRF		11		3[B]				
29. Easily frustrated	2	10			1[Y]		1	<1[W]
30. Easily jealous	6	5					<1	<1[Nf]
31. Eats nonfood	9	4				3[Y]		
32. Fears	(1)	1			1[Y]			
33. Feelings easily hurt	(1[f])						2	
34. Accident-prone	14	5					1	
35. Gets in fights	6	4		3[B]			<1[f]	
36. Gets into things	<1[f]	5	1[Bf]	1[B]	8[Y]		2	
37. Upset when separated	3				1[Y]		<1	
38. Trouble sleeping-CBCL	10				<1[Yf]			
Explosive-C-TRF		9		3[B]				
39. Headaches	9				3[O]			
40. Hits others	3	5		4[B]	4[Y]		2	

PROBLEM ITEM SCORES

Table 10-1 (cont.)

Item	Ref Stat[a] CBCL	C-TRF	Gender[b] CBCL	C-TRF	Age[c] CBCL	C-TRF	SES[d] CBCL	Ethnicity[e] CBCL
41. Holds breath	13	2			3[O]			
42. Hurts unintentionally	3	6		2[B]	2[Y]		<1	<1[Wf]
43. Looks unhappy	9	2						
44. Angry moods	4	11					2	
45. Nausea	12				6[O]			1[N]
46. Twitches	4	1[f]						
47. Nervous	8	10					<1	
48. Nightmares-CBCL	4							
Fails to finish-C-TRF		8		2[B]				
49. Overeating-CBCL	3							1[N]
Fears school-C-TRF								
50. Overtired	1[f]	3						2[W]
51. Panics-CBCL	1[f]							
Fidgets-C-TRF		8						
52. Painful BM-CBCL	2							
Is teased-C-TRF		1						
53. Attacks people	7	7		2[B]			<1[f]	
54. Picks skin	1	1[f]						2[W]
55. Plays with sex parts	9				<1[Of]			
56. Clumsy	3	4				1[Yf]	2	
57. Eye problems	2							<1[N]
58. Punishment doesn't change behavior	3	10		3[B]	<1[Yf]		2	
59. Quickly shifts	1	6		1[B]		1[Yf]		
60. Skin problems	7				2[O]			
61. Won't eat					2[Y]			
62. Refuses active games	4	1[f]						
63. Rocks head or body	4	2						
64. Resists bed-CBCL	<1[f]				1[Y]		1	
Inattentive-C-TRF		8		4[B]				
65. Resists toilet training-CBCL	6				2[Y]			
Lying, cheating-C-TRF		3				3[O]		
66. Screams	5	7			4[Y]		1	
67. Unresponsive to affection	11	2		1[B]	<1[O]			
68. Self-conscious		3			2[O]			
69. Selfish		7			1[Y]		1	
70. Little affection	9	2		2[B]	<1[Of]			<1[Nf]
71. Little interest	2						2	
72. Little fear		4		3[B]	1[Y]	1[Yf]		
73. Shy, timid	2				<1[Of]			
74. Sleeps little-CBCL	5							
Not liked-C-TRF		4		1[Bf]				
75. Smears BM-CBCL	8				1[O]			
Overactive-C-TRF		9		3[B]				
76. Speech problem	7	3			<1[Y]	2[Y]	1	
77. Stares	7	2	1[B]					
78. Stomachaches	3				2[O]			
79. Shifts between sad-excite-CBCL	5							
Overconforms-C-TRF		1[f]						
80. Strange behavior	11	4						

Table 10-1 (cont.)

Item	Ref Stat[a] CBCL	Ref Stat[a] C-TRF	Gender[b] CBCL	Gender[b] C-TRF	Age[c] CBCL	Age[c] C-TRF	SES[d] CBCL	Ethnicity[e] CBCL
81. Stubborn	3	10					2	
82. Sudden mood change	17	12					<1	
83. Sulks a lot	7	3			1[O]			
84. Talks, cries in sleep-CBCL	4							
Teases a lot-C-TRF		6		1[Bf]				
85. Temper	6	9			2[Y]		2	
86. Too concerned with neatness	3				2[O]			1[N]
87. Fearful		2					<1	
88. Uncooperative	5	10	1[B]				<1[f]	
89. Underactive	13				4[O]			
90. Unhappy, sad, depressed	5	7						
91. Loud	2	8	1[Bf]				1	
92. Upset by new	7	3						
93. Vomits	6							1[N]
94. Wakes often-CBCL	5				3[Y]		<1	1[W]
Unclean-C-TRF								
95. Wanders away	3	4	2[B]			2[Yf]		
96. Wants attention		12			2[Y]		3	
97. Whining	4	3						
98. Withdrawn	12	1			1[O]			
99. Worries	3	2			3[O]	1[Of]		
100. Other problems								
Total Problems	22	17	2[B]				2	

Note. N = 1,126 CBCL and N = 606 C-TRF, equally divided between referred and nonreferred children. Items are designated with summary labels for their content. Analyses were referral status x gender ANCOVAs with age in years, lower middle-upper SES, and nonLatino white vs. other ethnicity as covariates. Effects of interactions for both instruments and SES and ethnicity for C-TRF are omitted because they did not exceed chance expectations of 5 significant effects in 101 analyses.

[a]All significant effects of referral status reflected higher scores for referred than nonreferred except items *32* and *33* on the CBCL (indicated by parentheses).
[b]B = boys scored higher; G = girls scored higher.
[c]O = older scored higher; Y = younger scored higher.
[d]All significant effects of SES reflected higher scores for lower SES, except CBCL item *1*, which is superscripted U to indicate higher scores for upper SES. SES effects on the C-TRF did not exceed chance expectations.
[e]N = nonwhite; W = white. Ethnicity effects on the C-TRF did not exceed chance expectations.
[f]Not significant when corrected for number of analyses.

found for the Total Problems score, where the higher scores obtained by referred than nonreferred children accounted for 22% of the variance on the CBCL and 17% on the C-TRF. Referral status also had large effects on the following CBCL items: *1. Aches or pains (without medical cause)* (16%); *34. Gets hurt a lot, accident prone* (14%); and *82. Sudden changes in mood or feelings* (17%). On the C-TRF, the largest effects for individual items were: *15.*

Defiant (13%); *16. Demands must be met immediately* (13%); and *96. Wants a lot of attention* (12%).

DEMOGRAPHIC DIFFERENCES IN PROBLEM SCORES

In addition to the significant effects of referral status, Table 10-1 displays effect sizes for significant associations with gender and age on both instruments, plus SES and ethnicity on the CBCL. (These effects did not exceed chance expectations on the C-TRF.)

Gender Differences

With none exceeding 2% of variance, the 7 significant CBCL gender effects were barely above the chance expectation of 5 significant effects. Four reflected higher scores for boys, while 3 reflected higher scores for girls. On the C-TRF, by contrast, 32 items and the Total Problems score showed significant gender effects, all reflecting higher scores for boys except item *10. Clings to adults or too dependent* (2%). The largest gender effects accounted for 4% of variance on the following C-TRF items: *5. Can't concentrate, can't pay attention for long; 24. Difficulty following directions; 40. Hits others;* and *64. Inattentive, easily distracted.* Boys obtained significantly higher C-TRF Total Problems scores, accounting for 2% of variance.

Age Differences

The only demographic effects that reached Cohen's (1988) criterion for medium effects reflected the tendency for younger children to score higher on CBCL item *36. Gets into everything* (8% of variance) and for older children to score higher on *1. Aches or pains (without medical cause)* (6%) and *45. Nausea, feels sick (without medical cause)* (6%). On the CBCL, 23 age effects reflected higher scores for older children, while 24 reflected higher scores for younger children. On the C-TRF, there were far fewer age effects, with 7 reflecting higher scores for younger children and 2 reflecting higher scores for older children. Age was not significantly associated with Total Problems on either instrument. There was thus no consistent tendency for problem scores to increase or decrease with age.

SES Differences

SES differences exceeded chance expectations only on the CBCL, where lower SES parents tended to rate their children higher on 33 items and Total Problems. Upper SES parents tended to rate their children higher only on item *1. Aches or pains (without medical cause).* All SES effects were very small by Cohen's criteria, with only item *96. Wants a lot of attention* reaching 3% of variance.

Ethnic Differences

Ethnic differences exceeded chance expectations only on the CBCL, where nonLatino white parents tended to rate their children higher on 5 items and parents of other ethnic groups tended to rate their children higher on 10 items. All effects were very small, with only items *50. Overtired* and *54. Picks nose, skin, or other parts of body* reaching 2% of variance, both reflecting higher scores for nonLatino white children. Ethnic differences had no significant effect on Total Problems scores.

GRAPHS OF PREVALENCE RATES

To provide a detailed picture of the prevalence rate for each problem item, Figure 10-1 displays the percent of children for whom each problem was reported (i.e., was scored 1 or 2). The data points in the graphs correspond to the cells of the ANCOVAs, with children grouped according to referral status and gender, separately for the CBCL and C-TRF. (Mean scale scores were displayed for Total Problems and all other scales in Figure 9-1.)

PROBLEM ITEM SCORES

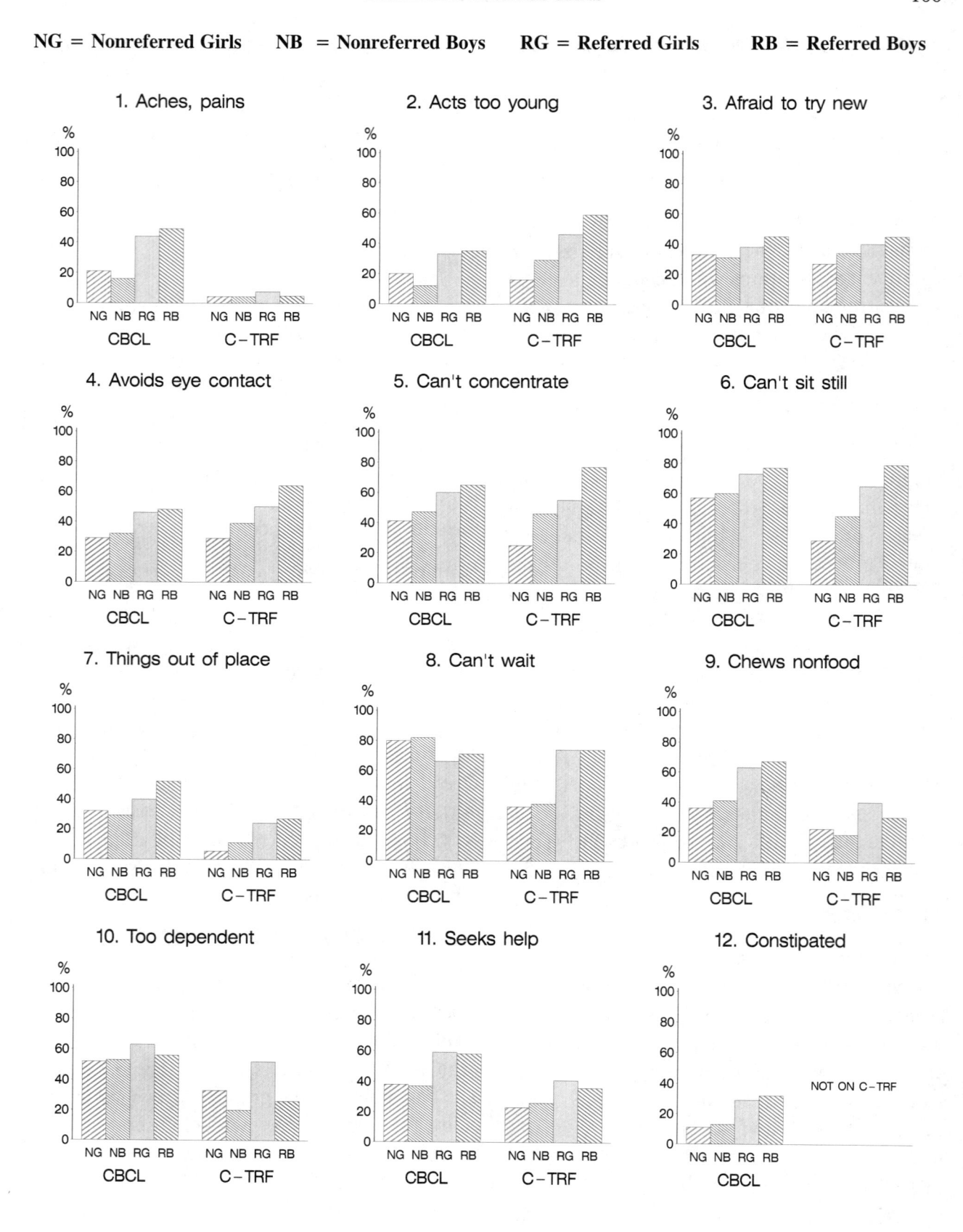

NG = Nonreferred Girls   NB = Nonreferred Boys   RG = Referred Girls   RB = Referred Boys

Figure 10-1. Percent of children for whom each problem was reported.

PROBLEM ITEM SCORES

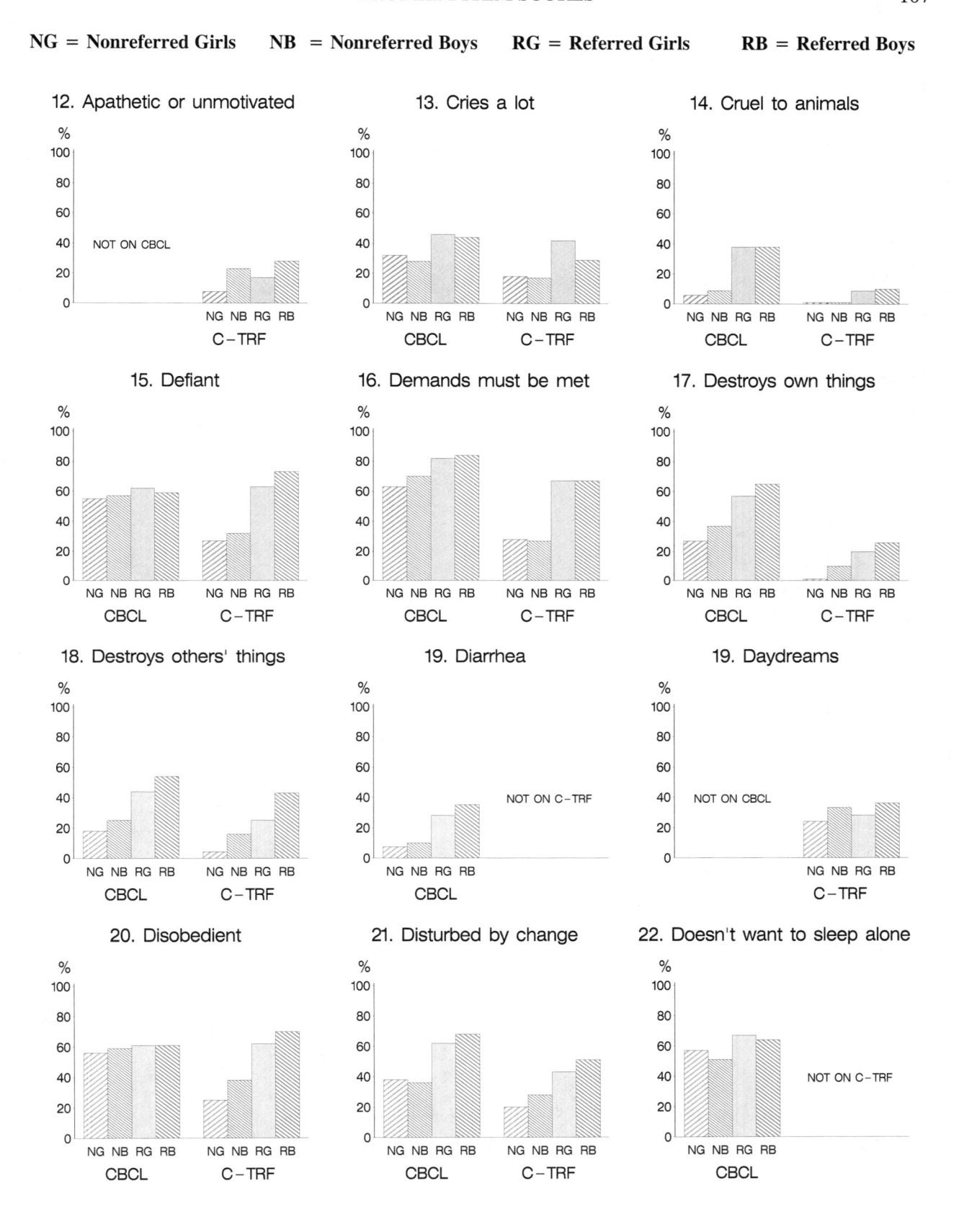

NG = Nonreferred Girls   NB = Nonreferred Boys   RG = Referred Girls   RB = Referred Boys

Figure 10-1 (cont.). Percent of children for whom each problem was reported.

PROBLEM ITEM SCORES

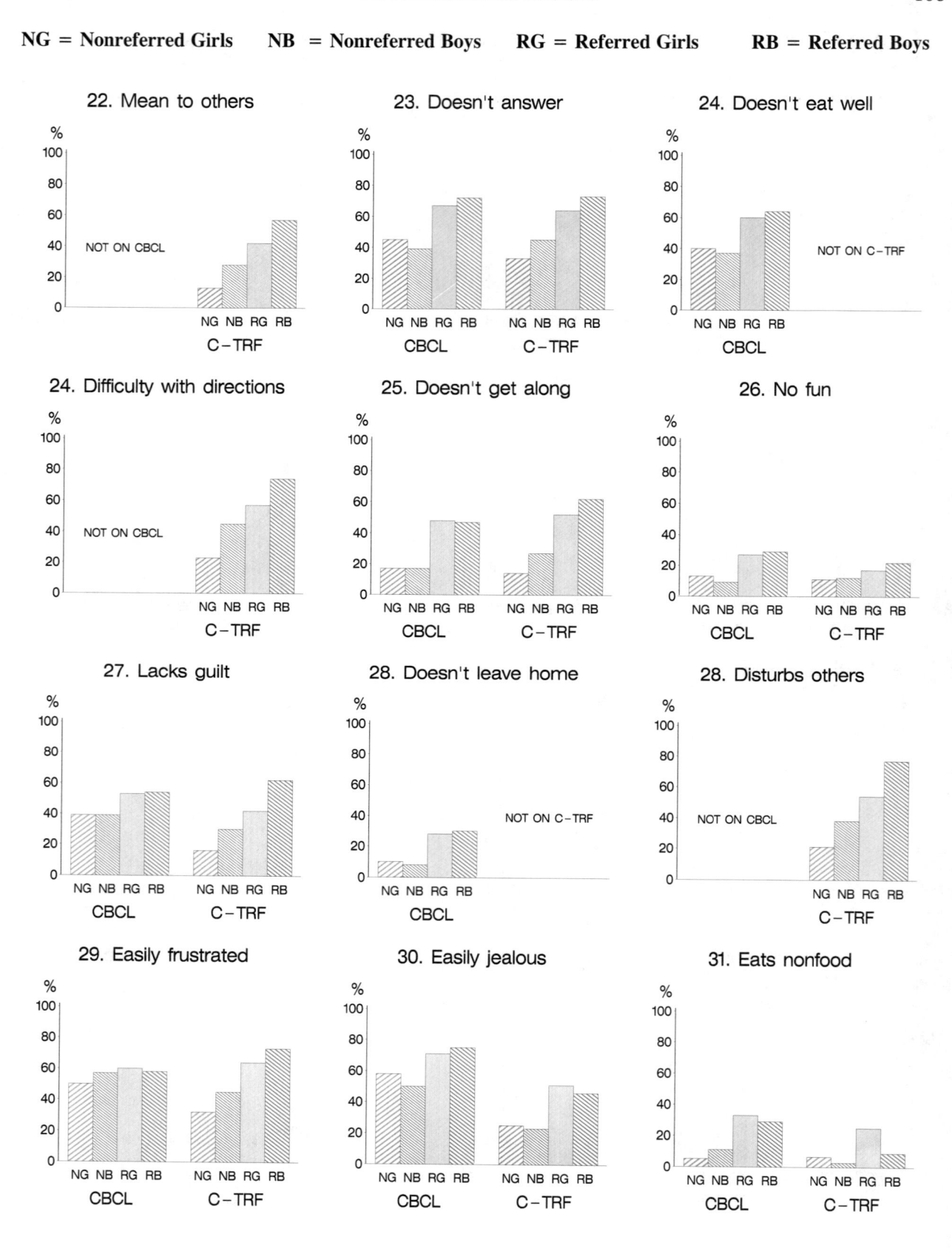

NG = Nonreferred Girls   NB = Nonreferred Boys   RG = Referred Girls   RB = Referred Boys

Figure 10-1 (cont.). Percent of children for whom each problem was reported.

PROBLEM ITEM SCORES

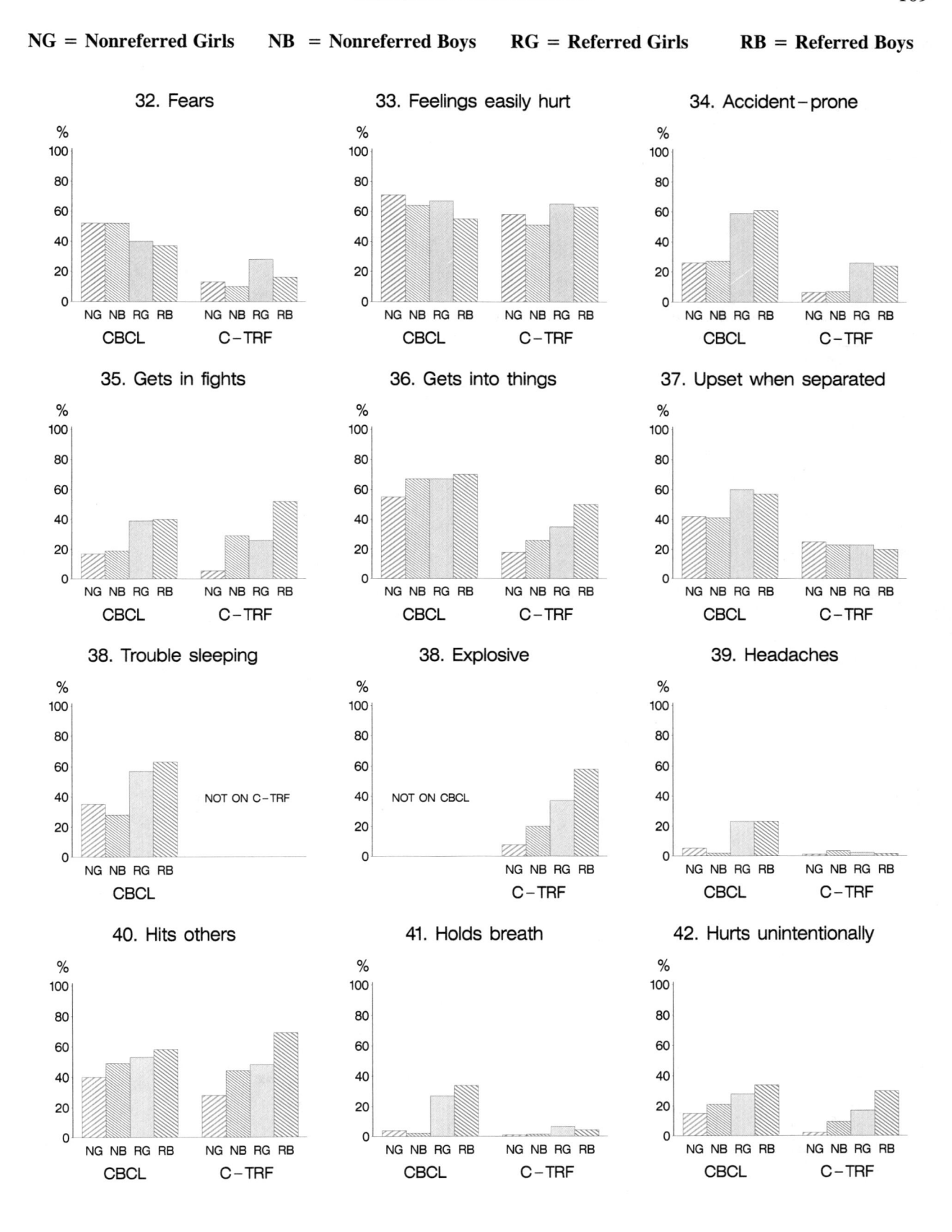

NG = Nonreferred Girls   NB = Nonreferred Boys   RG = Referred Girls   RB = Referred Boys

Figure 10-1 (cont.). Percent of children for whom each problem was reported.

PROBLEM ITEM SCORES

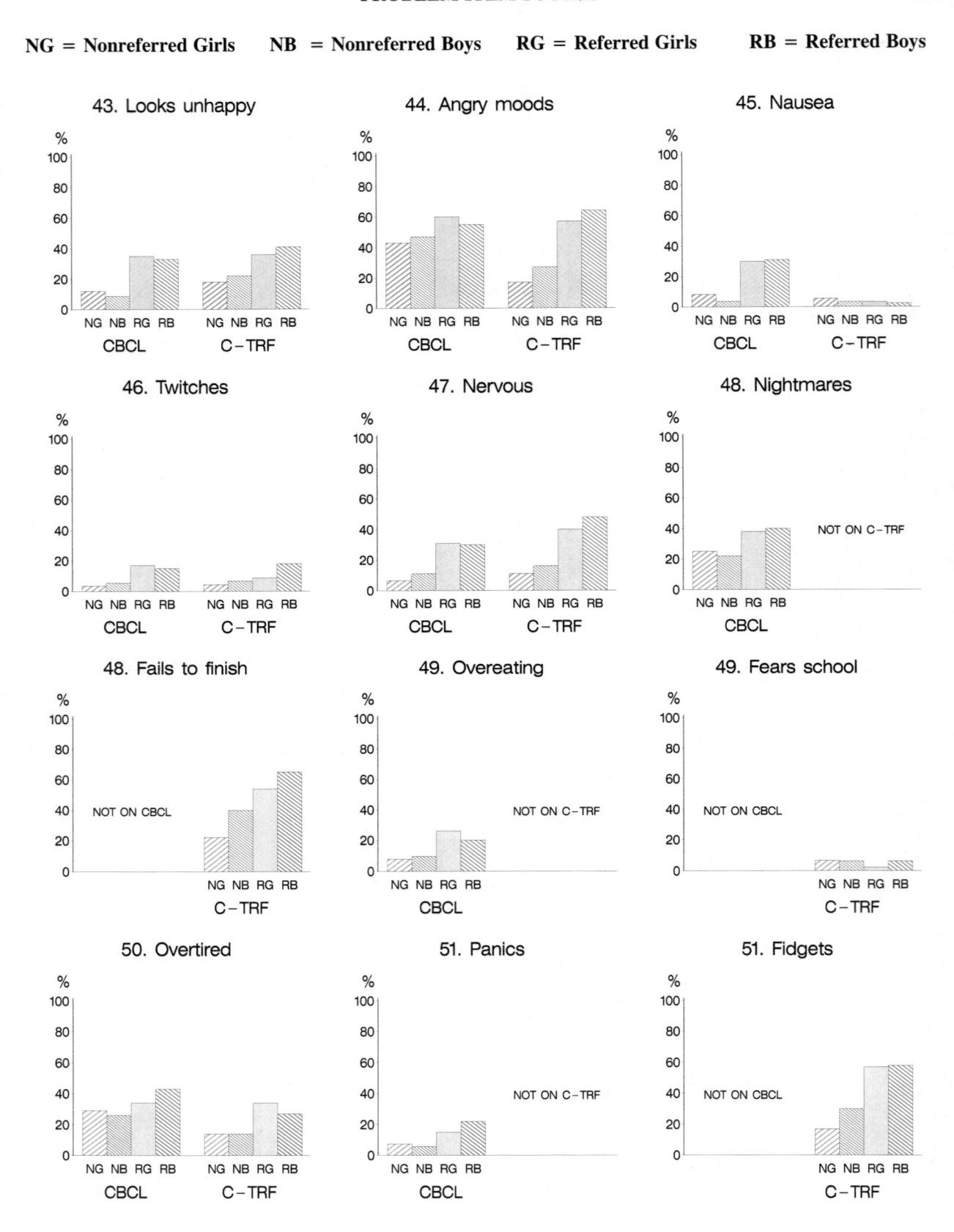

NG = Nonreferred Girls   NB = Nonreferred Boys   RG = Referred Girls   RB = Referred Boys

Figure 10-1 (cont.). Percent of children for whom each problem was reported.

PROBLEM ITEM SCORES 111

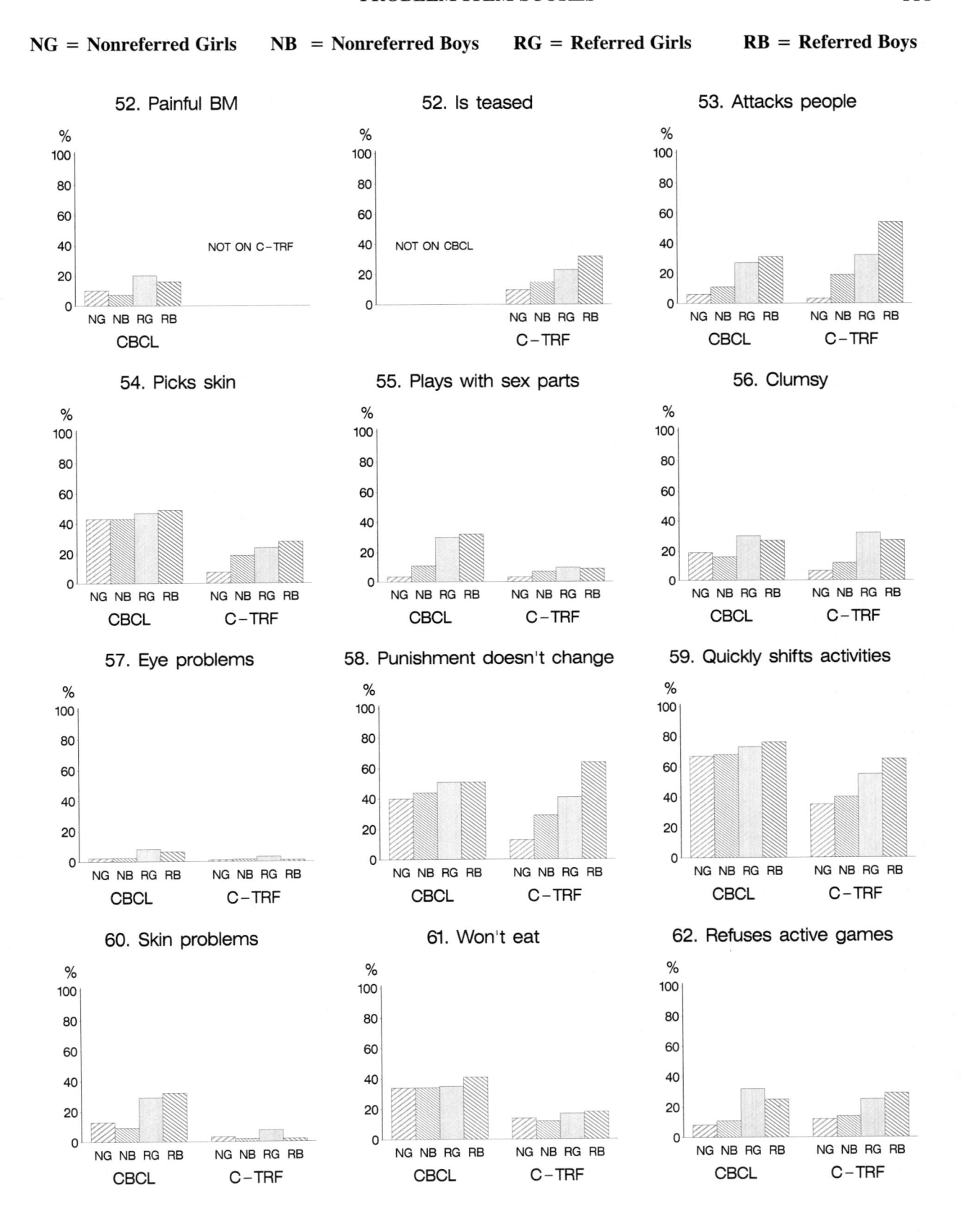

NG = Nonreferred Girls   NB = Nonreferred Boys   RG = Referred Girls   RB = Referred Boys

Figure 10-1 (cont.). Percent of children for whom each problem was reported.

PROBLEM ITEM SCORES

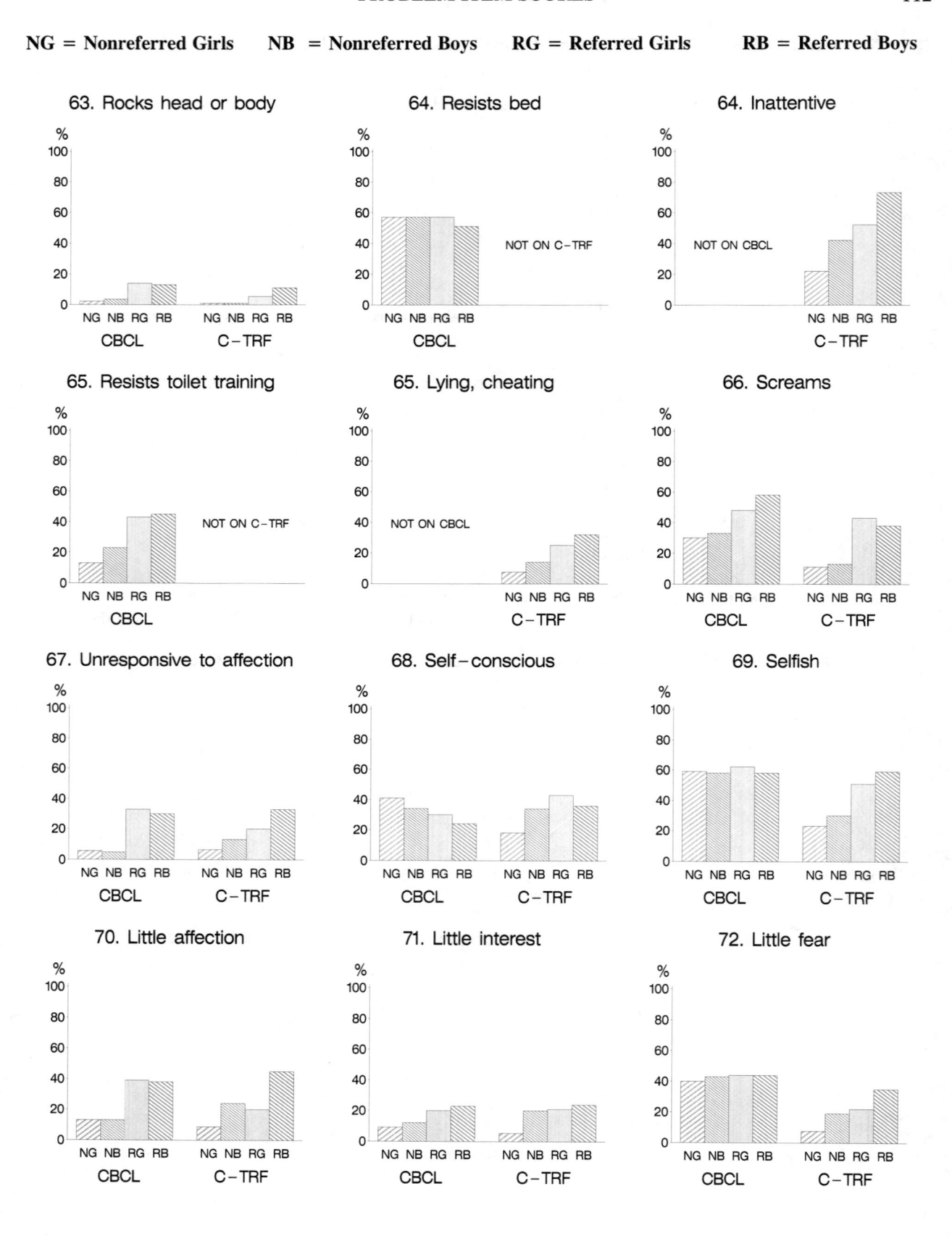

NG = Nonreferred Girls   NB = Nonreferred Boys   RG = Referred Girls   RB = Referred Boys

Figure 10-1 (cont.). Percent of children for whom each problem was reported.

PROBLEM ITEM SCORES

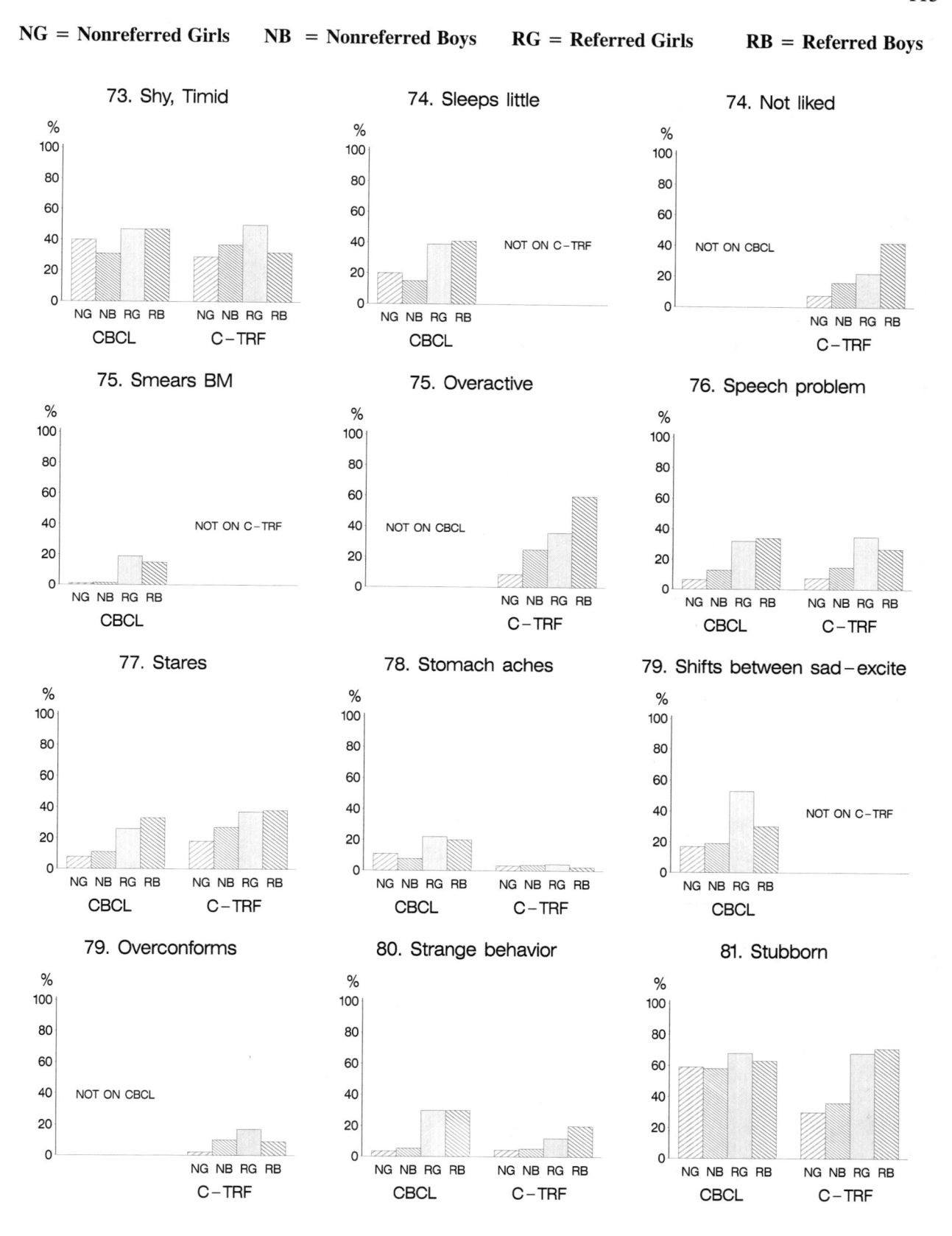

NG = Nonreferred Girls   **NB** = Nonreferred Boys   **RG** = Referred Girls   **RB** = Referred Boys

Figure 10-1 (cont.). Percent of children for whom each problem was reported.

PROBLEM ITEM SCORES 114

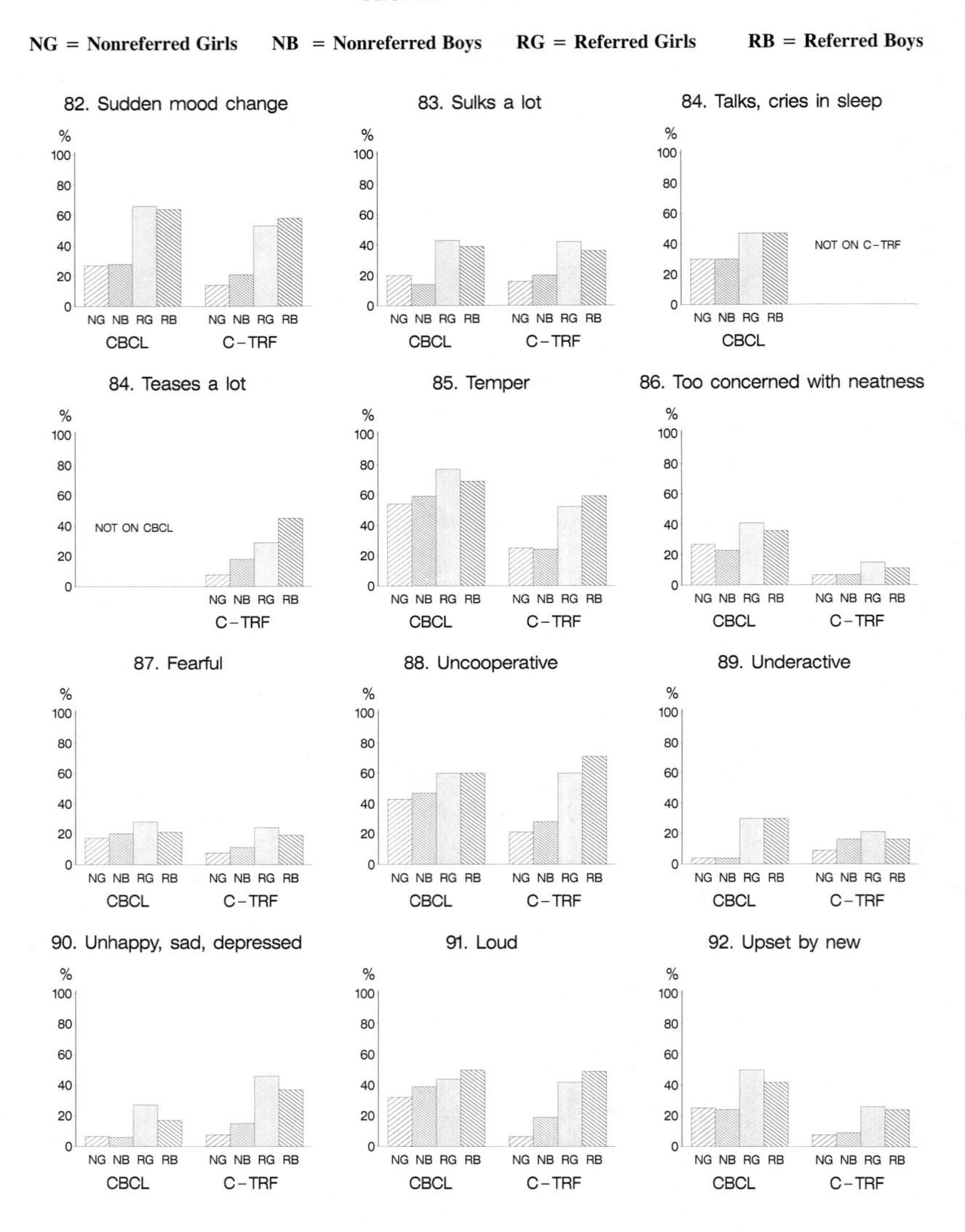

NG = Nonreferred Girls   NB = Nonreferred Boys   RG = Referred Girls   RB = Referred Boys

82. Sudden mood change
83. Sulks a lot
84. Talks, cries in sleep (NOT ON C-TRF)
84. Teases a lot (NOT ON CBCL)
85. Temper
86. Too concerned with neatness
87. Fearful
88. Uncooperative
89. Underactive
90. Unhappy, sad, depressed
91. Loud
92. Upset by new

Figure 10-1 (cont.). Percent of children for whom each problem was reported.

PROBLEM ITEM SCORES 115

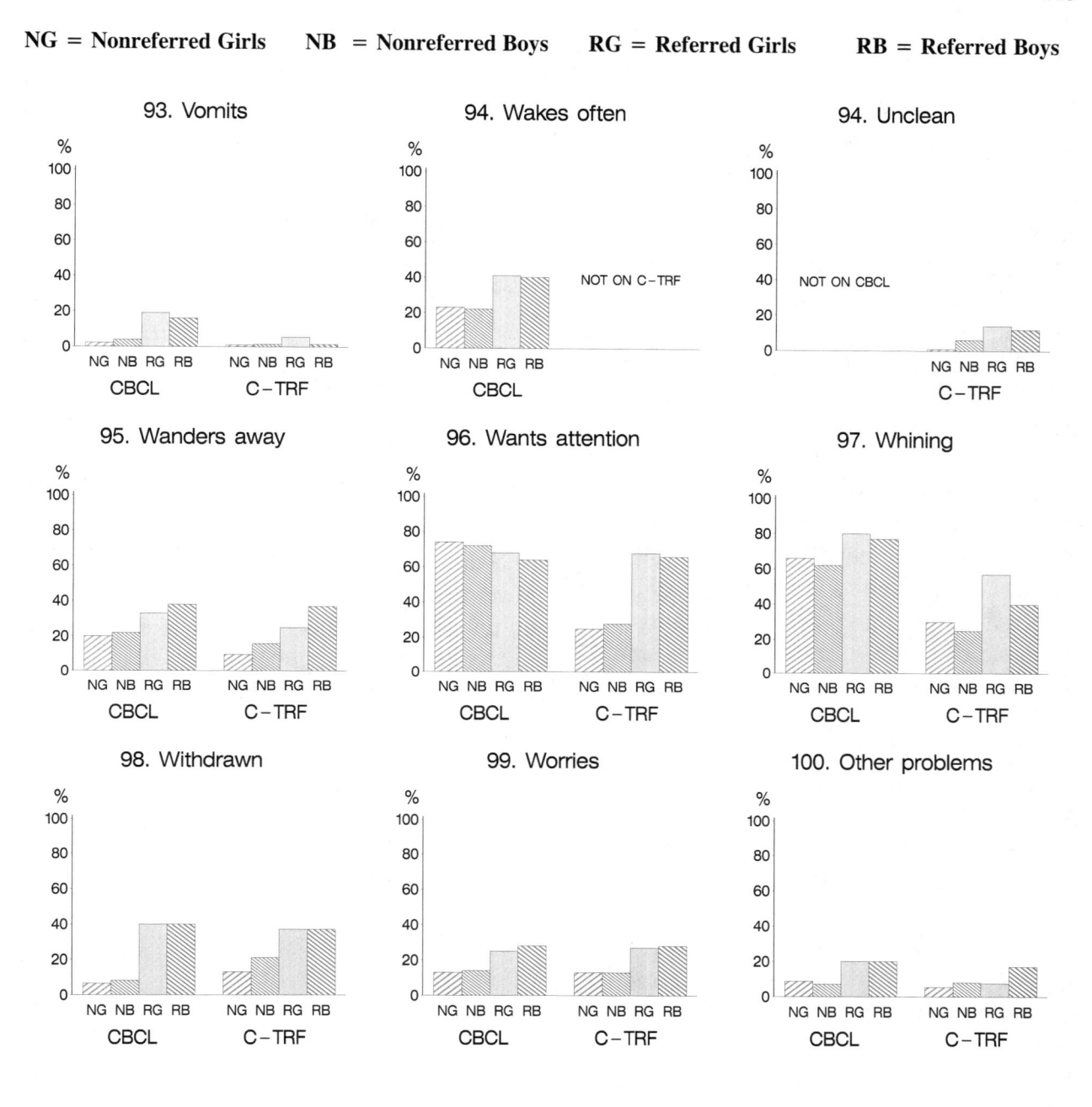

NG = Nonreferred Girls   NB = Nonreferred Boys   RG = Referred Girls   RB = Referred Boys

Figure 10-1 (cont.). Percent of children for whom each problem was reported.

Note that in some of the bar graphs in Figure 10-1, the percentage of referred children who were reported to have a particular kind of problem appears to be less than or equal to the percentage of nonreferred children reported to have the problem. In these cases, the dichotomous classification of children as either having or not having the problem masks the fact that more of the referred children received scores of 2. As a result, there was an overall tendency for referred children to obtain higher scores, which was reflected in higher mean scores for referred than nonreferred children. By looking in Appendix F at the actual distributions of 1 and 2 scores, as well as the mean scores, you can see that referred children obtained higher scores than nonreferred children on the following CBCL items, despite the appearance of the bar graphs to the contrary: *64. Resists going to bed at night; 69. Selfish or won't share;* and *72. Shows too little fear of getting hurt.*

SUMMARY

This chapter reported ANCOVAs of scores obtained by demographically matched referred and nonreferred children on the CBCL and C-TRF problem items and Total Problems. Of the items that appear on both forms, all but items *33* and *61* and the open-ended item *100* were scored significantly ($p \leq .01$) higher for referred than nonreferred children on at least one form. Although it was scored significantly higher for nonreferred than referred children in the CBCL sample, item *33. Feelings are easily hurt* obtained significant loadings on the CBCL and C-TRF Anxious/Depressed syndrome. This suggests that item 33 may contribute to the identification of children who are vulnerable to negative affect, even though it was not scored higher in our very heterogeneous sample of referred children.

The higher scores obtained by referred than nonreferred children accounted for 22% of the variance in Total Problems on the CBCL and 17% on the C-TRF, both exceeding Cohen's (1988) criterion for large effects.

Demographic effects were considerably smaller, with SES and ethnic differences not exceeding chance expectations on the C-TRF. Gender effects were most numerous on the C-TRF, where 31 of the 32 effects on item scores, plus the effect on Total Problems, reflected higher scores for boys than girls. Age effects were most numerous on the CBCL, where they were about equally divided between items on which younger vs. older children scored higher, but there were no significant age differences in Total Problems scores.

SES effects primarily reflected tendencies for lower SES parents to rate their children higher on the CBCL problem items, while ethnic effects were more evenly divided between items on which nonLatino white vs. other parents rated their children higher on the CBCL problem items. Ethnic differences had no significant effects on Total Problems scores. Figure 10-1 graphically displays the prevalence rate for each problem item by gender, referral status, and instrument.

Chapter 11
Relations Between the New ASEBA Scales and Previous Versions

In this chapter, we present similarities and differences between the new ASEBA scales and the previous scales that were scored from the CBCL/2-3 (Achenbach, 1992) and the C-TRF (Achenbach, 1997). We also present correlations between scores on the new scales and scores on their previous counterparts.

Other than minor changes in wording, the main innovations in the current ASEBA forms, scales, and profiles are as follows:

1. On the CBCL/1½-5, items *51. Shows panic for no good reason* and *79. Rapid shifts between sadness and excitement* replace items that were not scored on the CBCL/2-3 scales.

2. The new syndrome scales, as well as the Internalizing and Externalizing scales, were derived on larger, more representative samples of children by using combinations of exploratory and confirmatory factor analytic methodology to test similar factor structures for the CBCL/1½-5 and C-TRF.

3. DSM-oriented scales were constructed from ASEBA items rated by experienced psychiatrists and psychologists as being very consistent with DSM-IV diagnostic categories.

4. The new ASEBA scales were normed on new national samples of children.

5. The borderline clinical range on the syndrome scales was changed from *T* scores of 67 through 70 to *T* scores of 65 through 69.

6. The computer-scoring program now displays side-by-side item and scale scores, plus cross-informant correlations, for any combination of up to eight CBCL/1½-5 and C-TRF forms per child.

7. The LDS is now included on the same form as the CBCL/1½-5.

CHANGES IN SYNDROME SCALES

Our use of larger, more representative samples and more advanced analyses that were coordinated between the CBCL/1½-5 and C-TRF yielded some syndromes that are quite similar to the previous versions and some that are different. The new syndromes having predecessors with similar names on both instruments are Aggressive Behavior and Somatic Complaints. On the CBCL, the syndromes having predecessors with similar names are Anxious/Depressed, Sleep Problems, and Withdrawn. And on the C-TRF, the Attention Problems syndrome has a predecessor with a similar name. In addition, the CBCL now has an Attention Problems syndrome, while the C-TRF now has Anxious/Depressed and Withdrawn syndromes.

A new syndrome, designated as Emotionally Reactive, was found in all factor analyses of the CBCL/1½-5. The new CBCL/1½-5 items *51. Shows panic for no good reason* and *79. Rapid shifts between sadness and excitement* obtained high loadings on all versions of this factor (.62 to .81 for item *51*; .47 to .50 for item *79*). These two items are not on the C-TRF. However, as described in Chapter 6, the C-TRF counterparts of the other items of the Emotionally Reactive syndrome were found to form a factor that was successfully integrated into the C-TRF factor structure. In addition to CBCL/1½-5 items *51* and *79*, the items comprising this factor on both instruments are: *21. Disturbed by any change in routine; 46. Nervous movements or twitching; 82. Sudden changes in mood or feelings; 83. Sulks a lot; 92. Upset by new people or situations; 97. Whining;* and *99. Worries*. This syndrome may reflect early manifestations of mood disorders.

INTERNALIZING AND EXTERNALIZING

The new Internalizing and Externalizing groupings were constructed by performing second-order factor analyses of the correlations among the new syndrome scales, as described in Chapter 7. We performed separate factor analyses for each gender on the CBCL/1½-5 and C-TRF. The loadings obtained by each syndrome on each second-order factor in the four analyses (each gender on each instrument) were averaged to determine which syndromes were most strongly associated with each other. We found that the Aggressive Behavior and Attention Problems syndromes had their highest mean loadings on one factor, which we designated as Externalizing. The Emotionally Reactive, Anxious/Depressed, Somatic Complaints, and Withdrawn syndromes had their highest mean loadings on the other factor, which we designated as Internalizing. The CBCL Sleep Problems syndrome had low loadings on both second-order factors.

Like the previous C-TRF version, the new Externalizing grouping includes the Aggressive Behavior and Attention Problems syndromes. Like the previous version for both the CBCL and C-TRF, the new Internalizing grouping includes syndromes involving anxiety, depression, and withdrawal. However, the new Internalizing grouping also includes the Emotionally Reactive and Somatic Complaints syndromes. The CBCL Sleep Problems syndrome remains separate from the Internalizing and Externalizing groupings.

TOTAL PROBLEMS SCALE

The Total Problems scale for the CBCL now includes the new items *51* and *79* that replace the previous items *51* and *79*. The previous items *51* and *79* were not included in the Total Problems score on the CBCL/2-3, because they were not found to discriminate between referred and nonreferred children. The C-TRF Total Problems score comprises the same items as the previous version.

STATISTICAL RELATIONS BETWEEN THE NEW ASEBA SCALES AND PREVIOUS VERSIONS

Table 11-1 displays Pearson correlations between the scores for the new scales and their closest counterparts among the previous versions. Both sets of scores were computed from the ASEBA forms completed for our matched referred and nonreferred samples described in Chapter 9. These correlations can provide guidance for users who wish to relate findings obtained with the previous scales to findings likely to be obtained with the new scales.

As Table 11-1 shows, most correlations between the new and previous empirically based scales were > .90. These correlations indicate high consistency in the rank ordering of scores that children would obtain on the counterpart scales. However, users should keep in mind that children will not usually obtain the same raw total scores on counterpart scales, because of differences in some of the items included in the scales.

The new Emotionally Reactive syndrome correlated .79 with the Total Problems scales on both instruments and also with the C-TRF Immature syndrome. These correlations and the lower correlations for CBCL Attention Problems ($r = .75$) and for C-TRF Anxious/Depressed ($r = .74$) and Somatic Complaints ($r = .56$) suggest that these new syndromes tap constructs that were not tapped in quite the same way by the previous syndrome scales.

DSM-Oriented Scales

The correlations for the DSM-oriented scales suggest that the constructs tapped by the Pervasive Developmental Problems ($r = .87$)

Table 11-1
Pearson Correlations Between the New ASEBA Scales and Previous Versions

New Scales	CBCL	C-TRF
	N = 1,126	N = 606
Syndromes		
Emotionally Reactive[a]	.79	.79
Anxious/Depressed[b]	.94	.74
Somatic Complaints	.97	.56
Withdrawn[c]	.91	.92
Sleep Problems	1.00	NA
Attention Problems[d]	.75	.96
Aggressive Behavior	.96	.99
Internalizing	.86	.95
Externalizing	.93	.99
Total Problems	1.00	1.00
DSM-Oriented Scales		
Affective Problems[e]	.79	.84
Anxiety Problems[f]	.79	.72
Pervasive Developmental Problems[g]	.85	.87
Attention Deficit/Hyperactivity Problems[h]	.81	.98
Oppositional Defiant Problems[i]	.89	.95

Note: Samples were equally divided between referred and nonreferred children. All *r*s were significant at *p* < .01. Superscripts indicate scales whose highest correlation was with a previous scale having a different name than the new scale.

[a]Emotionally Reactive *r* for CBCL and C-TRF is with Total Problems and also with Immature for C-TRF.

[b]Anxious/Depressed *r* for C-TRF is with Internalizing.

[c]Withdrawn *r* for C-TRF is with Depressed/Withdrawn.

[d]Attention Problems *r* for CBCL is with Destructive Behavior.

[e]Affective Problems *r* for CBCL is with Total Problems; *r* for C-TRF is with Depressed/Withdrawn.

[f]Anxiety Problems *r* for CBCL is with Anxious/Depressed; *r* for C-TRF is with Anxious/Obsessive.

[g]Pervasive Developmental Problems *r* for CBCL is with Withdrawn; *r* for C-TRF is with Internalizing.

[h]Attention Deficit/Hyperactivity Problems *r* for CBCL is with Externalizing.

[i]Oppositional Defiant Problems *r* for CBCL and C-TRF is with Aggressive Behavior.

and Attention Deficit/Hyperactivity Problems ($r = .98$) scales were well measured by previous C-TRF scales, and that the construct tapped by the Oppositional Defiant Problems scale was well measured by previous scales of both the CBCL ($r = .89$) and C-TRF ($r = .95$). The lowest correlations of DSM-oriented scales on the CBCL were .79 for the DSM-Oriented Affective and Anxiety Problems scales. As shown in Appendix E, the DSM-oriented scales correlate with the new empirically based scales at about the same level as with the previous CBCL/2-3 and C-TRF scales. However, the DSM-oriented Anxiety Problems scale correlates .87 with the new C-TRF Anxious/Depressed syndrome among nonreferred children and .80 among referred children, compared with its correlation of .72 with the previous C-TRF Anxious/Depressed syndrome.

SUMMARY

This chapter presented similarities and differences between the new ASEBA preschool scales and previous scales scored from the CBCL/2-3 and the C-TRF. Innovations include: Replacement of items *51* and *79* on the CBCL; new syndromes and Internalizing and Externalizing groupings were derived on larger, more representative samples via advanced factor analytic methodology coordinated between the CBCL and C-TRF; DSM-oriented scales have been added; the borderline range on the syndrome scales now spans from $T = 65$ through 69; the computer-scoring program now displays side-by-side item and scale scores, plus cross-informant correlations, for any combination of up to eight CBCL/1½-5 and C-TRF forms per child; and the LDS is now included with the CBCL/1½-5.

High correlations between most of the new empirically based scales and their predecessors indicate that children would have similar rank orders on the old and new scales. However, they would not usually obtain the same raw scale scores, because of differences in some items included in the scales. The new Emotionally Reactive syndrome on both instruments, the CBCL Attention Problems syndrome, and the C-TRF Anxious/Depressed and Somatic Complaints syndromes had moderate correlations of .56 to .79 with previous scales. These moderate correlations indicated greater differences between these scales and previous scales than for the scales that had correlations in the .80's and .90's. Correlations between the new DSM-oriented scales and previous scales ranged from .72 to .98, indicating moderate to very high correspondence.

Chapter 12
Research Use of ASEBA Preschool Forms

Chapter 5 outlined ways in which ASEBA preschool forms can help users make practical decisions about particular children and situations. In this chapter, we outline applications to research, which seeks testable knowledge that can be extended beyond a particular case or situation. ASEBA forms are designed to advance research and to link it with practical applications by providing cost-effective means for quickly obtaining scores on a broad range of items and scales under diverse conditions. This chapter is designed to be helpful for students as well as for experienced researchers.

There is growing awareness of needs for systematic research on adaptive and maladaptive functioning during the preschool period. This awareness is spurred by concerns such as the following: Use of psychoactive medications with preschoolers despite a paucity of studies of the effects of these drugs on young children; widespread impressions that Pervasive Developmental Disorders (PDD) are becoming much more common; the need to improve services for helping abused children; mandates for early screening of preschoolers to identify problems and to provide appropriate services; prevention of problems at early ages before they impair children's social and educational development; and applications of developmental perspectives to understanding relations between early and later adaptive and maladaptive functioning.

As research on preschoolers advances, specialized procedures are being developed for assessing limited aspects of children's functioning in particular studies. However, excessive reliance on specialized assessment procedures may impede integration and applications of knowledge. To facilitate integration and applications of findings from different studies, it is important that different studies employ a common set of standardized procedures in addition to specialized procedures that are tailored to particular aims. Standardized procedures that have norms based on large representative samples of children provide a common data language for integrating findings from diverse studies that may each include specialized procedures.

In this chapter, we first present guidelines for research applications of ASEBA instruments. These guidelines concern *(a)* use of raw scores vs. *T* scores; *(b)* standardization of scores within research samples; and *(c)* developmental perspectives on longitudinal research. We then outline applications of ASEBA forms to research areas such as epidemiology, diagnosis, etiology, and outcomes. Thereafter, we consider research focused on particular populations, such as children living in different cultures, abused children, children with medical conditions, and children whose parents have particular characteristics or conditions.

Because creative research blends ideas, challenges, opportunities, and methods in innovative ways, readers are likely to think of additional possibilities. To facilitate access to research studies and findings, our *Bibliography of Published Studies Using ASEBA Instruments* is updated annually. The 2000 edition lists over 3,500 publications by some 6,000 authors on over 300 topics (Bérubé & Achenbach, 2000), with 400 to 500 new publications being added annually. In addition, our website offers periodic updates on ASEBA research around the world at http://ASEBA.uvm.edu.

GUIDELINES FOR USE OF ASEBA FORMS IN RESEARCH

Scientific knowledge advances best when

results can be compared and synthesized across many studies. The following sections provide guidelines designed to facilitate comparisons of findings from different studies.

Use of Raw Scores vs. *T* Scores

Chapter 6 described the computation of raw scale scores and the assignment of *T* scores to the scales of the preschool forms. The main function of the *T* scores is to facilitate comparisons of the degree of deviance indicated by children's standing on the different scales of a form. The *T* scores also facilitate comparisons with children's standing on each of the preschool forms. The *T* scores from 50 to 70 are similarly based on percentiles for the syndrome scales of both forms. A *T* score of 70 on both the CBCL/1½-5 and C-TRF, for example, indicates that a child scored at approximately the 98th percentile of the relevant normative samples. If a child obtains a *T* score of 70 on the CBCL/1½-5 Withdrawn scale and 60 on the C-TRF Withdrawn scale completed by a preschool teacher, the child is less deviant in terms of withdrawal according to the teacher's report than the parent's report.

By being based on percentiles for the normative samples, the *T* scores provide convenient ways to quickly judge whether parents, teachers, and caregivers report relatively many problems compared to the problems reported for non-referred children. However, because we truncated the assignment of *T* scores at *T* = 50 on the syndrome scales, raw scores may reflect greater differentiation than *T* scores among children who obtain low scores on these scales. This is not the case for the Internalizing, Externalizing, and Total Problems scales, however, where the *T* scores were not truncated at 50.

For statistical analyses of the syndrome scales, it is usually preferable to use the raw scale scores rather than the *T* scores in order to take account of the full range of variation in these scales. Because *T* scores are not truncated for the Internalizing, Externalizing, and Total Problems scales, statistical analyses using the *T* scores for these scales should yield results similar to analyses using the raw scores. In any case, the obtained distributions of scores to be analyzed should be checked for compatibility with the statistics to be used. If the obtained distributions depart much from the statistical assumptions, other statistical procedures or transformations of the scores may be needed.

Standardization of Scale Scores within Research Samples

For the reasons outlined in the preceding section, we do not recommend using our *T* scores for statistical analyses of the syndrome scales. However, researchers may wish to convert raw scale scores to standard scores within their own samples. For example, if they wish to include boys' and girls' scores or CBCL and C-TRF scores in the same analyses, it is desirable to take account of possible differences in the means and standard deviations of scores for each gender or instrument within the researcher's own sample.

Raw scores can be converted to standard scores within a sample as follows: Using statistical programs such as SPSS (2000) or SAS (1999), you can convert all the boys' scores on a particular scale to standard scores. You can also separately convert all the girls' scores on that scale to standard scores having the same mean and standard deviation as the standard scores for boys. You can choose a convenient mean, such as 100, and standard deviation, such as 15. You can also elect to convert raw scores to *z*-scores (mean = 0, *SD* = 1), although the *z*-score mean of 0 may cause confusion, because children who score below the mean will have negative scores.

If scores for both genders from both the CBCL and C-TRF are to be combined in the same analysis, you can separately standardize the boys' CBCL scores, boys' C-TRF scores, girls' CBCL scores, and girls' C-TRF scores to give each of the four sets of scores the same mean and standard deviation. These scores can then be combined in a single analysis that will be unaffected by the fact that the means and standard deviations of the raw scores may have differed by gender and instrument.

Developmental Perspectives on Longitudinal Research

The items of the preschool forms were chosen to be developmentally appropriate for ages 1½-5. However, to facilitate longitudinal research beyond age 5, we have ensured considerable continuity between the ASEBA preschool and school-age forms, for which revised profiles will be published in 2001. The problem items of the ASEBA school-age forms completed by parents and teachers employ the same 0-1-2 scoring as the preschool forms. In addition, many items of the preschool forms have counterparts among the problem items of the corresponding forms for school-age children.

The numerous counterpart items and several counterpart scales on ASEBA instruments for preschool and school-age children facilitate developmental research on behavioral/emotional problems across the age span from 1½ to 18 years. A great deal remains to be learned about relations between early problems, risk factors, and interventions, on the one hand, and long-term outcomes on the other. Consequently, almost any longitudinal studies of children from preschool to school ages that use adequate samples, developmentally appropriate standardized assessment procedures, and appropriate statistics can contribute important new knowledge.

Relations Between Preschool Scores and Later Scores. Table 9-5 displayed longitudinal correlations between ASEBA scores at ages 2 and 3 and ASEBA scores through age 9. Also, as reported in Chapter 9, LDS scores at age 2 have significantly predicted a variety of language measures at age 13 (Rescorla, 2000).

For longitudinal and other studies, researchers may wish to link scores for children who are 5 and children who are 6. If a sample consists mostly of 5-year-olds, plus a few children who are no older than about 6½ years, it would usually be better to use the ASEBA preschool forms for all children, rather than using the preschool forms for most and the school-age forms for a few. Conversely, if most of the children are 6 years old, with only a few 5-year-olds, it would be preferable to use the school-age forms for all of them.

If a sample contains large proportions of preschool and school-age children, it would be preferable to use the age-appropriate forms and then to stratify the statistical analyses by age. To control for possible age differences in scores, the scores can be transformed to standard scores separately for each age group, as well as for each gender and instrument, as outlined in the section on standardization of scores. By standardizing within age, the effects of differences in the composition of the preschool vs. school-age scales, as well as possible developmental differences, can be controlled, if desired.

To perform correlational, regression, and structural modeling analyses of relations between children's scores on the preschool instruments and the same children's later scores on the school-age instruments, researchers can use raw scores from both the preschool and school-age instruments, because correlational statistics are not affected by possible differences in the magnitude of the earlier vs. later scores.

EPIDEMIOLOGICAL RESEARCH

Epidemiology is the study of the rate and distribution of disorders in populations. It is especially concerned with the *incidence* (rate of onset) of new disorders, and the *prevalence* (percent of the population having disorders) at particular points in time. Knowledge of the incidence, prevalence, and distribution of disorders is important for planning services, developing hypotheses about causal factors, and identifying changes in rates over time. Such knowledge is also helpful for interpreting findings on particular research samples in light of data from samples of large populations. The ASEBA cutpoints for discriminating between the normal and clinical range are based on epidemiological data.

Population Studies

Population studies are typically designed to estimate the prevalence of disorders or problems in a large population at a particular point in time. The target population may be defined as all the children of certain ages living in a particular geographical area, such as a city, county, state, region, or country. Because it is seldom feasible to assess every child in the target population, *samples* of children are assessed as a basis for estimating prevalence rates in the entire population.

Sampling procedures must be carefully designed to obtain samples that are as representative as possible of the population. That is, every child in the population must have an equal chance of being selected for assessment. However, it is not only the sampling procedure, but completion rates in the selected sample and the quality of the assessment procedures that determine whether the obtained data validly represent the entire population.

For assessing the behavioral/emotional problems of children in particular samples, parents are usually a key source of data. To maximize our chance of obtaining representative data from parents, we need standardized assessment procedures that are economical, acceptable to parents, easy to administer, brief, reliable, and efficiently scored. To maximize the utility of the data, the instruments should not be narrowly restricted to predetermined concepts of disorders that are apt to change. The need to improve diagnostic constructs for preschool disorders makes it especially important to obtain data that can be aggregated in multiple ways. The instruments should also be usable in a similar fashion with different kinds of samples, such as children referred for mental health or special education services.

ASEBA instruments are applicable to a variety of population studies, as well as to research on clinical samples. They have been used to assess our own samples from the general population, as described in Chapter 6. The methodology used to assess these samples can be applied to population samples almost anywhere.

Data obtained in new studies using the same methodology can be rigorously compared with data obtained in previous studies to identify similarities and differences between populations and from one time to another within a population. Population studies can also be used to determine base rates for problems. Base rates for different kinds of behavioral/emotional problems can be determined via the CBCL/1½-5, while the base rate for delayed language in children up to 35 months of age can be determined via the LDS.

Comparisons can be made to determine whether rates of behavioral/emotional problems or language delay differ for particular groups, such as children from certain ethnic groups, or disadvantaged children, or children with disabilities. Different cutpoints on the LDS and problem scales can also be tested in relation to various external criteria for different groups of children.

DIAGNOSTIC AND TAXONOMIC RESEARCH

Much research on behavioral/emotional problems is oriented toward DSM diagnostic categories, such as ADHD. However, because the DSM's categories and criteria are based largely on older children and adults, more research is needed on diagnoses of behavioral/emotional problems in preschoolers. The DSM-oriented scales for scoring the CBCL/1½-5 and C-TRF are designed to facilitate research on relations between empirically based syndromes and ASEBA items that are judged to correspond to DSM categories, as explained in Chapter 4.

Even when studies focus primarily on a single diagnostic category such as ADHD, children who qualify for the diagnosis often have other kinds of problems as well. Known as *comorbidity*, the co-occurrence of different kinds of problems argues for assessing diverse problems in addition to those that comprise particular diagnostic categories. By using ASEBA forms, researchers can easily assess diverse problems for analysis in relation to particular diagnostic categories.

Diagnosis of Behavioral/Emotional Problems

The term "diagnosis" is widely used in reference to children's behavioral/emotional problems, and diagnostic labels are often required for purposes of record keeping and third party payment. For physical diseases that are known to be caused by a specific identifiable agent, the concept of diagnosis is clear. For example, the bacterium that causes diphtheria can be inferred from a pattern of symptoms and confirmed by laboratory tests. The symptoms serve as observable clues to an underlying condition that can be rigorously assessed by the appropriate laboratory tests. However, when applied to children's behavioral/emotional problems, the concept of diagnosis is much less clear than when referring to the diphtheria bacterium.

No specific cause is known for most behavioral/emotional problems of childhood. It is an open question whether causes as specific as the diphtheria bacterium will ever be found for many behavioral/emotional problems. Although physical factors may contribute to such problems, these factors may be multiple and may involve variations in constitutional parameters, rather than specific pathogenic agents. Furthermore, learning experiences and environmental stresses may affect the probability, the timing, and the form of such problems among children who have the physical risk factors.

In the absence of evidence for specific physical abnormalities, the diagnosis of behavioral/emotional problems does not have the same meaning as the diagnosis of well-understood physical illnesses. Because little is known about the causes of most behavioral/emotional problems of childhood, it is not clear whether they should be construed as disease entities like diphtheria or whether other conceptual models are more appropriate. Even if some behavioral/emotional problems are ultimately found to constitute disease entities, these entities and the borders between them have not yet been clearly identified. This is especially true for preschoolers, for whom there has been less diagnostic research than for older ages.

Assessment and Taxonomy

It is helpful to separate two aspects of the process of distinguishing among different groups of behavioral/emotional problems. One aspect is *assessment*, which is the identification of the distinguishing features of individual cases. The second aspect is *taxonomy*, which is the use of distinguishing features to construct groups of similar problems, disorders, or cases.

Having been tested for reliability, stability, and discriminative power, the ASEBA preschool forms provide a basis for empirically identifying groups of co-occurring problems. We have done this by factor analyzing problem items, as described in Chapter 6. The empirically based syndromes provide a *taxonomy* of problem patterns. That is, users can form groups of children who score high on a particular syndrome. Furthermore, syndrome profiles can be used to form a taxonomy of patterns of high and low scores across all the syndromes. For example, children who are high on one particular combination of syndromes and low on other syndromes can be grouped together.

The DSM-Oriented ASEBA Scales

The DSM-oriented scales for scoring the ASEBA preschool forms offer opportunities for linking empirically based scales with scales for scoring the pre-school instruments in terms of items judged by mental health researchers to be consistent with DSM diagnostic categories. The construction of the scales, their content, and profiles for scoring them were described in Chapter 4, while the methodological details are provided by Achenbach et al. (2000). Because the DSM-oriented scales do not include all the specific criteria for DSM diagnoses, high scale scores are not equivalent to DSM diagnoses. Consequently, one line of research would be to test associations between scores on our DSM-oriented scales and DSM diagnoses.

Because the DSM does not specify assessment procedures nor methods for combining data from different informants, the diagnostic results may differ according to the assessment procedures, the sources of data, how the data are combined, and how judgments of each DSM criterion are made. Consequently, the degree of agreement between the DSM-oriented scales and DSM diagnoses will depend on diverse methodological factors.

It would also be worth testing associations between empirically based scales, on the one hand, and the DSM-oriented scales, on the other. Appendix E reports correlations between our DSM-oriented and empirically-based scales. By looking at Appendix E, you can see that many of the correlations are fairly high. However, findings may differ for children having different kinds of disorders, as well as for children selected, assessed, diagnosed, and analyzed in different ways.

The DSM-oriented and empirically based scales scored from the same instruments can facilitate comparisons of the correlates and predictive power of the two approaches. For example, genetic studies of over 7,000 Dutch twins have shown high heritability and negligible effects of rater bias in mothers' and fathers' ratings of the empirically based scales (van der Valk et al., 2000). Now that the same data can be analyzed in terms of DSM-oriented scales, it would be worth comparing the heritability and rater bias effects for these scales with the van der Valk et al. findings for the empirically based scales. It would also be worth comparing the ability of the DSM-oriented and empirically based scales to predict long-term outcomes for children who receive various interventions vs. children who do not receive the interventions.

Classification of Children with Language Delays

Young children with language delays detected by the LDS are a heterogeneous group. Some children have pure expressive language delays, others have delays in both expressive and receptive language, others have general developmental delays characteristic of mental retardation, and still others have delays that are pervasive across cognitive, adaptive, and social/emotional domains, such as are found in autism and other forms of PDD. Research is needed to examine the distributions of these subgroups within different samples of children who are identified as delayed on the LDS. For example, children with delayed language who differ in SES, family history, or medical risk factors may have quite different distributions of other disorders.

ETIOLOGICAL RESEARCH

Etiological research aims to identify the causes of disorders. The behavioral/emotional disorders of childhood are likely to involve many different kinds of causal factors, such as cultural and genetic influences, temperament, interactions with parents, and traumatic experiences. Some factors may not be causal in themselves, but may raise the risk of behavioral/emotional problems under particular conditions. Children who are cognitively either much more or less advanced than their peers, for example, may face frustrations that spawn behavioral/emotional problems, even though there is nothing pathological about their cognitive functioning per se.

Because the determinants of behavioral/emotional disorders are likely to be complex, it is important to triangulate multiple variables from multiple sources. Etiological research should therefore employ data from different informants whenever possible, as well as from other sources, such as observations, interviews, tests, laboratory measures, and biomedical assays.

For some purposes, parents are the only feasible informants about children's typical behavior. For children who do not attend preschool or daycare, parents' reports on the CBCL may be the most practical way to assess everyday behavioral/emotional problems. If children attend preschool or daycare, the C-TRF can be used to obtain data from personnel who see the children in those settings. Data from all available informants can be combined in regression analyses and structural models to optimize associations between ratings and underlying variables that may be etiologically important.

Examples of etiological research using the ASEBA preschool forms include the following:

1. Identify children who all manifest a particular profile pattern and compare them with children who manifest a different profile pattern with respect to hypothesized differences in etiology.

2. If a potential etiological factor, such as a particular type of brain damage, can be identified, compare scale scores and profile patterns for children who do and do not have the etiological factor to determine whether they differ in behavioral/emotional problems reported on the preschool forms. If they do differ, this would be evidence in favor of a causal role for the identified etiological factor. Similarly, because language and learning disorders tend to run in families, we could use the LDS to compare early vocabulary development and word combinations in children with or without a sibling or parent who had been a late talker.

3. If hypothesized etiological factors can be experimentally manipulated, the preschool forms can be completed following different experimental conditions to determine whether problems perceived by raters change in response to the manipulations. For example, suppose that a particular food additive is hypothesized to cause sleep problems. To test this hypothesis, we could have parents complete CBCLs after a 2-month period when their children received food containing the additive and also after a 2-month period when the children's food was free of the additive. We should counterbalance the experimental order so that some children receive the food additive first, while other children receive the food additive second. We can then compare scores obtained at the end of each experimental condition to determine whether they differ significantly.

4. If an hypothesized etiological factor is present during a child's early years, we can administer the preschool forms periodically to compare children who have the hypothesized etiological factor with children who do not. For example, suppose we want to determine whether recurrent ear infections affect early language development, which is a subject of much controversy in the research literature. We could repeatedly administer the LDS from age 18 to 35 months to compare children with differing numbers of ear infections. We could also track language growth and behavior problems in youngsters before and after receiving myringotomy tubes. If assessment of behavior problems continues beyond age 5, we can use ASEBA school-age forms, which have many counterparts of ASEBA preschool items and scales.

OUTCOME RESEARCH

If we knew the typical outcome for each childhood disorder following no intervention and following various intervention options, we could make better decisions about how to help each child. Furthermore, if we could identify problem patterns that typically lead to poor outcomes following all available interventions as well as following no intervention, these problem patterns should receive high priority for research designed to improve interventions.

If we find that particular patterns of ASEBA scale scores are typically followed by much worse outcomes than other patterns of scores, we can select children who initially have scores that predict poor outcomes for participation in studies to improve their outcomes. We could also determine whether preschool children with certain patterns of problem scores on the CBCL/1½-5 have worse outcomes if their language is delayed according to the LDS. Other variables, such as observational data, family constellation, developmental measures, and biomedical conditions, might also be found to predict outcomes. These variables could then be used in conjunction with ASEBA scores to identify children expected to have poor outcomes and then to develop better ways of helping them.

Just as information from other measures may augment prediction of outcomes from initial characteristics, the outcomes themselves should be evaluated using criteria in addition to ASEBA scores whenever possible. For example, children identified as language delayed on the LDS should be assessed with standardized tests of receptive and expressive language. For young children identified as deviant on the CBCL or LDS, outcomes should be assessed in terms of variables such as adaptation to school, cognitive functioning, achievement test scores, emergence of new problems, and referral for various services.

Groups at Risk

Outcome research can be useful for determining relative risk rates among children thought to be predisposed to poor outcomes by certain identifiable background conditions. Children whose family members are alcoholic, schizophrenic, or depressed, for example, may be at elevated risk for behavioral/emotional problems. To determine whether such children are reported to have elevated rates of problems in general or problems tapped by certain syndrome scales in particular, the ASEBA preschool forms can be used to compare children having each of several risk factors with children not having the risk factors. Each child in the risk groups could be rated by their parent who does not have the target condition. However, it would also be important to obtain data from other sources as well, such as preschool and daycare personnel. Similarly, family history of language or reading problems, low SES, bilingual rearing conditions, and daycare environments could be tested as risk factors for language delay.

Outcomes of Services

Financial and policy considerations are requiring increasing accountability for outcomes of all kinds of services, including psychotherapy, family counseling, early intervention, and speech-language therapy. This means that providers, agencies, and schools are obliged to systematically document the effectiveness of their efforts.

A basic way to evaluate outcomes is to use the same standardized procedures to assess children's functioning before and after services are provided. If we assess children only after they receive services, we cannot know whether their functioning after the services is better, worse, or the same as before the services. To test for significant changes, we need to apply the same standardized assessment procedures before and after the services. However, improvement in scores from before to after services does not prove that the services were responsible for the improvement. Other explanations are possible, such as: *(a)* Children's problems may tend to decrease as they grow older; *(b)* the people providing the data may report improvements because they believe that the services helped; *(c)* the *test-retest attenuation effect* (a general tendency for people to report fewer problems at a second assessment) may account for apparent improvements.

To make valid outcome evaluations, it is helpful to obtain pre-service and post-service data from a variety of people, at least some of whom are not directly involved in the services. For example, if the services involve work with the children's parents, such as parent training, it would be desirable to obtain pre-service and post-service ratings from teachers and/or caregivers, as well as from the participating parents. Conversely, if the services involve teachers, it would be desirable to obtain pre-service and post-service ratings from parents and caregivers, as well as from the participating teachers.

To control for general developmental declines in problems, as well as to control for test-retest attenuation effects, it is desirable to compare children who are assessed in the same way over the same intervals before and after services but who receive different services or no services. The results can then be compared to determine whether Service A had better outcomes than Service B or no services. However, to determine whether the different outcomes were really produced by the different services, experimental intervention studies are needed, as described in the following section.

Experimental Intervention Studies

If outcome research identifies case characteristics that predict poor outcomes, this argues for active efforts to improve outcomes for these cases. The most rigorous way to determine whether a particular intervention can improve outcomes is to experimentally test the intervention. Experimental studies require a large enough supply of appropriate cases to be assigned to different experimental conditions, such as by randomized assignment to Intervention A versus Intervention B vs. no intervention. For example, a highly structured behavioral intervention could be compared with a more child-centered, play-based approach for promoting vocabulary and phrase development, as assessed by the LDS. For some types of interventions, such as drugs or manipulation of specific behaviors, it may be possible to apply each intervention to the same children in counterbalanced sequences, such as ABAB and BABA.

To warrant the effort and cost of experimental intervention studies, children must be assessed in a uniform fashion to identify those who have the target characteristics and to exclude those who do not. If deviant scores on particular ASEBA scales were previously found to predict poor outcomes, then these scores could be used to select children for an intervention study. Children who are not deviant on the target scales or who are deviant on additional scales could be excluded from the study. Moreover, the initial ASEBA scores can be used as a baseline against which to measure change by readministering the ASEBA forms again after the experimental conditions and comparing pre- vs. post-intervention scores for children receiving the different conditions. Other measures, such as direct observations and tests, could also be used to evaluate the intervention effects.

CROSS-CULTURAL RESEARCH

To advance our understanding of child psychopathology, it is important to calibrate assessment procedures across different countries and cultures. If similar procedures produce similar results in different cultures, this supports the cross-cultural robustness of the findings and the possibilities for integrating results from the different cultures. If different results are obtained from different cultures, by contrast, the findings may provide clues as to causal factors related to cultural differences.

At this writing, we know of translations of ASEBA forms into the 58 languages listed in Table 12-1. The *Bibliography* (Bérubé & Achenbach, 2000) lists published studies using ASEBA forms in some 50 cultures. Crijnen, Achenbach, and Verhulst (1997, 1999) have published comparisons of ASEBA scores for over 13,000 children from 12 cultures.

RESEARCH ON CHILD ABUSE

Professionals who work with children are expected to detect and report child abuse. When abuse has been detected, the abused children usually need to be assessed for forensic and evaluation purposes. ASEBA forms can be useful at all stages of assessment related to abuse. CBCLs from different informants, for example, may be especially discrepant from each other when one of the informants is involved in or has knowledge of abuse.

As with other risk factors, it is important for research on abuse to take account of multiple possibilities. Rather than merely searching for unique symptoms of abuse, for example, we should test whether abuse exacerbates pre-existing problems or has different effects on different children. For studies of children known to be abused, comparisons with clinical samples of nonabused children are needed to identify ways in which particular subgroups of abused children may differ from other referred children. ASEBA forms can also be used in conjunction with other assessment procedures to study the progress of abused children receiving different intervention conditions, such as individual therapy, family therapy, or foster placement.

RESEARCH ON PARENTAL CHARACTERISTICS

Various characteristics of parents may be related to data obtained with the CBCL in various ways. For example, mothers may have a particular condition, such as depression, that is found to be associated with their children's scores on the CBCL. Associations between maternal depression and CBCL scores may occur for reasons such as the following:

1. The children are responding to the same environmental stressors as their mothers, such as abusive fathers.

2. The children share their mothers' genetic vulnerability to the same depressive disorders.

3. The children are temperamentally like their mothers in displaying proportionally more Internalizing than Externalizing problems.

4. The children are responding to the stress created by their mothers' depression.

Table 12-1
Translations of ASEBA Forms[a]

Afrikaans	German	Portuguese
Albanian	Greek	Portuguese Creole
American Sign Language	Gujerati (India)	Romanian
Amharic (Ethiopia)	Haitian Creole	Russian
Arabic	Hebrew	Samoan
Armenian	Hindi	Samy (Norwegian Laplanders)
Bahasa-Indonesia	Hungarian	Sepedi (South Africa)
Bahasa-Malaysia	Icelandic	Serbo-Croatian
Bengali	Iranian (Farsi, Persian)	Slovenian
Bosnian	Italian	Sotho (South Africa)
Bulgarian	Japanese	Spanish
Cambodian	Kiembu (Kenya)	(Castilian & Latin American)
Catalan (Spain)	Korean	Swahili
Chinese	Latvian	Swedish
Czech	Lithuanian	Tagalog (Philippines)
Danish	Maltese	Thai
Dutch	Norwegian	Tibetan
Finnish	Papiamento-Aruba	Turkish
Flemish	Papiamento-Curacao	Vietnamese
French	Polish	Zulu
(Canadian & Parisian)		

[a] Languages into which at least one ASEBA form has been translated.

5. The children model their own behavior on their mothers' depressive behavior.

6. The mothers' behavior toward their children evokes problem behaviors by the children.

7. The children's behavior problems contribute to their mothers' depression.

8. Mothers' depression affects their ratings of their children's behavior.

Correlations between mothers' problems and their ratings of their children have sometimes been interpreted as reflecting parental "biases." However, parental bias is only one of the many factors that may be at work. When data on the children of depressed mothers were obtained from sources beside the mothers, for example, the other sources also indicated more problems than among control children (Richters, 1992). These findings indicated that elevated problem scores in mothers' ratings were not explained by maternal biases.

Parents' characteristics may well affect their ratings of their children. However, a full understanding of the relations between parent and child problems requires research on multiple parent, child, environmental, and biological factors that may be contributory. In addition, causation may run from child to parent, as well as from parent to child. Rigorous research on associations between child and parent problems therefore requires data from multiple sources, including but not limited to the parents themselves.

For many parental conditions, research is needed to determine whether there is any association at all between parent and child problems. If so, do such associations involve similar or different problems in the parents and their children? And do these associations vary with factors such as the gender of the parent and the gender and age of the child? The *Bibliography of Published Studies Using ASEBA Instruments* (Bérubé & Achenbach, 2000) lists over 200 published references to research on parental perceptions and parental characteristics such as psychopathology in relation to ASEBA instruments.

RESEARCH ON MEDICAL CONDITIONS

Certain behavioral/emotional problems may accompany particular medical conditions. In some cases, a medical condition or a medical treatment may specifically cause problems such as sleep disturbance, depression, lethargy, or overactivity. In other cases, a medical condition may cause stress that raises the risk of behavioral/emotional problems. To determine whether particular behavioral/emotional problems tend to accompany particular medical conditions, ASEBA forms can be used to compare children having a particular medical condition with children having other medical conditions and with physically healthy children. By comparing children having different medical conditions, we can avoid erroneously attributing elevated rates of problems to a particular condition, when they may actually accompany multiple conditions.

ASEBA forms can be used as outcome measures in interventions aimed at reducing behavioral/emotional problems associated with medical conditions. Afflicted children can be assessed with ASEBA forms before and after receiving a particular intervention vs. a control condition to determine whether children have fewer behavioral/emotional problems after the intervention than after the control condition. To illustrate the range of possibilities for using the ASEBA forms in research on medical conditions, Table 12-2 summarizes medically related topics from the *Bibliography of Published Studies Using ASEBA Instruments* (Bérubé & Achenbach, 2000).

SUMMARY

ASEBA forms, scales, and profiles are products of extensive research, and they can be used in many ways to expand our knowledge through research. The lack of well-established diagnostic traditions for assessment of preschool problems offers opportunities for basing research on an empirical approach to assessment, taxonomy, and diagnosis.

Like practical applications, research should use multiple sources of data about children's functioning. However, parents' are usually the most available sources of data about preschoolers' functioning, and the importance of parents' perceptions makes parents' reports a key focus for research. Daycare providers and preschool teachers also play increasingly important roles in children's lives. Because ASEBA is not confined to a single theoretical viewpoint, it can be applied to research involving many types of questions, theories, and other assessment procedures.

In this chapter, we presented reasons for using raw scale scores rather than T scores for most statistical analyses. We also outlined ways of using a developmental longitudinal research paradigm by linking ASEBA preschool scores with scores obtained on the school-age ASEBA forms. We then addressed applications to research areas including epidemiology, diagnosis, etiology, and outcomes. Lastly, we discussed research on cross-cultural comparisons, abused children, parental characteristics, and medical conditions. Because parental characteristics may be associated with CBCL scores for many different reasons, it is important to rigorously test the various possibilities rather than merely attributing associations to "biases" in parents' reports about their children.

Table 12-2
Examples of Medical Conditions for Which Research has Employed ASEBA[a]

Abdominal pain	Fibromyalgia	Neurofibromatosis
Adrenal hyperplasia	Headaches	Neuropathology
Allergy	Hearing impairment	Obesity
Alopecia areata	Heart disease	Opsoclonus-myoclonus syndrome
Amniocentesis	Hemodialysis	Pain
Anemia	Hemolytic uremic syndrome	Phenylketonuria
Angelman syndrome	Hemophilia	Post-viral fatigue syndrome
Apert syndrome	Hermaphroditism	Prader-Willi syndrome
Arthritis	Hirschsprung's disease	Precocious puberty
Asphyxia	HIV	Prematurity
Asthma	Hydrocephalus	Reyes syndrome
Beta-thalassaemia	Hydroxyprolinemia	Rheumatic disease
Birth defects	Hypercholesterolemia	Rubinstein-Taybi syndrome
Bone marrow transplant	Hypo- & epispadias	Serotonin
Brain damage	Hypothyroidism	Short stature
Bronchopulmonary dysplasia	Inflammatory bowel disease	Sickle cell anemia
Burns	Language disorders	Sleep disturbance
Cancer	Lead toxicity	Smith-Magenis syndrome
Cerebral palsy	Legg Perthes disease	Sotos syndrome
Chronic fatigue syndrome	Leukemia	Spina bifida
Cleft palate	Limb deficiency	Sudden infant death syndrome
Colitis	Liver transplant	Tourette's syndrome
Crohn's disease	Low birthweight	Toxoplasmosis
Cyclic vomiting syndrome	Lung disease	Trauma
Cystic fibrosis	Lung transplant	Tracheostomy
Diabetes	Mastocytosis	Turner's syndrome
Ear disease	Melatonin	Velocardiofacial syndrome
Epilepsy	Meningitis	Visual impairment
Epstein-Barr virus	Mental retardation	Williams syndrome
Esophageal atresia	Metabolism	
Fetal alcohol syndrome	Migraine	

[a] From Bérubé & Achenbach (2000) *Bibliography of Published Studies Using ASEBA Instruments.*

Chapter 13
Answers to Commonly Asked Questions

This chapter answers questions that may arise about the preschool forms and profiles. The questions are grouped according to whether they refer mainly to the rating forms, to scoring the forms, to the profiles on which the scores are displayed, or to the LDS. If you have a question that is not found under one heading, look under the other headings. The Table of Contents and Index may also help you find answers to questions not listed here.

QUESTIONS ABOUT THE CBCL/1½-5 AND C-TRF FORMS

1. Can the CBCL/1½-5 be filled out by people other than parents?

Answer: The CBCL/1½-5 is designed to be filled out by people who know the child well and interact with the child as parents do. Adoptive parents, foster parents, relatives, and other adults who live with a child are appropriate respondents. For children in residential care and other institutional settings, child care workers who know the children well would be appropriate respondents.

2. In daycare and preschool settings, who should be asked to fill out the C-TRF on a particular child?

Answer: Staff members who have the most experience with the child over the longest periods are the best candidates. Because completion of the C-TRF requires no special training, it can be completed by assistants and trainees, as well as by experienced personnel. Because different staff members may have different samples and views of a child's behavior, it is desirable to have as many staff as possible complete separate C-TRFs for the child.

3. If multiple staff members are available to complete the C-TRF, should they collaborate in completing a single C-TRF, or should they independently complete separate C-TRFs?

Answer: Each informant should independently complete a separate C-TRF to reflect his/her own views of the child.

4. Can homecare providers and babysitters fill out the C-TRF?

Answer: Homecare providers and babysitters who see a child's behavior in a group of at least four children would usually be appropriate for completing the C-TRF. Because four C-TRF items specifically refer to relations with other children, caregivers and babysitters who do not see a child's interactions with other children would not have a basis for rating these items, but could probably rate most other items adequately. For homecare providers and babysitters who do not see children in groups but who can report on their sleeping and toileting problems, the CBCL/1½-5 may be an appropriate alternative.

5. What if daycare or preschool staff say they don't know enough about a child to score certain items?

Answer: If a staff member has known a child for at least 2 months, he/she should be encouraged to complete the C-TRF, even if guessing is necessary. The user can point out to the respondent that a score of *0* does not require complete certainty that the problem does not occur, but only that the respondent does not know that it occurs—i.e., the instructions state: *0 = Not True (as far as you know).*

6. What if a respondent can't read well enough to complete a form?

Answer: The forms require only fifth grade reading skills. They can also be administered orally by an interviewer who completes the form on the basis of the respondent's answers. If there is some doubt about a respondent's reading skill, embarrassment can be avoided by handing the form to the respondent and having the interviewer read each item aloud and record the answers on another copy of the form. Respondents who can read will usually start answering spontaneously, without waiting for the questions to be read.

7. What if a respondent can't read English but can read a different language?

Answer: At this writing, we know of translations of our forms into the 58 languages listed in Table 12-1. For the current status of translations into a particular language, check our website or send us your questions about translations via fax or e-mail.

8. Don't certain items involve subjective judgments, such as *27. Doesn't seem to feel guilty after misbehaving* and *33. Feelings are easily hurt*?

Answer: Subjectivity is involved in all ratings of any person by another person. Some items are less subjective than others, but we recognize that the scores obtained on all items reflect judgments about what to report. However, parents, caregivers, and teachers are usually able to judge and report children's expressions of feelings.

9. Can social desirability, lying, and other informant characteristics such as depression cause biases in scores?

Answer: Many informant characteristics may be associated with scores on all kinds of questionnaires. Studies have shown, for example, that CBCL problem scores are correlated with maternal depression. Such correlations do not necessarily indicate a "bias" in parents' reports, however, because other sources of data have also indicated that the children of depressed mothers have more problems than children of nondepressed mothers (Conrad & Hammen, 1989; Richters & Pellegrini, 1989; Richters, 1992). Because any reports by any informants may be affected by characteristics of the informants, as well as by their own particular knowledge of the child's behavior, no single informant's reports can provide a complete picture. It is the user's task to construct a comprehensive picture of the child from multiple sources and types of data. The answers to questions in the section of this chapter dealing with profiles provide guidelines for evaluating scores that are so low or high as to suggest gross distortions or errors. Chapter 8 of this *Manual* provides data on reliability and cross-informant agreement, while the computer program displays comparisons and correlations between informants' reports for a particular child.

10. Can the forms be used for ages below 1½ and above 5?

Answer: For children who are a few months younger than 1½ or older than 5, there is not likely to be much error in using the forms and their norms. However, the greater the deviation in age from the norms, the less appropriate they will be. If children are to be reassessed over periods that are mainly within the 1½-5-year range but include one or two assessments that are no more than about 4 months outside this range, it may be better to use the preschool forms at all assessment points to maintain complete continuity of item and scale scores, rather than using other instruments.

11. The forms instruct the respondent to base ratings on the previous 2 months. What if a form is to be readministered over intervals of less than 2 months?

Answer: The 2-month instruction can be shortened to suit the interval being used. If the interval is shortened much below 2 months, this may slightly reduce scores on some problem items and scales. Low frequency behaviors may also be missed if the rating interval is too short. However, if reassessments are planned at intervals of less than 2 months, respondents should use the same shortened interval for the initial ratings as well as for each follow-up rating. For example, if follow-up ratings are to be done after a 1-month interval, the initial rating should also be based on a 1-month period, so that the initial scores will not be higher than the follow-up scores merely because they span a longer rating period. To allow time for behavioral changes to stabilize and to become clearly evident, reassessment intervals should generally span at least a month.

12. Are there short forms that take less time to fill out?

Answer: There are no short forms. Most respondents can complete the forms in about 10 minutes. Furthermore, data from subsets of items cannot be compared to our reliability, validity, and normative data. Consequently, it would not make sense to abbreviate the forms. However, if time is at a premium, respondents can omit the open-ended items at the bottom of page 2.

13. Are there machine-readable versions of the forms?

Answer: Check our website, or e-mail or fax us your questions about machine-readable forms.

14. If respondents fill out the forms, won't this cause them to focus on the child's problems instead of the family system?

Answer: When people seek help for a child, they expect to provide information about the child. The forms are not likely to instigate an exclusive focus on the child, because data on the family will typically be obtained as well. The practitioner's own approach and the specific referral problems usually outweigh the forms in determining the degree of focus on the child vs. the family system.

15. Can other assessment procedures—such as play sessions, tests, behavioral observations, and family assessment—be used with the ASEBA forms?

Answer: The ASEBA forms can be used in conjunction with any other assessment procedures. Our Windows® software enables users to enter other data along with ASEBA data.

QUESTIONS ABOUT SCORING THE CBCL/1½-5 AND C-TRF

Appendix A contains detailed scoring instructions, including criteria for items the respondent is asked to describe.

1. What if the respondent scores two different items when his/her comments indicate that they refer to exactly the same problem?

Answer: Score only the item that most specifically describes the behavior. For example, if the respondent circled a 1 for item *2. Acts too young for age* and also circled a 1 for item *80. Strange behavior*, describing the behavior as "acts babyish," only item *2* should be counted.

2. What if the respondent circles two scores for a particular item or otherwise indicates that the item is true of the child but does not clearly indicate a score of 1 or 2?

Answer: Score the item 1.

3. On item *100. Please write in any problems the child has that were not listed above*, what should be done if a respondent describes behavior that is specified elsewhere on the problem list?

Answer: Score the item *only* where it is most precisely specified on the problem list, whether or not the respondent has scored it there as well as in item *100*. For example, if the respondent wrote "very jealous of younger sister," and scored it 2 for item *100*, only item *30. Easily jealous* should be scored 2, rather than item *100*, whether or not the respondent had also scored item *30*.

4. How is item *100* figured in the total score?

Answer: If the respondent enters on item *100* a problem that is not clearly covered by another item, obtain the Total Problems score by adding the 1 or 2 scored by the respondent to the sum of 1s and 2s for all other items. If the respondent enters more than one additional problem, count only the problem that received the highest score. For example, if a respondent circles *1* for one problem in item *100* and circles *2* for another problem in item *100*, add 2 to the Total Problems score. (Adding a maximum of 2 points for item *100* is intended to limit the amount of variance contributed by problems that are not stated for other respondents to rate.)

5. Should forms that have many unanswered items be scored?

Answer: The scoring instructions (Appendix A) give rules for dealing with unanswered items. In brief, if more than 8 items are left blank (excluding item *100*), do not compute problem scale scores or total scores, unless it is clear that the respondent intended the blanks to be zeroes.

6. How is the Total Problems score used?

Answer: The Total Problems score provides a global index of the child's problems, as seen by the respondent. We have found that a Total Problems *T* score of 60 provides a good cutpoint for discriminating between clinically referred and nonreferred children (see Chapter 2 for details of cutpoints). The Total Problems score can also be used as a basis for comparing problems in different groups and for assessing change as a function of time or interventions.

QUESTIONS ABOUT THE CBCL/1½-5 AND C-TRF PROFILES

1. How do the profiles differ from the previous editions?

Answer: Chapter 2 describes the current profile scales in detail. Briefly, the main innovations include *(a)* the age span has been increased to 1½-5; *(b)* the LDS has been added to the CBCL/1½-5; *(c)* the borderline clinical range has been changed to span *T* scores 65-69 (93rd to 97th percentiles); *(d)* the syndrome scales have been revised; *(e)* the CBCL/1½-5 and C-TRF scales are more similar, which facilitates direct comparisons between scores from both instruments; and *(f)* DSM-oriented scales have been added.

2. Can hand-scoring be made quicker and easier?

Answer: We offer scoring templates that fit over the forms to indicate the syndrome and DSM-oriented scales on which the problem items are scored. The time taken to score profiles usually decreases with experience. However, we recommend using our Windows® software to computer score the forms whenever possible, as this is quicker and more accurate. The software stores scores for subsequent analysis, as well as printing hard-copy profiles whenever desired. In addition, the software displays comparisons of item scores, scale scores, and cross-informant correlations for up to 8 CBCL/1½-5 and C-TRF forms per child.

3. Why are there no norms for the "Other Problems" listed on the profile?

Answer: The "Other Problems" on the profile do *not* constitute a scale. They are merely the items that our factor analyses did not identify as belonging to any single syndrome. There are thus no associations among them to warrant treating them as a scale. However, each of these problems may be important in its own right, and they are all included in the Total Problems score. To facilitate computing the Total Problems score by hand, a space is provided below the list of Other Problems to enter the sum of their scores. This sum is then added to the syndrome scale scores to obtain the Total Problems score.

4. Should raw scores or *T* scores be used to report results?

Answer: For evaluating a particular child, *T* scores are helpful for indicating the degree to which the child deviates from normative samples of peers on each scale. However, for statistical analyses of syndrome scales and DSM-oriented scales, raw scores should be used because the *T* scores are truncated at 50. For statistical analyses of Internalizing, Externalizing, and Total Problems, raw scores and *T* scores will usually produce similar results. Chapter 12 discusses the different uses of raw scores and *T* scores in detail.

5. Should extremely low scores be considered deviant?

Answer: Extremely low scores merely reflect the absence of reported problems. The profile compresses the low end of the syndrome scales, so that a *T* score of 50 is the minimum obtainable on any scale. However, nearly all children have at least some problems. On the CBCL/1½-5, the mean Total Problems score for nonreferred children in our normative sample was 33.3. On the C-TRF it was 23.1 for boys and 19.6 for girls. Total Problems scores ≤2 were obtained by only 2% of our normative sample on the CBCL/1½-5. And Total Problems scores of 0 were obtained by 2% of our normative sample on the C-TRF. Such low scores suggest that the respondent has not understood the form, is poorly informed about the child, or is not being candid. Total Problems scores of 3 and 4 on the CBCL/1½-5 are also low enough to be questionable.

6. Should there be separate norms for mothers' and fathers' CBCL/1½-5 ratings or for different ethnic groups?

Answer: As detailed in Chapter 8, differences between the mean scale scores obtained from mothers' and fathers' ratings did not exceed chance expectations. As detailed in Chapter 9, ethnic differences on scale scores did not exceed chance expectations. Socioeconomic differences were somewhat larger, but were too small compared to the differences between referred and nonreferred children to warrant separate norms.

7. Why are there gaps between successive raw scores on some scales of the profiles?

Answer: Most gaps directly reflect the distributions of scores in the normative samples, where skewed distributions or clusters of individuals at a particular raw score caused a large change in percentiles from one score to the next. Gaps between scores in the clinical range occur in scales where there were only a few possible scores available for assignment to *T* scores in equal intervals.

8. How are clinical interpretations of the profiles made?

Answer: The profiles are intended as standardized *descriptions* of behavior, as seen by the person filling out the form and compared to reports by other respondents. The information from the profile should be *integrated* with other data to provide a picture of the child consisting partly of the child's standing on dimensions assessable for children in general and partly of unique characteristics of the child and family.

Specific guidelines and clinical illustrations are provided in Chapter 5. The Windows® software prints narrative summaries of the findings.

9. Is there a "lie" scale for the profiles?

Answer: Deliberate lying is only one factor that can lead to excessively low or high scores, depending on whether the respondent denies or exaggerates problems. Social desirability sets, over-scrupulousness, and misunderstandings can also affect ratings. Because of the variety of possible influences and our goal of using only items that are meaningful in themselves, we did not add items designed to detect all such influences. Instead, we stress that profile scores should never be used to make clinical judgments in isolation from other information about the child and the respondent. Instead, the scores should always be compared with other data in order to identify major distortions and to determine the possible reasons for distortions. Extremely low or high Total Problems scores should always be followed up to determine whether they accurately reflect the respondent's view of the child. If extremely low or high Total Problems scores do reflect the respondent's view, the user should then determine whether this view differs markedly from other people's view of the child.

In our answer to a previous question, we listed Total Problems scores that are so low as to invite further inquiry (scores of 0 to 2 on the CBCL and 0 on the C-TRF). Total Problems scores > 102 on the CBCL/1½-5 and > 108 on the C-TRF are so *high* as to raise questions about exaggeration or misunderstanding, because these scores are higher than 98% of the scores in our factor analytic samples.

10. What are the "DSM-oriented" scales?

Answer: Questions are often raised about relations between empirically based assessment and the diagnostic categories of the American Psychiatric Association's (1994) *Diagnostic and Statistical Manual* (DSM-IV). The DSM-oriented scales scored from the CBCL/1½-5 and C-TRF are based on experienced psychiatrists' and psychologists' ratings of the consistency of our problem items with DSM diagnostic categories that are relevant to preschoolers. By scoring our items in terms of the DSM-oriented scales, users can see how children compare with normative samples on problems that correspond to DSM diagnostic categories, as detailed in Chapter 4. To determine whether children meet criteria for DSM diagnoses, users need to consult the DSM itself.

11. What is the difference between a profile and a template?

Answer: A hand-scored *profile* is an 8½ x 14" sheet of paper on which the problem items of the CBCL/1½-5 or C-TRF are displayed for each syndrome. The 0-1-2 scores for each item are copied onto the profile from the CBCL/1½-5 or C-TRF completed for a child. The 0-1-2 scores for the items of a syndrome are summed to obtain the total score for the syndrome. The score for each syndrome is marked in a graphic display and the user draws lines between the marked scores to form a profile. One profile is needed for each form that is hand scored. If you use our computer-scoring program, you do not need hand-scored profiles.

A *template* is a reusable cardboard cutout that helps you transfer the 0-1-2 item scores from the completed CBCL/1½-5 or C-TRF to a hand-scored profile. When a template is placed on a completed CBCL/1½-5 or C-TRF, it indicates the syndrome scales and DSM-oriented scales on which the 0-1-2 item scores should be copied.

12. How much of a change in a child's score on a scale should be considered a "real" change?

Answer: Changes that are being measured in research designed to compare the effects of different interventions with each other or with no interventions can be tested as follows: Scores for groups of children receiving the different conditions should be statistically analyzed to see whether there are *(a)* significant changes from pre-intervention to post-intervention, and *(b)* whether there are significant group differences in changes. Statistical analyses of group data thus provide a basis for determining whether changes are "real" according to statistical criteria for chance vs. nonchance changes.

A rough approximation to statistical criteria can be applied to scale scores for individual children by comparing the changes with the standard error of measurement for each scale, as follows: *(a)* On the righthand side of Appendix D, locate the column headed *SE of Meas*; *(b)* If you are assessing a child who is considered for mental health services, look in the column headed *Ref*; *(c)* if you are assessing a child who is not considered for mental health services, look in the column headed *Nonref*; *(d)* look down the column until you reach the scale on which you wish to evaluate change; *(e)* if a child's score on a scale has changed more than twice the amount indicated in the appropriate column for the relevant scale, the change exceeds the change that is likely to occur by chance. It should be remembered, however, that the standard error of measurement provides only a rough guideline for judging whether changes in an individual's scale scores are likely to exceed chance expectations.

RELATIONS OF THE CBCL/1½-5 AND C-TRF PRESCHOOL FORMS TO THE SCHOOL-AGE CBCL AND TRF

1. If the preschool forms are completed for a child and the school-age CBCL or TRF is completed when the child is older, how can the scores from the earlier and later assessments be compared?

Answer: Several scales of the preschool forms are fairly comparable to scales of the school-age forms. However, their precise content differs to reflect age differences and to reflect our findings on the covariation among items from the different instruments. The preschool scales that have the clearest counterparts on the school-age CBCL and TRF are: Anxious/Depressed, Withdrawn, Somatic Problems, Attention Problems, Aggressive Behavior, Internalizing, Externalizing, and Total Problems. To directly compare a child's standing on the corresponding scales, the profiles scored from the different instruments can be viewed side-by-side. Because the T scores indicate a child's standing relative to the child's agemates, the user can determine whether a child has become less deviant or more deviant from the earlier assessment to the later assessment, compared to the child's agemates at each point.

2. For longitudinal research, how can correlations be computed between the preschool scores and subsequent scores on the school-age forms?

Answer: Because correlational and regression statistics are not affected by the absolute magnitudes of the scores at each assessment point, they can be used to compute longitudinal associations between the raw scores or T scores obtained from each instrument. For syndrome scales and DSM-oriented scales, raw scores provide more differentiated analyses than T scores do, because the T scores are truncated at 50. For the Internalizing, Externalizing, and Total Problems scales, T scores can be used with no loss of differentiation, because they are not truncated at 50. To provide a more precise measure of longitudinal associations between the corresponding sets of items on the preschool and school-age forms, correlations can be computed between the sum of scores on the CBCL/1½-5 items that have counterparts on the school-age CBCL and the sum of scores on their counterparts for older ages. Likewise, correlations can be computed between the sum of scores for the items that have counterparts on the C-TRF and TRF.

3. For longitudinal research, how can deviance on the preschool scales be analyzed in relation to deviance on the school-age scales scored later for the same children?

Answer: The profiles for all the instruments provide criteria for classifying scores as being in the normal, borderline, or clinical range. If children are grouped into these categories according to their preschool scores and their subsequent school-age scores, relations between the earlier and later classifications can be analyzed via chi square, kappa, odds ratios, and correlational statistics.

QUESTIONS ABOUT THE LDS

1. Can daycare providers fill out the LDS?

Answer: The LDS is designed to be filled out by parents and parent surrogates. However, caregivers who spend many hours each day with a child should have enough information about the child's language skills to complete the LDS accurately.

2. Should the LDS be used if a language other than English is spoken in the home?

Answer: Parents who can read English can complete the LDS by circling any word the child says in English. For words the child says in another language, the parent can add a letter next to the English version of the word denoting the child's other language. (For example, the parent can write an "S" next to "dog" to indicate that the child uses the Spanish word "perro"). We also offer a Spanish version of the CBCL/1½-5 and LDS.

3. Can the parent include words the child says imitatively?

Answer: No, the LDS is intended to reflect the child's spontaneous vocabulary, not words the child understands or can say only in imitation. However, parents should include words the child mispronounces or says in baby talk (such as "blankie" for "blanket") or words that have a somewhat different meaning than is customary in adult usage (e.g., the child says "doggie" to include wolves as well as dogs).

4. What if the child uses a word such as "brush" to indicate an action, but the word is listed under the category of "Personal" words?

Answer: Many words in early vocabularies can be used as either nouns (object labels) or verbs (references to actions). When the child uses just one word at a time, the part of speech cannot be clearly determined. We have placed each LDS word in the category that seems most appropriate, but if the child seems to use an object word as a verb or vice versa, circle the word wherever it appears on the vocabulary list.

5. Can the LDS be used for children older than 35 months?

Answer: Children with normal language development "outgrow" the LDS by age 3, because they typically have vocabularies exceeding 300 words. However, the LDS can be used for language-delayed children older than 3 to track emerging vocabulary and sentence development.

QUESTIONS ABOUT SCORING THE LDS

1. What if the parent writes down words that are not among the 310 on the vocabulary list?

Answer: For purposes of calculating the vocabulary score, add a maximum of 5 additional words to the number of words circled on the list.

2. What if the parent writes that the child produces phrases or sentences but does not give any examples?

Answer: If no examples of phrases or sentences are provided, the average length of phrases cannot be computed. Consequently, language delay will have to be decided on the basis of the vocabulary score only. Most children who use at least 50 words also produce word combinations.

3. Do repeated words such as "choochoo" or "beepbeep" count as valid phrases?

Answer: No, duplicated syllables or words, rote phrases (such as "thank you"), and contractions (such as "he's") all count as single words in scoring the average length of phrases.

QUESTIONS ABOUT INTERPRETING THE LDS

1. What is the earliest age at which expressive language delays can be identified?

Answer: There is great variation in vocabulary development before 24 months. Many children who have almost no words at 20 months are speaking well by 24 months. A large vocabulary on the LDS from 18 to 23 months indicates that a child is making good progress, but a small vocabulary in that period does not necessarily indicate a significant delay. However, by 24 months, most toddlers say at least 50 words and produce some word combinations. A child who fails either of these milestones may therefore have a significant language delay.

2. Why are there separate cutpoints for boys vs. girls for the vocabulary score but not for average length of phrases?

Answer: In our normative sample, vocabulary scores were significantly lower for boys than girls in all three age periods, but average length of phrases did not show significant gender differences. Consequently, we recommend using gender-specific cutpoints for vocabulary scores but not for phrase length scores.

3. How accurate are parents' reports of vocabulary?

Answer: As reported in Chapter 9, correlations between LDS vocabulary scores and other measures of language development have been high in numerous studies. Test-retest correlations and internal consistency as measured by Cronbach's (1951) *alpha* have also been very high, as reported in Chapter 8.

REFERENCES

Abramowitz, M., & Stegun, I.A. (1968). *Handbook of mathematical functions*. Washington, D.C.: National Bureau of Standards.

Achenbach, T.M. (1965). *A factor-analytic study of juvenile psychiatric symptoms*. Paper presented at Society for Research in Child Development, Minneapolis, MN.

Achenbach, T.M. (1966). The classification of children's psychiatric symptoms: A factor-analytic study. *Psychological Monographs, 80,* (No. 615).

Achenbach, T.M. (1991a). *Manual for the Child Behavior Checklist/4-18 and 1991 Profile*. Burlington, VT: University of Vermont, Department of Psychiatry.

Achenbach, T.M. (1991b). *Manual for the Teacher's Report Form and 1991 Profile*. Burlington, VT: University of Vermont, Department of Psychiatry.

Achenbach, T.M. (1992). *Manual for the Child Behavior Checklist/2-3 and 1992 Profile*. Burlington, VT: University of Vermont, Department of Psychiatry.

Achenbach, T.M. (1997). *Guide for the Caregiver-Teacher Report Form for Ages 2-5*. Burlington, VT: University of Vermont, Department of Psychiatry.

Achenbach, T.M., Dumenci, L., & Rescorla, L.A. (2000) Ratings of relations between DSM-IV diagnostic categories and items of the CBCL/1½-5 and C-TRF. Burlington, VT: University of Vermont, Department of Psychiatry. Available at: http://ASEBA.uvm.edu

Achenbach, T.M., & Edelbrock, C. (1978). The classification of child psychopathology: A review and analysis of empirical efforts. *Psychological Bulletin, 85,* 1275-1301.

Achenbach, T.M., & Edelbrock, C. (1981). Behavioral problems and competencies reported by parents of normal and disturbed children aged four to sixteen. *Monographs of the Society for Research in Child Development, 46*(1, Serial No. 188).

Achenbach, T.M., Edelbrock, C., & Howell, C.T. (1987). Empirically based assessment of the behavioral/emotional problems of 2-3-year-old children. *Journal of Abnormal Child Psychology, 15,* 629-650.

Achenbach, T.M., Howell, C., Aoki, M., & Rauh, V. (1993). Nine-year outcome of the Vermont Intervention Program for Low Birthweight Infants. *Pediatrics, 91,* 45-55.

Achenbach, T.M., & Lewis, M. (1971). A proposed model for clinical research and its application to encopresis and enuresis. *Journal of the American Academy of Child Psychiatry, 10,* 535-554.

Achenbach, T.M., McConaughy, S.H., & Howell, C.T. (1987). Child/adolescent behavioral and emotional problems: Implications of cross-informant correlations for situational specificity. *Psychological Bulletin, 101,* 213-232.

Achenbach, T.M., & Ruffle, T.M. (2000). *Medical practitioners' guide to the Achenbach System of Empirically Based Assessment (ASEBA)*. Burlington, VT: University of Vermont Department of Psychiatry.

American Psychiatric Association. (1994). *Diagnostic and statistical manual of mental disorders* (4th ed.). Washington, D.C.: American Psychiatric Association.

REFERENCES

Arend, R., Lavigne, J.V., Rosenbaum, D., Binns, H.J., & Christoffel, K.K. (1996). Relation between taxonomic and quantitative diagnostic systems in preschool children: Emphasis on disruptive disorders. *Journal of Clinical Child Psychology, 25,* 388-397.

Bayley, N. (1969). *Bayley Scales of Infant Development.* New York: Psychological Corporation.

Bayley, N. (1993). *Bayley Scales of Infant Development-II* (2nd ed.). New York: Psychological Corporation.

Behar, L.B., & Stringfield, S. (1974). A behavior rating scale for the preschool child. *Developmental Psychology, 10,* 601-610.

Benedict, H. (1979). Early lexical development: comprehension and production. *Journal of Child Language, 6,* 183-201.

Bérubé, R.L., & Achenbach, T.M. (2000). *Bibliography of published studies using ASEBA instruments: 2000 edition.* Burlington, VT: University of Vermont, Department of Psychiatry.

Briggs-Gowan, M.J., & Carter, A.S. (1998). Preliminary acceptability and psychometrics of the Infant-Toddler Social and Emotional Assessment (ITSEA): A new adult-report questionnaire. *Infant Mental Health Journal, 19,* 422-445.

Browne, N.W., & Cudeck, R. (1993). Alternative ways of assessing model fit. In K.A. Bollen & J.S. Long (Eds.), *Testing structural equation models* (pp.136-162). Newbury Park, CA: Sage.

Clarke, R.A., Murphy, D.L., Constantino, J.N. (1999). Serotonin and externalizing behavior in young children. *Psychiatry Research, 86,* 29-40.

Cohen, J. (1988). *Statistical power analysis for the behavioral sciences* (2nd ed.). New York: Academic Press.

Compas, B.E., Phares, V.S., Banez, G.A., & Howell, D.C. (1991). Correlates of internalizing and externalizing behavior problems: Perceived competence, causal attributions, and parental symptoms. *Journal of Abnormal Child Psychology, 19,* 197-218.

Conrad, M., & Hammen, C. (1989). Role of maternal depression in perceptions of child maladjustment. *Journal of Consulting and Clinical Psychology, 57,* 663-667.

Crijnen, A.A.M., Achenbach, T.M., & Verhulst, F.C. (1997). Comparisons of problems reported by parents of children in 12 cultures: Total Problems, Externalizing, and Internalizing. *Journal of the American Academy of Child and Adolescent Psychiatry, 36,* 1269-1277.

Crijnen, A.A.M., Achenbach, T.M., & Verhulst, F.C. (1999). Comparisons of problems reported by parents of children in twelve cultures: The CBCL/4-18 syndrome constructs. *American Journal of Psychiatry, 156,* 569-574.

Crocker, L., & Algina, J. (1986). *Introduction to classical and modern test theory.* New York: Holt, Rinehart, & Winston.

Cronbach, L.J. (1951). Coefficient alpha and the internal structure of tests. *Psychometrika, 16,* 297-334.

Cronbach, L.J., & Meehl, P.E. (1955). Construct validity in psychological tests. *Psychological Bulletin, 52,* 281-302.

Crowther, J.H., Bond, L.A., & Rolf, J.E. (1981). The incidence, prevalence, and severity of behavior disorders among preschool-age children in day care. *Journal of Abnormal Child Psychology, 9,* 23-42.

REFERENCES

Dromi, E. (1987). *Early lexical development.* New York: Cambridge University Press.

Edelbrock, C., & Costello, A.J. (1988). Convergence between statistically derived behavior problem syndromes and child psychiatric diagnoses. *Journal of Abnormal Child Psychology, 16,* 219-231.

Edelbrock, C., Costello, A.J., Dulcan, M.K., Kalas, R., & Conover, N.C. (1985). Age differences in the reliability of the psychiatric interview of the child. *Child Development, 56,* 265-275.

Evans, W.R., (1975). The Behavior Problem Checklist. Data from an inner city population. *Psychology in the Schools, 12,* 301-303.

Fenson, L., Dale, P.S., Reznick, J.S., Bates, E., Thal, D., Hartung, J., Pethick, S., & Reilly, J.S. (1993). *Guide and technical manual for the MacArthur Communicative Development Inventories.* San Diego, CA: Singular Press.

Ferdinand, R.F., Verhulst, F.C., & Wiznitzer, M. (1995). Continuity and change of self-reported problem behaviors from adolescence into young adulthood. *Journal of the American Academy of Child and Adolescent Psychiatry, 34,* 680-690.

Fleiss, J.L. (1981). *Statistical methods for rates and proportions* (2nd ed.). New York: Wiley.

Frankenburg, W.K., Dodds, J., Archer, P., Shapiro, H., & Bresnick, B. (1992). The Denver II: A major revision and restandardization of the Denver Development Screening Test. *Pediatrics, 89,* 91-97.

Goodman, R. (1997). The Strengths and Difficulties Questionnaire: A research note. *Journal of Child Psychology and Psychiatry, 38,* 581-586.

Gove, P. (Ed.). (1971). *Webster's third new international dictionary of the English language.* Springfield, MA: Merriam.

Guilford, J.P. (1965). *Fundamental statistics in psychology and education* (4th ed.). New York: McGraw-Hill.

Guze, S. (1978). Validating criteria for psychiatric diagnosis: The Washington University approach. In M.S. Akiskal & W.L. Webb (Eds.), *Psychiatric diagnosis: Exploration of biological predictors* (pp. 49-59). New York: Spectrum.

Hay, D.F., Pawlby, S., Sharp, D., Schmucker, G., Mills, A., Allen, H., & Kumar, R. (1999). Parents' judgements about young children's problems: Why mothers and fathers might disagree yet still predict later outcomes. *Journal of Child Psychology and Psychiatry, 40,* 1249-1258.

Heinstein, M. (1969). *Behavior problems of young children in California.* Berkeley, CA: California Department of Public Health.

Hollingshead, A.B. (1975). *Four factor index of social status.* New Haven, CT: Unpublished paper, Yale University, Department of Sociology.

Ireton, H. (1984). *The Preschool Development Inventory.* Minneapolis, MN: Behavior Science Systems.

Ireton, H., & Thwing, E.J. (1974). *Minnesota Child Development Inventory.* Minneapolis, MN: Behavior Science Systems.

Junker, D.A. *Expressive vocabulary of German-English bilinguals.* M.A. thesis, Michigan State University, 1999.

REFERENCES

Kasius, M.C., Ferdinand, R.F., van den Berg, H., & Verhulst, F.C. (1997). Associations between different diagnostic approaches for child and adolescent psychopathology. *Journal of Child Psychology and Psychiatry, 38*, 625-632.

Kazdin, A.E., & Heidish, I.E. (1984). Convergence of clinically derived diagnoses and parent checklists among inpatient children. *Journal of Abnormal Child Psychology, 12*, 421-435.

Keenan, K., Shaw, D., Walsh, B., Delliquadri, E., & Giovannelli, J. (1997). DSM-III-R disorders in preschool children from low-income families. *Journal of the American Academy of Child and Adolescent Psychiatry, 36*, 620-627.

Keenan, K., & Wakschlag, L.S. (2000). More than the terrible twos: The nature and severity of behavior problems in clinic-referred preschool children. *Journal of Abnormal Child Psychology, 28,* 33-46.

Klee, T., Carson, D.K., Gavin, W.J., Hall, L., Kent, A., & Reece, S. (1998). Concurrent and predictive validity of an early language screening program. *Journal of Speech, Language, and Hearing Research, 41*, 627-641.

Kohn, M., & Rosman, B.L. (1972). A social competence scale and symptom checklist for the preschool child: Factor dimensions, their cross-instrument generality, and longitudinal persistence. *Developmental Psychology, 6*, 430-44.

Koot, H., van den Oord, J., Verhulst, F.C., & Boomsma, D. (1997). Behavioral and emotional problems in young preschoolers: Cross-cultural testing of the validity of the Child Behavior Checklist/2-3. *Journal of Abnormal Child Psychology, 25*, 183-196.

Leopold, W. F. (1949) *Speech development of a bilingual child.* Evanston, IL: Northwestern University Press.

Loehlin, J.C. (1998). *Latent variable models: An introduction to factor, path, and structural analysis* (3rd ed.). Mahwah, NJ: Lawrence Erlbaum Associates.

McCarthy, D. (1972). *McCarthy Scales of Children's Abilities.* New York: Psychological Corporation.

McConaughy, S.H., Achenbach, T.M., & Gent, C.L. (1988). Multiaxial empirically based assessment: Parent, teacher, observational, cognitive, and personality correlates of Child Behavior Profiles for 6-11-year-old boys. *Journal of Abnormal Child Psychology, 16*, 485-509.

Mesman, J., & Koot, H.M. (2000) Common and specific correlates of preadolescent internalizing and externalizing psychopathology. *Journal of Abnormal Psychology*, in press.

Messick, S. (1993). Validity. In R.L. Linn (Ed.), *Educational measurement* (3rd ed.). Washington, D.C.: American Council on Education.

Milich, R., Roberts, M., Loney, J., & Caputo, J. (1980). Differentiating practice effects and statistical regression on the Conners Hyperkinesis Index. *Journal of Abnormal Child Psychology, 8,* 549-552.

Miller, L.C. (1967). Louisville Behavior Checklist for males, 6-12 years of age. *Psychological Reports, 21,* 885-896.

Miller, L.C., Hampe, E., Barrett, C.L., & Noble, H. (1972). Test-retest reliability of parent ratings of children's deviant behavior. *Psychological Reports, 31,* 249-250.

Mish, F.C. (Ed.). (1988). *Webster's ninth new collegiate dictionary.* Springfield, MA: Merriam-Webster.

REFERENCES

Mouton-Simien, P., McCain, A.P., & Kelley, M.L. (1997). The development of the Toddler Behavior Screening Inventory. *Journal of Abnormal Child Psychology, 25*, 59-64.

Mullen, E.M. (1993). *Mullen Scales of Early Learning.* Circle Pines, MN: American Guidance Service.

Nelson, K. (1973). Structure and strategy in learning to talk. *Monographs of the Society for Research in Child Development, 38*(1-2, Serial Number 149).

NICHD Early Child Care Research Network (1994). Child care and development: The NICHD Study of Early Child Care. In S.L. Friedman & H.C. Haywood (Eds.), *Developmental follow-up: Concepts, domains, and methods* (pp. 377-395). New York: Academic Press.

Patterson, J.L. (1998). Expressive vocabulary development and word combinations of Spanish-English bilingual toddlers. *Journal of Speech and Language Pathology, 7*, 46-56.

Petersen, N.S., Kolen, M.J., & Hoover, H.D. (1993). Scaling, norming, and equating. In R.L. Linn (Ed.), *Educational measurement* (3rd ed., pp. 221-262). Washington, D.C.: American Council on Education.

Peterson, D.R. (1961). Behavior problems of middle childhood. *Journal of Consulting Psychology, 25*, 205-209.

Rescorla, L. (1980). Overextension in early language development. *Journal of Child Language, 7*, 321-335.

Rescorla, L. (1989). The Language Development Survey: A screening tool for delayed language in toddlers. *Journal of Speech and Hearing Disorders, 54*, 587-599.

Rescorla, L. (2000). Do late-talking toddlers turn out to have reading difficulties a decade later? *Annals of Dyslexia*, in press.

Rescorla, L., & Alley, A. (2000). Validation of the Language Development Survey (LDS): A parent report tool for identifying language delay in toddlers. *Journal of Speech, Language, and Hearing Research*, in review.

Rescorla, L., Alley, A., & Book, J. (2000). Word frequencies in toddlers' lexicons. *Journal of Speech, Language, and Hearing Research*, in review.

Rescorla, L., Hadicke-Wiley, M., & Escarce, E. (1993). Epidemiological investigation of expressive language delay at age two. *First Language, 13*, 5-22.

Rescorla, L., Mirak, J., & Singh, L. (2000). Vocabulary acquisition in late talkers: Lexical development from 2;0 to 3;0. *Journal of Child Language, 27*, 293-311.

Reynell, J., & Gruber, C. (1985). *Reynell Developmental Language Scales.* Los Angeles: Western Publishing Co.

Richman, N. (1977). Is a behaviour checklist for preschool children useful? In P.J. Graham (Ed.), *Epidemiological approaches to child psychiatry* (pp. 125-136). London: Academic Press.

Richman, N., Stevenson, J., & Graham, P.J. (1982). *Pre-school to school: A behavioural study.* London and New York: Academic Press.

Richters, J.E. (1992). Depressed mothers as informants about their children: A critical review of the evidence for distortion. *Psychological Bulletin, 112*, 485-499.

REFERENCES

Richters, J.E., & Pellegrini, D. (1989). Depressed mothers' judgments about their children: An examination of the depression-distortion hypothesis. *Child Development, 60,* 1068-1075.

Robins, L.N. (1985). Epidemiology: Reflections on testing the validity of psychiatric interviews. *Archives of General Psychiatry, 42,* 918-924.

Sakoda, J.M., Cohen, B.H., & Beall, G. (1954). Test of significance for a series of statistical tests. *Psychological Bulletin, 51,* 172-175.

SAS (1999). *SAS/STAT User's Guide, Version 8, Volumes 1, 2, and 3.* Cary, NC: SAS Institute.

Schmitz, S., Fulker, D.W., & Mrazek, D.A. (1995). Problem behavior in early and middle childhood: An initial behavior genetic analysis. *Journal of Child Psychology and Psychiatry, 36,* 1443-1458.

Sparrow, S., Cicchetti, D.V., & Balla, D. (1984). *Vineland Adaptive Behavior Scales-Revised.* Circle Pines, MN: American Guidance Service.

Spiker, D., Kraemer, H.C., Constantine, N.A., & Bryant, D. (1992). Reliability and validity of behavior problem checklists as measures of stable traits in low birth weight, premature preschoolers. *Child Development, 63,* 1481-1496.

SPSS (2000). *SPSS Base 10.0 User's Guide.* Chicago: SPSS.

Stelzer, S.C. (1995). *Adaptacion, normalizacion, y estudios de validez del "sondeo del desarrollo de lenguaje" (SDL) para la deteccion de retraso de lenguaje expresivo en niños Mexicanos de 15 a 31 meses de edad.* Mexico City: Universidad de las Americas.

Swets, J.E., & Pickett, R.M. (1982). *Evaluation of diagnostic systems: Methods from signal detection theory.* New York: Academic Press.

Thorndike, R.L., Hagen, E.P., & Sattler, J.M. (1986). *Stanford-Binet Intelligence Scale* (4th ed.). Chicago, IL: Riverside Press.

van den Oord, E.J.C.G., Verhulst, F.C., & Boomsma, D.I. (1996). A genetic study of maternal and paternal ratings of problem behaviors in three-year-old twins. *Journal of Abnormal Psychology, 105,* 349-357.

van der Valk, M.A., van den Oord, E.J.C.G., Verhulst, F.C., & Boomsma, D.I. (2000). Using parental ratings to study the etiology of 3-year-old twins' problem behaviors: different views or rater bias? *Journal of Child Psychology and Psychiatry,* in review.

Wechsler, D.C. (1989). *Wechsler Preschool and Primary Scale of Intelligence-Revised.* San Antonio: Psychological Corporation.

Weiss, S.J., Goebel, P., Page, A., Wilson, P., & Warda, M. (1999). The impact of cultural and familial context on behavioral and emotional problems of preschool Latino children. *Child Psychiatry and Human Development, 29,* 287-301.

Zahn-Waxler, C., Schmitz, S., Fulker, D., Robinson, J., & Emde, R. (1996). Behavior problems in 5-year-old monozygotic and dizygotic twins: Genetic and environmental influences, patterns of regulation, and internalization of control. *Development and Psychopathology, 8,* 103-122.

Zimmerman, I., Steiner, V., & Evatt, R. (1969). *Preschool Language Scale.* Columbus, OH: Charles E. Merrill.

APPENDIX A
INSTRUCTIONS FOR HAND SCORING
THE ASEBA PRESCHOOL FORMS

To score the Language Development Survey (LDS), read the instructions on the LDS Scoring Form.

Scoring the CBCL/1½-5 and C-TRF Problem Scales

Do *not* score the problem scales if data are missing for more than 8 items, not counting item *100*.

TRANSFERRING PROBLEM ITEM SCORES TO THE PROFILES

Templates. Templates are available to aid in transferring data from the preschool forms to the profiles. Different templates are needed for the CBCL/1½-5 and C-TRF. To transfer problem item scores onto the profile, place the Page 1 template on Page 1 of the form. For each problem item, the template indicates whether the item's score is to be entered on a syndrome scale or on the *OTHER PROBLEMS* list of the profile of empirically based syndromes. The template also indicates which DSM-oriented scale to score each item on. Repeat using the Page 2 template on Page 2 of the form.

Item Scores. For each problem item, print the respondent's 0, 1, or 2 response in the appropriate space beside the item on the profile form. If the respondent circled two numbers for an item, print 1 beside the item on the profile form. Comments written by the respondent should be used in judging whether items deserve to be scored, with the following guidelines:

1. For each problem reported by the respondent, only the item that most specifically describes the problem should be scored. If the respondent's comments show that more than one item has been scored for a particular problem, or if the respondent wrote in a problem for item *100* that is specifically covered elsewhere, score only the most specific item.

2. For items on which the respondent noted "used to do this," score as the respondent scored it, unless it clearly occurred earlier than the 2 months specified in the instructions.

3. When in doubt, score the item the way the respondent scored it, except on the following items:
   Item 31, eats or drinks things that are not food—score *0* for sweets or junk food.
   Item 46, nervous movements—if "can't sit still" or anything entirely covered by item *6* is entered here, score only item *6*.
   Item 57, problems with eyes—score *0* for "wears glasses," "near-sighted," and other visual problems having a physical basis.
   Item 80, strange behavior—if what the respondent described is specifically covered by another item, score the more specific item instead.
   Item 100, additional problems—score only if *not* specifically covered by another item; if respondent entered more than 1 problem here, count only the highest rating toward the Total Problems score (e.g., if any problem listed in item *100* is rated *2*, add *2* to Total Problems score; if the highest rating in item *100* is *1*, add *1* to total score). The open-ended items following item *100* are clinically useful but are not scored.

Syndrome and DSM-Oriented Scale Scores. To obtain the total raw score for each scale, sum the 1s and 2s you have entered for the scale. The *OTHER PROBLEMS* do not form a scale, but should be summed to help in computing the Total Problems score, as described later.

APPENDIX A (cont.)

GRAPHIC DISPLAY AND T SCORES

To complete the graphic displays for the syndrome and DSM-oriented scales, circle the number above each scale that equals the total score obtained for that scale. ***On the C-TRF, be sure to circle the number in the column appropriate for boys vs. girls.*** Then draw a line to connect the circled numbers. Percentiles based on the normative sample can be read from the left side of the graphic display. *T* scores can be read from the right side.

INTERNALIZING, EXTERNALIZING, TOTAL PROBLEMS

Computation of Scores. On the profile of syndrome scales, look to the right of the graphic display. You will see a column headed *Computations*. Under *Computations*, enter the raw scores that you have obtained for each of the syndrome scales and for the OTHER PROBLEMS as follows:

1. (a) Enter the score for the leftmost syndrome scales in the spaces provided.
   (b) Enter their sum in the box marked *Internal.*

2. (a) Enter the scores for the rightmost syndrome scales in the spaces provided.
   (b) Enter their sum in the box marked *External.*

3. (a) Enter the total score for *OTHER PROBLEMS* and the score for the middle syndrome scale (CBCL only) in the spaces provided.
   (b) Sum the scores from *3(a)* plus the scores from the boxes marked *Internal* and *External* and enter this sum in the box marked *Tot Prob*.

T Scores. Obtain *T* scores for Internalizing, Externalizing, and Total Problems as follows:

1. Look in the appropriate columns of the large box on the right side of the profile form.

2. In the appropriate column under the heading *Internalizing,* circle the raw score that corresponds to the score you have entered in the box beside *Internal.*

3. Look to the right in the *Internalizing* column headed *T* and circle the *T* score that corresponds to the Internalizing raw score that you have obtained.

4. Enter this *T* score in the box marked *Internal T* under the *Computations* heading.

5. Look under the *Externalizing* and *Total Problems* headings to obtain *T* scores in the same way as was done for Internalizing; enter the *Externalizing* and *Total Problems T* scores in the appropriate boxes.

APPENDIX B
LOADINGS OF ITEMS ON SYNDROME SCALES IN FINAL WEIGHTED LEAST SQUARES FACTOR ANALYSES OF TETRACHORIC CORRELATIONS

Items on Syndromes	Loadings CBCL	C-TRF
EMOTIONALLY REACTIVE		
21. Disturbed by change	.47	.49
46. Twitches	.57	.39
51. Panics	.73	NA
79. Shifts between sad-excite	.48	NA
82. Sudden mood change	.61	.82
83. Sulks a lot	.64	.66
92. Upset by new	.46	.36
97. Whining	.33	.53
99. Worries	.61	.41
ANXIOUS/DEPRESSED		
10. Too dependent	.27	.40
33. Feelings easily hurt	.21	.36
37. Upset when separated	.42	.39
43. Looks unhappy	.76	.81
47. Nervous	.66	.68
68. Self-conscious	.38	.34
87. Fearful	.50	.65
90. Unhappy, sad, depressed	.70	.83
SOMATIC COMPLAINTS		
1. Aches, pains	.68	.67
7. Can't stand things out of place	.47	.55
12. Constipated	.59	NA
19. Diarrhea	.48	NA
24. Doesn't eat well	.38	NA
39. Headaches	.87	.77
45. Nausea	.96	.94
52. Painful B.M.	.46	NA
78. Stomachaches	.59	.80
86. Too concerned with neatness	.66	.55
93. Vomits	.66	.45
WITHDRAWN		
2. Acts too young	.41	.44
4. Avoids eye contact	.42	.61
12. Apathetic	NA	.60
19. Daydreams	NA	.31
23. Doesn't answer	.28	.70
62. Refuses active games	.61	.59
67. Unresponsive to affection	.86	.80
70. Little affection	.76	.71
71. Little interest	.59	.74
98. Withdrawn	.84	.56

Note: All loadings were significant at $p < .01$.

APPENDIX B (cont.)

Items on Syndromes	Loadings CBCL	C-TRF
SLEEP PROBLEMS		
22. Doesn't want to sleep alone	.53	NA
38. Trouble sleeping	.76	NA
48. Nightmares	.60	NA
64. Resists bed	.61	NA
74. Sleeps little	.54	NA
84. Talks, cries in sleep	.44	NA
94. Wakes often	.54	NA
ATTENTION PROBLEMS		
5. Can't concentrate	.59	.80
6. Can't sit still	.53	.86
24. Difficulty with directions	NA	.78
48. Fails to finish	NA	.79
51. Fidgets	NA	.69
56. Clumsy	.53	.35
59. Quickly shifts	.39	.65
64. Inattentive	NA	.81
95. Wanders away	.55	.72
AGGRESSIVE BEHAVIOR		
8. Can't stand waiting	.77	.72
14. Cruel to animals	NA	.58
15. Defiant	.65	.82
16. Demands must be met	.41	.77
17. Destroys own things	NA	.77
18. Destroys others' things	.16[a]	.85
20. Disobedient	.79	.73
22. Mean to others	NA	.80
27. Lacks guilt	.46	.74
28. Disturbs others	NA	.79
29. Easily frustrated	.64	.54
35. Gets in fights	.21	.81
40. Hits others	.61	.80
42. Hurts unintentionally	.50	.65
44. Angry moods	.44	.71
53. Attacks people	.51	.83
58. Punishment doesn't change behavior	.64	.77
66. Screams	.34	.75
69. Selfish	.40	.65
74. Not Liked	NA	.66
81. Stubborn	.50	.71
84. Teases	NA	.68
85. Temper	.53	.80
88. Uncooperative	.58	.82
96. Wants attention	.61	.54

Note: All loadings were significant at $p < .01$.

[a]Despite loading $< .20$, item 18 was retained for the CBCL Aggressive Behavior syndrome because it was the highest loading item on the C-TRF Aggressive Behavior syndrome.

APPENDIX C
PROBLEM SCALE SCORES FOR NORMATIVE SAMPLES

Scale	CBCL	C-TRF Boys	C-TRF Girls	Scale	CBCL	C-TRF Boys	C-TRF Girls
	$N = 700$	588	604		$N = 700$	588	604
Emotionally Reactive				**Attention Problems**			
Raw Score				Raw Score			
Mean	2.4	1.5	1.3	Mean	2.5	3.6	2.6
SD	2.2	1.9	1.9	SD	1.9	3.7	3.4
SE[a]	0.1	0.1	0.1	SE[a]	0.1	0.2	0.1
T Score				T Score			
Mean	54.0	53.9	54.0	Mean	54.1	54.3	54.4
SD	5.7	5.8	6.3	SD	5.6	6.2	6.4
SE[a]	0.2	0.2	0.3	SE[a]	0.2	0.3	0.3
Anxious/Depressed				**Aggressive Behavior**			
Raw Score				Raw Score			
Mean	2.9	2.1	2.2	Mean	10.4	6.9	5.3
SD	2.3	2.2	2.4	SD	6.4	8.5	7.6
SE[a]	0.1	0.1	0.1	SE[a]	0.2	0.4	0.3
T Score				T Score			
Mean	54.2	54.4	54.4	Mean	54.2	54.1	54.2
SD	5.7	5.9	6.2	SD	6.0	6.3	6.4
SE[a]	0.2	0.2	0.3	SE[a]	0.2	0.3	0.3
Somatic Complaints				**Internalizing**			
Raw Score				Raw Score			
Mean	1.8	0.5	0.7	Mean	8.6	6.8	6.4
SD	1.9	1.0	1.2	SD	6.2	6.6	6.9
SE[a]	0.1	0.1	0.1	SE[a]	0.2	0.3	0.3
T Score				T Score			
Mean	54.0	52.9	53.6	Mean	50.0	50.2	50.1
SD	5.8	5.5	6.0	SD	9.9	9.9	10.0
SE[a]	0.2	0.2	0.2	SE[a]	0.4	0.4	0.4
Withdrawn				**Externalizing**			
Raw Score				Raw Score			
Mean	1.5	2.8	2.3	Mean	12.9	10.5	8.0
SD	1.7	3.2	2.9	SD	7.7	11.3	10.1
SE[a]	0.1	0.1	0.1	SE[a]	0.3	0.5	0.4
T Score				T Score			
Mean	54.1	54.5	53.7	Mean	50.0	50.3	50.3
SD	5.8	6.3	5.7	SD	9.9	9.7	9.6
SE[a]	0.2	0.3	0.2	SE[a]	0.4	0.4	0.4
Sleep Problems				**Total Problems**			
Raw Score				Raw Score			
Mean	2.8	NA	NA	Mean	33.3	23.1	19.6
SD	2.4	NA	NA	SD	18.7	20.9	20.9
SE[a]	0.1	NA	NA	SE[a]	0.7	0.9	0.8
T Score				T Score			
Mean	54.2	NA	NA	Mean	50.1	50.2	50.3
SD	5.7	NA	NA	SD	9.9	10.0	10.2
SE[a]	0.2	NA	NA	SE[a]	0.4	0.4	0.4

[a] SE = standard error of the mean.

APPENDIX C (cont.)

		C-TRF	
Scale	CBCL	Boys	Girls
	N = 700	588	604

DSM-Oriented Scales

Affective Problems
Raw Score

Mean	2.1	1.2	1.2
SD	2.0	2.0	1.9
SE[a]	0.1	0.1	0.1

T Score

Mean	54.4	54.2	54.2
SD	5.7	6.1	6.5
SE[a]	0.2	0.3	0.3

Anxiety Problems
Raw Score

Mean	3.4	1.1	1.3
SD	2.5	1.6	1.9
SE[a]	0.1	0.1	0.1

T Score

Mean	54.2	54.2	53.9
SD	5.9	5.7	6.3
SE[a]	0.2	0.2	0.3

Pervasive Developmental Problems
Raw Score

Mean	2.8	3.2	2.6
SD	2.4	3.2	3.0
SE[a]	0.1	0.1	0.1

T Score

Mean	54.1	54.3	54.5
SD	5.7	5.9	6.0
SE[a]	0.2	0.2	0.2

Attention Deficit/Hyperactivity Problems
Raw Score

Mean	5.0	5.5	4.1
SD	2.8	5.5	4.9
SE[a]	0.1	0.2	0.2

T Score

Mean	54.3	54.3	54.5
SD	5.6	6.7	6.6
SE[a]	0.2	0.3	0.3

Oppositional Defiant Problems
Raw Score

Mean	3.6	2.1	1.7
SD	2.5	3.0	2.7
SE[a]	0.1	0.1	0.1

T Score

Mean	54.2	54.1	54.3
SD	5.8	6.0	7.2
SE[a]	0.2	0.2	0.3

[a]SE = standard error of the mean.

APPENDIX D
MEAN CBCL SCALE SCORES FOR MATCHED REFERRED CHILDREN AND NONREFERRED CHILDREN

Scale	T Score Ref Mean	(SD)	T Score Nonref Mean	(SD)	Raw Score Ref Mean	(SD)	Raw Score Nonref Mean	(SD)	SE of Mean[a] Ref	SE of Mean[a] Nonref	SE of Meas[b] Ref	SE of Meas[b] Nonref	Cronbach's Alpha
Syndromes													
Emotionally Reactive	60.1	(8.3)	54.1	(5.8)	4.7	(3.1)	2.4	(2.2)	.13	.09	1.12	0.79	.73
Anxious/Depressed	57.3	(8.1)	54.3	(5.7)	4.1	(2.9)	3.0	(2.3)	.12	.10	1.64	1.30	.66
Somatic Complaints	62.6	(11.1)	54.2	(5.9)	4.9	(4.2)	1.9	(1.9)	.18	.08	1.68	0.76	.80
Withdrawn	62.3	(10.0)	54.2	(5.9)	3.9	(3.0)	1.7	(1.7)	.13	.07	1.34	0.76	.75
Sleep Problems	60.2	(11.6)	54.3	(5.7)	4.8	(3.6)	2.9	(2.4)	.15	.10	1.02	0.68	.78
Attention Problems	58.4	(8.2)	54.2	(5.6)	3.9	(2.4)	2.6	(1.9)	.10	.08	1.13	0.89	.68
Aggressive Behavior	60.6	(12.5)	54.3	(6.0)	15.1	(9.7)	10.5	(6.4)	.41	.27	3.50	2.31	.92
Internalizing	61.2	(10.9)	50.2	(10.0)	17.5	(10.2)	8.7	(6.3)	.43	.27	3.23	1.99	.89
Externalizing	57.3	(13.4)	50.2	(9.9)	19.0	(11.1)	13.1	(7.8)	.47	.33	4.00	2.81	.92
Total Problems	61.7	(11.1)	50.1	(9.9)	58.8	(26.5)	33.4	(18.8)	1.12	.79	8.38	5.95	.95

155

APPENDIX D (cont.)
CBCL SCALE SCORES (cont.)

	T Score				Raw Score				SE of Mean[a]		SE of Meas[b]		Cronbach's
Scale	Ref Mean	(SD)	Nonref Mean	(SD)	Ref Mean	(SD)	Nonref Mean	(SD)	Ref	Nonref	Ref	Nonref	Alpha
DSM-Oriented Scales													
Affective Problems	62.4	(9.3)	54.5	(5.8)	4.9	(3.1)	2.1	(2.1)	.13	.09	1.42	0.96	.69
Anxiety Problems	58.0	(8.2)	54.4	(6.1)	4.9	(3.1)	3.5	(2.6)	.13	.11	1.20	1.01	.63
Pervasive Developmental Problems	64.3	(10.4)	54.2	(5.7)	7.2	(4.5)	2.8	(2.4)	.19	.10	1.68	0.90	.80
Attention Deficit/ Hyperactivity Problems	57.9	(8.3)	54.3	(5.7)	6.4	(3.3)	5.0	(2.8)	.14	.12	1.68	1.43	.78
Oppositional Defiant Problems	59.4	(10.1)	54.2	(5.9)	5.3	(3.7)	3.6	(2.6)	.16	.11	1.33	0.94	.86

Note. $N = 563$ each in demographically-matched referred and nonreferred samples described in Chapter 9, where statistical analyses are presented.

[a] Standard error of mean raw scores.

[b] Standard error of measurement = $SD \sqrt{1-\text{reliability}}$ (Guilford, 1965) computed from reliability of raw scores shown in Table 8-1.

APPENDIX D (cont.)
MEAN C-TRF SCALE SCORES FOR MATCHED REFERRED CHILDREN AND NONREFERRED CHILDREN

Scale	T Score Ref Mean	(SD)	T Score Nonref Mean	(SD)	Raw Score Ref Mean	(SD)	Raw Score Nonref Mean	(SD)	SE of Mean[a] Ref	SE of Mean[a] Nonref	SE of Meas[b] Ref	SE of Meas[b] Nonref	Cronbach's Alpha
Syndromes													
Emotionally Reactive	60.2	(8.6)	53.8	(6.0)	3.4	(2.7)	1.4	(1.9)	.15	.11	1.41	1.01	.71
Anxious/ Depressed	58.8	(8.2)	54.6	(6.6)	3.8	(3.0)	2.2	(2.6)	.17	.14	1.67	1.39	.76
Somatic Complaints	53.9	(6.2)	52.2	(4.9)	0.7	(1.2)	0.4	(0.9)	.08	.05	0.35	0.27	.52
Withdrawn	58.4	(7.0)	54.5	(7.1)	4.9	(3.6)	2.7	(3.5)	.21	.20	1.72	1.67	.83
Attention Problems	61.6	(10.8)	54.5	(6.4)	7.2	(4.7)	3.4	(3.9)	.27	.22	1.88	1.54	.89
Aggressive Behavior	63.7	(10.9)	54.6	(6.5)	18.4	(12.6)	7.0	(8.7)	.72	.50	4.17	2.90	.96
Internalizing	58.5	(9.2)	49.7	(10.6)	12.7	(8.0)	6.6	(7.1)	.46	.41	3.84	3.41	.89
Externalizing	62.7	(10.6)	50.6	(10.1)	25.6	(15.9)	10.5	(11.7)	.91	.67	5.27	3.89	.96
Total Problems	62.1	(9.6)	50.0	(10.6)	50.3	(27.6)	22.6	(21.8)	1.59	1.25	9.58	7.55	.97

APPENDIX D (cont.)
C-TRF SCALE SCORES (cont.)

	T Score				Raw Score				SE of Mean[a]		SE of Meas[b]		Cronbach's
Scale	Ref Mean	(SD)	Nonref Mean	(SD)	Ref Mean	(SD)	Nonref Mean	(SD)	Ref	Nonref	Ref	Nonref	Alpha
DSM-Oriented Scales													
Affective Problems	58.1	(7.4)	54.6	(7.1)	2.5	(2.5)	1.3	(2.3)	.14	.13	1.21	1.11	.78
Anxiety Problems	57.7	(7.5)	54.0	(6.0)	2.2	(2.2)	1.5	(1.8)	.13	.10	1.47	1.15	.68
Pervasive Developmental Problems	60.4	(8.0)	54.1	(5.9)	6.3	(4.2)	2.9	(3.2)	.24	.19	1.71	1.33	.80
Attention Deficit/ Hyperactivity Problems	62.6	(11.3)	54.5	(6.8)	11.3	(6.9)	5.3	(5.6)	.39	.32	3.14	2.57	.92
Oppositional Defiant Problems	62.9	(9.9)	54.7	(6.3)	6.1	(4.3)	2.3	(3.2)	.24	.18	1.53	1.13	.93

Note. $N = 303$ each in demographically-matched referred and nonreferred samples described in Chapter 9, where statistical analyses are presented.

[a] Standard error of mean raw scores.

[b] Standard error of measurement $= SD \sqrt{1-\text{reliability}}$ (Guilford, 1965) computed from reliability of raw scores shown in Table 8-1.

APPENDIX E
PEARSON CORRELATIONS AMONG T SCORES FOR CBCL
REFERRED CHILDREN ABOVE DIAGONAL, NONREFERRED CHILDREN BELOW DIAGONAL

	Syndromes											DSM-Oriented Scales				
	Emot. Anx./Dep.	Som.	Withd.	Sleep	AttProb.	Aggress.	Int.	Ext.	Total	Aff.	Anx.	Perv. Devel.	ADHP	Opp.
Syndromes														
Emotionally Reactive	.52	.53	.63	.28	.38	.29	.84	.31	.75	.60	.58	.78	.26	.31
Anxious/Depressed	.62	.11	.40	.42	.40	.43	.59	.45	.64	.61	.79	.45	.38	.42
Somatic Complaints	.37	.39	.51	.00	.13	-.22	.72	-.23	.40	.35	.30	.57	-.14	-.22
Withdrawn	.47	.48	.28		.15	.41	.13	.78	.15	.64	.57	.39	.84	.17	.14
Sleep Problems	.40	.32	.30	.17		.26	.51	.25	.52	.53	.63	.56	.20	.37	.48
Attention Problems	.40	.35	.23	.41	.34		.48	.41	.50	.65	.40	.40	.44	.77	.44
Aggressive Behavior	.54	.40	.26	.40	.35	.67		.19	.93	.63	.40	.36	.20	.75	.92
Internalizing	.73	.75	.61	.66	.41	.45	.51		.22	.80	.66	.62	.83	.22	.20
Externalizing	.51	.40	.28	.42	.41	.73	.86	.59		.76	.47	.44	.30	.82	.89
Total Problems	.67	.63	.48	.56	.56	.67	.76	.84	.88		.75	.69	.73	.61	.61
DSM-Oriented Scales														
Affective Problems	.52	.51	.46	.43	.64	.42	.49	.60	.47	.66		.59	.56	.34	.40
Anxiety Problems	.61	.78	.37	.46	.50	.35	.37	.67	.39	.62	.48		.49	.34	.35
Perv. Devel. Probs.	.67	.56	.41	.76	.24	.36	.42	.72	.40	.60	.41	.55		.24	.20
ADH Problems	.38	.34	.21	.32	.31	.82	.73	.41	.68	.66	.38	.33	.31		.68
Oppositional Probs.	.52	.39	.21	.36	.40	.54	.86	.47	.77	.68	.47	.35	.38	.57	

Note: CBCL $N = 563$ in each sample; all $rs > .11$ are $p < .01$.

159

APPENDIX E (cont.)
PEARSON CORRELATIONS AMONG T SCORES FOR C-TRF
REFERRED CHILDREN ABOVE DIAGONAL, NONREFERRED CHILDREN BELOW DIAGONAL

	Syndromes										DSM-Oriented Scales				
	Emot.	Anx/Dep.	Som.	Withd.	AttProb.	Aggress.	Int.	Ext.	Total	Aff.	Anx.	Perv. Devel.	ADHP	Opp.
Syndromes														
Emotionally Reactive		.65	.41	.46	.35	.56	.81	.55	.72	.61	.63	.64	.41	.59
Anxious/Depressed	.68		.32	.40	.17	.34	.78	.32	.56	.70	.80	.46	.20	.37
Somatic Complaints	.30	.32		.22	−.03	.13	.46	.10	.28	.23	.42	.42	.02	.19
Withdrawn	.42	.66	.15		.37	.40	.76	.43	.62	.60	.35	.83	.38	.40
Attention Problems	.44	.41	.09	.65		.60	.35	.75	.67	.21	.21	.35	.93	.46
Aggressive Behavior	.54	.27	.10	.39	.64		.51	.95	.87	.38	.29	.48	.74	.87
Internalizing	.72	.84	.39	.77	.56	.48		.53	.78	.75	.70	.79	.39	.54
Externalizing	.54	.36	.11	.48	.76	.88	.62		.91	.38	.30	.49	.84	.82
Total Problems	.65	.61	.25	.66	.74	.77	.85	.91		.59	.52	.68	.76	.79
DSM-Oriented Scales														
Affective Problems	.57	.79	.22	.81	.52	.36	.78	.44	.64		.47	.50	.24	.42
Anxiety Problems	.66	.87	.35	.54	.39	.26	.74	.34	.56	.62		.46	.22	.30
Perv. Devel. Probs.	.62	.72	.25	.87	.59	.46	.81	.52	.69	.73	.63		.38	.50
ADH Problems	.42	.28	.08	.50	.90	.78	.47	.80	.73	.38	.27	.48		.58
Oppositional Probs.	.58	.32	.12	.39	.58	.92	.52	.84	.75	.40	.31	.46	.68	

Note: C-TRF $N = 303$ in each sample; all rs $> .14$ are $p < .01$.

APPENDIX F
SCORES FOR REFERRED AND NONREFERRED CHILDREN ON EACH CBCL AND C-TRF ITEM

		CBCL					C-TRF				
Item	Group[a]	% 1	% 2	% 1+2	Mean	SE[b]	% 1	% 2	% 1+2	Mean	SE[b]
1. Aches, pains	RB	14	34	49	.83	.05	04	<01	05	.05	.02
	RG	14	30	44	.74	.06	04	03	08	.11	.04
	NB	14	03	16	.19	.03	04	00	04	.04	.01
	NG	19	02	21	.23	.03	04	00	04	.04	.02
2. Acts too young	RB	26	09	35	.45	.04	43	16	59	.75	.05
	RG	27	07	33	.40	.04	34	12	46	.58	.07
	NB	11	01	12	.14	.02	23	06	29	.35	.04
	NG	17	03	20	.23	.03	14	02	16	.18	.05
3. Afraid to try new	RB	38	07	45	.52	.03	37	08	45	.53	.04
	RG	31	07	38	.45	.04	32	09	40	.49	.07
	NB	27	04	31	.35	.03	28	06	34	.40	.04
	NG	31	02	33	.35	.03	24	03	27	.30	.06
4. Avoids eye contact	RB	39	08	48	.56	.04	43	21	64	.85	.05
	RG	37	10	46	.56	.04	39	11	50	.61	.07
	NB	28	05	32	.37	.03	32	07	39	.45	.04
	NG	28	01	29	.30	.03	24	05	29	.35	.06
5. Can't concentrate	RB	44	22	65	.87	.04	49	28	77	1.05	.05
	RG	41	19	60	.79	.05	38	17	55	.73	.08
	NB	40	08	47	.55	.03	31	15	46	.61	.05
	NG	36	05	41	.46	.04	21	04	25	.29	.06
6. Can't sit still	RB	38	39	77	1.16	.04	42	37	79	1.16	.05
	RG	41	31	73	1.04	.05	42	23	65	.88	.08
	NB	42	18	60	.78	.04	27	18	45	.64	.05
	NG	45	12	57	.69	.04	24	05	29	.35	.06
7. Can't stand things out of place	RB	33	19	52	.70	.04	20	07	27	.34	.04
	RG	23	17	40	.57	.05	17	07	24	.30	.06
	NB	23	05	29	.34	.03	09	03	11	.14	.03
	NG	25	07	32	.40	.04	02	03	05	.09	.04
8. Can't stand waiting	RB	31	40	71	1.11	.05	39	35	74	1.09	.05
	RG	30	36	66	1.02	.06	42	32	74	1.05	.08
	NB	48	34	82	1.17	.04	27	11	38	.49	.05
	NG	53	27	80	1.07	.05	27	09	36	.45	.07
9. Chews nonfood	RB	41	26	67	.93	.04	23	08	30	.38	.04
	RG	30	33	63	.97	.06	18	22	40	.62	.09
	NB	30	11	41	.53	.04	15	02	18	.20	.03
	NG	31	05	36	.41	.04	20	02	22	.24	.05
10. Too dependent	RB	39	17	56	.74	.04	20	06	26	.32	.04
	RG	40	23	63	.86	.05	33	20	52	.72	.08
	NB	41	12	53	.65	.04	16	04	20	.24	.04
	NG	37	14	52	.66	.05	28	04	33	.37	.06

[a]RB = referred boys; RG = referred girls; NB = nonreferred boys; NG = nonreferred girls. For CBCL, RB and NB=333; RG and NG=230 each; for C-TRF, RB and NB = 211 each; RG and NG = 92 each. [b]SE = standard error of the mean.

		CBCL					C-TRF				
Item	Group[a]	% 1	% 2	% 1+2	Mean	SE[b]	% 1	% 2	% 1+2	Mean	SE[b]
11. Seeks help	RB	45	13	58	.71	.04	29	07	36	.44	.04
	RG	44	14	59	.73	.05	32	10	41	.51	.07
	NB	34	02	37	.39	.03	19	06	26	.32	.04
	NG	34	04	38	.42	.04	22	01	23	.24	.05
12. Constipated-CBCL Apathetic-C-TRF	RB	28	05	32	.37	.03	24	04	28	.33	.04
	RG	19	10	29	.39	.04	13	04	17	.22	.05
	NB	11	02	13	.15	.02	19	04	23	.27	.04
	NG	09	02	11	.13	.03	03	04	08	.12	.05
13. Cries a lot	RB	32	13	44	.57	.04	22	08	29	.37	.04
	RG	30	16	46	.62	.05	38	04	42	.47	.06
	NB	25	03	28	.31	.03	13	04	17	.20	.03
	NG	27	05	32	.37	.04	15	03	18	.22	.05
14. Cruel to animals	RB	27	11	38	.48	.04	07	03	10	.13	.03
	RG	29	09	38	.47	.04	08	01	09	.10	.03
	NB	08	01	09	.10	.02	01	00	01	.01	.07
	NG	05	04	06	.06	.02	00	00	00	.00	.00
15. Defiant	RB	32	27	59	.86	.04	43	30	73	1.02	.05
	RG	37	26	62	.88	.05	41	22	63	.85	.08
	NB	47	10	57	.66	.04	27	06	32	.38	.04
	NG	48	07	55	.62	.04	26	01	27	.28	.05
16. Demands must be met	RB	44	41	84	1.25	.04	38	29	67	.97	.05
	RG	36	46	82	1.27	.05	37	30	67	.98	.08
	NB	54	16	70	.86	.04	19	08	27	.35	.04
	NG	50	13	63	.75	.04	26	02	28	.30	.05
17. Destroys own things	RB	38	28	65	.93	.04	18	08	26	.34	.04
	RG	31	26	57	.83	.05	12	08	20	.27	.06
	NB	31	07	37	.44	.03	08	02	10	.12	.03
	NG	24	03	27	.30	.03	00	00	00	.00	.00
18. Destroys others' things	RB	38	16	54	.70	.04	28	15	43	.58	.05
	RG	29	15	44	.60	.05	15	10	25	.35	.07
	NB	20	05	25	.30	.03	12	04	16	.19	.03
	NG	16	03	18	.21	.03	03	01	04	.05	.03
19. Diarrhea-CBCL Daydreams-C-TRF	RB	26	09	35	.45	.04	27	09	36	.45	.05
	RG	21	07	28	.34	.04	20	09	28	.37	.07
	NB	09	01	10	.11	.02	27	06	33	.39	.04
	NG	07	<01	07	.08	.02	21	03	24	.27	.05
20. Disobedient	RB	40	21	61	.81	.04	46	24	70	.94	.05
	RG	42	20	61	.81	.05	47	15	62	.77	.07
	NB	54	05	59	.63	.03	32	07	38	.45	.04
	NG	52	04	56	.60	.04	25	00	25	.25	.05

[a]RB = referred boys; RG = referred girls; NB = nonreferred boys; NG = nonreferred girls. For CBCL, RB and NB=333 each; RG and NG=230 each; for C-TRF, RB and NB = 211 each; RG and NG = 92 each.

[b]*SE* = standard error of the mean.

APPENDIX F

Item	Group[a]	CBCL % 1	% 2	% 1+2	Mean	SE[b]	C-TRF % 1	% 2	% 1+2	Mean	SE[b]
21. Disturbed by change	RB	46	22	68	.91	.04	33	18	51	.70	.05
	RG	46	17	62	.79	.05	32	12	43	.55	.07
	NB	33	03	36	.39	.03	25	04	28	.32	.04
	NG	35	04	38	.42	.04	18	01	20	.21	.05
22. Not sleep alone-CBCL	RB	35	29	64	.92	.04	31	26	57	.83	.06
Mean to others-C-TRF	RG	38	29	67	.95	.05	29	13	42	.55	.07
	NB	26	25	51	.76	.05	20	09	28	.37	.04
	NG	35	22	57	.78	.05	12	01	13	.14	.04
23. Doesn't answer	RB	46	26	72	.97	.04	51	22	73	.94	.05
	RG	53	13	67	.80	.04	49	15	64	.79	.07
	NB	37	02	39	.41	.03	37	08	45	.53	.04
	NG	42	03	45	.48	.04	27	05	33	.38	.06
24. Doesn't eat well-CBCL	RB	46	18	64	.81	.04	48	26	74	1.00	.05
Difficulty with directions-C-TRF	RG	42	17	60	.77	.05	42	14	57	.71	.07
	NB	31	06	37	.43	.03	36	09	45	.55	.05
	NG	31	09	40	.48	.04	18	04	23	.27	.06
25. Doesn't get along	RB	38	09	47	.56	.04	44	18	62	.79	.05
	RG	36	12	48	.60	.05	45	08	52	.60	.07
	NB	16	02	17	.19	.02	25	02	27	.30	.04
	NG	16	04	17	.17	.03	12	02	14	.16	.04
26. No fun	RB	25	04	29	.32	.03	16	06	22	.28	.04
	RG	23	05	27	.32	.04	13	04	17	.22	.05
	NB	07	02	09	.11	.02	11	01	12	.13	.02
	NG	11	02	13	.15	.03	09	02	11	.13	.04
27. Lacks guilt	RB	32	22	54	.77	.04	25	37	62	.99	.06
	RG	34	20	53	.73	.05	24	18	42	.61	.08
	NB	34	06	39	.45	.03	20	10	30	.39	.05
	NG	32	07	39	.46	.04	14	02	16	.18	.05
28. Doesn't leave home-CBCL	RB	21	10	30	.40	.04	41	36	77	1.13	.05
Disturbs others-C-TRF	RG	18	10	28	.38	.04	38	16	54	.71	.08
	NB	07	01	08	.09	.02	27	10	38	.48	.05
	NG	09	01	10	.11	.02	20	01	21	.22	.05
29. Easily frustrated	RB	33	25	58	.83	.04	40	33	73	1.06	.05
	RG	34	26	60	.85	.05	36	28	64	.92	.08
	NB	49	08	57	.65	.03	35	10	45	.54	.05
	NG	40	10	50	.60	.04	28	03	32	.35	.06
30. Easily jealous	RB	41	34	75	1.09	.04	30	16	46	.62	.05
	RG	43	28	71	.99	.05	34	17	51	.68	.08
	NB	38	13	50	.63	.04	19	04	23	.27	.04
	NG	47	11	58	.70	.04	22	03	25	.28	.05

[a]RB = referred boys; RG = referred girls; NB = nonreferred boys; NG = nonreferred girls.
For CBCL, RB and NB=333 each; RG and NG=230 each; for C-TRF, RB and NB = 211 each; RG and NG = 92 each.
[b]SE = standard error of the mean.

APPENDIX F

		CBCL					C-TRF				
Item	Group[a]	% 1	% 2	% 1+2	Mean	SE[b]	% 1	% 2	% 1+2	Mean	SE[b]
31. Eats nonfood	RB	21	08	29	.38	.03	04	05	09	.14	.03
	RG	21	12	33	.45	.05	11	14	25	.39	.08
	NB	09	02	11	.12	.02	02	<01	03	.03	.01
	NG	04	01	05	.07	.02	07	00	07	.07	.03
32. Fears	RB	30	07	37	.44	.03	13	03	16	.18	.03
	RG	27	13	40	.53	.05	18	10	28	.38	.07
	NB	40	12	52	.64	.04	09	10	10	.11	.02
	NG	42	10	52	.62	.04	10	03	13	.16	.05
33. Feelings easily hurt	RB	38	17	55	.73	.04	48	15	63	.77	.05
	RG	40	27	67	.93	.05	47	18	65	.84	.07
	NB	44	20	64	.83	.04	41	10	51	.61	.05
	NG	51	20	71	.92	.05	46	12	58	.70	.07
34. Accident-prone	RB	37	24	61	.84	.04	18	06	24	.30	.04
	RG	33	25	59	.84	.05	12	14	26	40	.08
	NB	22	05	27	.32	.03	06	01	07	.09	.02
	NG	23	03	26	.30	.03	03	03	07	.10	.04
35. Gets in fights	RB	29	11	40	.51	.04	29	23	52	.75	.06
	RG	31	08	39	.47	.04	16	10	26	.36	.07
	NB	16	03	19	.22	.03	23	06	29	.35	.04
	NG	14	02	17	.19	.03	04	01	05	.07	.03
36. Gets into things	RB	32	38	70	1.08	.05	28	22	50	.72	.06
	RG	37	29	67	.96	.05	20	15	35	.50	.08
	NB	36	31	67	.98	.04	20	05	26	.31	.04
	NG	34	21	55	.76	.05	14	04	18	.23	.05
37. Upset when separated	RB	35	22	57	.79	.04	15	05	20	.26	.04
	RG	39	21	60	.80	.05	17	05	23	.28	.06
	NB	30	11	41	.53	.04	19	03	23	.26	.04
	NG	33	09	42	.51	.04	22	03	25	.28	.05
38. Trouble sleeping-CBCL Explosive-C-TRF	RB	41	23	63	.86	.04	27	31	58	.89	.06
	RG	35	22	57	.79	.05	20	17	37	.54	.08
	NB	23	04	28	.32	.03	14	07	20	.27	.04
	NG	29	07	35	.42	.04	07	01	08	.09	.03
39. Headaches	RB	17	07	23	.30	.03	01	00	01	.01	.01
	RG	14	09	23	.31	.04	01	01	02	.03	.02
	NB	02	00	02	.02	.07	03	<01	03	.04	.01
	NG	04	01	05	.06	.02	01	00	01	.01	.01
40. Hits others	RB	34	24	58	.83	.04	39	30	69	1.00	.05
	RG	37	16	53	.69	.05	34	14	48	.62	.08
	NB	43	06	49	.55	.03	32	12	44	.56	.05
	NG	32	08	40	.48	.04	27	01	28	.29	.05

[a]RB = referred boys; RG = referred girls; NB = nonreferred boys; NG = nonreferred girls. For CBCL, RB and NB=333 each; RG and NG=230 each; for C-TRF, RB and NB = 211 each; RG and NG = 92 each.
[b]SE = standard error of the mean.

APPENDIX F

		CBCL					C-TRF				
Item	Group[a]	% 1	% 2	% 1+2	Mean	SE[b]	% 1	% 2	% 1+2	Mean	SE[b]
41. Holds breath	RB	23	11	34	.45	.04	04	<01	04	.05	.02
	RG	19	08	27	.35	.04	03	03	07	.10	.04
	NB	02	<01	02	.02	.01	01	00	01	.01	.01
	NG	03	01	04	.05	.02	00	00	00	.00	.00
42. Hurts unintentionally	RB	26	09	34	.43	.04	22	08	30	.37	.04
	RG	21	07	28	.35	.04	15	02	17	.20	.05
	NB	20	02	21	.23	.02	08	01	10	.10	.02
	NG	14	01	15	.16	.03	02	00	02	.02	.02
43. Looks unhappy	RB	25	08	33	.41	.03	33	08	41	.49	.04
	RG	27	08	35	.43	.04	32	04	36	.40	.06
	NB	08	<01	09	.09	.02	19	03	22	.25	.03
	NG	11	01	12	.13	.02	15	03	18	.22	.05
44. Angry moods	RB	35	21	55	.76	.04	40	24	64	.89	.05
	RG	42	18	60	.79	.05	38	18	57	.75	.08
	NB	42	05	47	.51	.03	21	07	27	.34	.04
	NG	38	05	43	.48	.04	17	00	17	.17	.04
45. Nausea	RB	22	09	31	.40	.04	02	00	02	.02	.01
	RG	20	10	30	.39	.04	03	00	03	.03	.02
	NB	04	00	04	.04	.01	03	00	03	.03	.01
	NG	08	<01	08	.09	.02	05	00	05	.05	.02
46. Twitches	RB	09	06	15	.21	.03	07	11	18	.29	.04
	RG	10	07	17	.23	.04	04	04	09	.13	.05
	NB	05	01	05	.06	.02	05	02	07	.09	.02
	NG	03	01	03	.04	.02	03	01	04	.05	.03
47. Nervous	RB	17	12	30	.42	.04	32	17	48	.65	.05
	RG	21	10	31	.41	.04	25	15	40	.55	.08
	NB	10	02	11	.13	.02	14	02	16	.18	.03
	NG	05	02	07	.08	.02	10	01	11	.12	.04
48. Nightmares-CBCL Fails to finish-C-TRF	RB	29	11	40	.50	.04	46	19	65	.84	.05
	RG	29	09	38	.47	.04	39	15	54	.70	.08
	NB	21	01	22	.22	.02	33	07	40	.46	.04
	NG	21	04	25	.29	.04	21	01	22	.23	.05
49. Overeating-CBCL Fears school-C-TRF	RB	17	04	20	.24	.03	06	<01	06	.07	.02
	RG	19	07	26	.33	.04	02	00	02	.02	.02
	NB	08	02	10	.11	.02	06	05	06	.07	.02
	NG	07	01	08	.09	.02	07	00	07	.07	.03
50. Overtired	RB	36	07	43	.50	.03	21	06	27	.33	.04
	RG	24	10	34	.45	.04	27	07	34	.40	.06
	NB	23	04	26	.30	.03	12	02	14	.16	.03
	NG	26	03	29	.32	.03	13	01	14	.15	.04

[a]RB = referred boys; RG = referred girls; NB = nonreferred boys; NG = nonreferred girls. For CBCL, RB and NB=333 each; RG and NG=230 each; for C-TRF, RB and NB = 211 each; RG and NG = 92 each.
[b]SE = standard error of the mean.

		CBCL					C-TRF				
Item	Group[a]	% 1	% 2	% 1+2	Mean	SE[b]	% 1	% 2	% 1+2	Mean	SE[b]
51. Panics-CBCL	RB	18	03	22	.25	.07	34	24	58	.82	.05
Fidgets-C-TRF	RG	15	00	15	.15	.06	35	22	57	.78	.08
	NB	05	01	06	.07	.02	22	08	30	.37	.04
	NG	06	01	07	.09	.02	15	02	17	.20	.05
52. Painful BM-CBCL	RB	13	03	16	.19	.03	27	05	32	.37	.04
Is teased-C-TRF	RG	14	06	20	.26	.04	18	04	23	.27	.06
	NB	06	01	07	.08	.02	14	01	15	.17	.03
	NG	09	02	10	.12	.02	09	01	10	.11	.04
53. Attacks people	RB	20	11	31	.42	.04	30	23	54	.77	.06
	RG	21	06	27	.32	.04	21	11	32	.42	.07
	NB	09	02	11	.12	.02	14	06	19	.25	.04
	NG	06	00	06	.06	.02	02	01	03	.04	.03
54. Picks skin	RB	30	19	49	.68	.04	18	10	28	.37	.04
	RG	32	15	47	.63	.05	21	03	24	.27	.05
	NB	36	07	43	.50	.03	15	04	19	.23	.04
	NG	38	06	43	.49	.04	04	03	08	.11	.04
55. Plays with sex parts	RB	21	11	32	.43	.04	06	03	09	.12	.03
	RG	20	10	30	.41	.04	05	04	10	.14	.05
	NB	09	02	11	.14	.02	05	02	07	.09	.03
	NG	03	<01	03	.04	.01	03	00	03	.03	.02
56. Clumsy	RB	19	08	27	.35	.03	19	08	27	.35	.04
	RG	23	07	30	.37	.04	21	11	32	.42	.07
	NB	14	01	16	.17	.02	10	02	12	.14	.03
	NG	15	03	19	.22	.03	05	01	07	.08	.03
57. Eye problems	RB	05	01	07	.08	.02	<01	<01	01	.01	.01
	RG	05	03	08	.12	.03	02	01	03	.04	.03
	NB	02	<01	02	.03	.01	01	00	01	.01	.01
	NG	01	01	02	.03	.01	01	00	01	.01	.01
58. Punishment doesn't change	RB	25	26	51	.77	.05	34	30	64	.94	.06
	RG	28	23	51	.74	.05	25	16	41	.58	.08
	NB	34	10	44	.53	.04	23	07	29	.36	.04
	NG	35	05	40	.44	.04	11	02	13	.15	.04
59. Quickly shifts	RB	41	35	76	1.11	.04	36	29	65	.94	.05
	RG	40	33	73	1.06	.05	33	23	55	.78	.08
	NB	43	25	68	.92	.04	30	10	40	.50	.05
	NG	47	20	67	.87	.05	32	03	35	.38	.06
60. Skin problems	RB	17	15	32	.48	.04	01	<01	02	.02	.01
	RG	17	12	29	.41	.05	04	03	08	.11	.04
	NB	08	01	09	.11	.02	01	01	02	.03	.01
	NG	10	03	13	.17	.03	02	01	03	.04	.03

[a]RB = referred boys; RG = referred girls; NB = nonreferred boys; NG = nonreferred girls. For CBCL, RB and NB=333 each; RG and NG=230 each; for C-TRF, RB and NB = 211 each; RG and NG = 92 each.

[b]SE = standard error of the mean.

… APPENDIX F

		CBCL					C-TRF				
Item	Group[a]	% 1	% 2	% 1+2	Mean	SE[b]	% 1	% 2	% 1+2	Mean	SE[b]
61. Won't eat	RB	33	08	41	.49	.04	15	04	18	.22	.03
	RG	27	08	35	.43	.04	15	02	17	.20	.05
	NB	30	04	34	.38	.03	10	02	12	.14	.03
	NG	29	05	34	.39	.04	12	02	14	.16	.04
62. Refuses active games	RB	21	04	25	.29	.03	25	05	29	.34	.04
	RG	25	07	32	.40	.04	24	01	25	.26	.05
	NB	10	01	11	.11	.02	13	<01	14	.14	.03
	NG	08	<01	08	.09	.02	08	04	12	.16	.05
63. Rocks head or body	RB	10	03	13	.17	.02	06	06	11	.17	.03
	RG	10	04	14	.19	.03	05	00	05	.05	.02
	NB	04	00	04	.04	.01	<01	00	<01	.05	<.01
	NG	02	<01	02	.03	.01	00	00	00	.00	.00
64. Resists bed-CBCL Inattentive-C-TRF	RB	25	26	51	.77	.05	37	36	73	1.09	.05
	RG	27	29	57	.86	.06	34	18	52	.71	.08
	NB	47	10	57	.68	.04	29	12	42	.54	.05
	NG	45	12	57	.68	.04	18	03	22	.25	.05
65. Resists toilet training-CBCL Lying, cheating-C-TRF	RB	27	18	45	.63	.04	22	10	32	.43	.05
	RG	21	22	43	.65	.05	22	03	25	.28	.05
	NB	15	08	23	.30	.03	11	02	14	.16	.03
	NG	09	04	13	.17	.03	08	00	08	.08	.03
66. Screams	RB	34	25	58	.83	.04	22	16	38	.55	.05
	RG	32	17	48	.65	.05	35	09	43	.52	.07
	NB	27	06	33	.40	.03	10	03	13	.16	.03
	NG	26	04	30	.35	.04	10	01	11	.12	.04
67. Unresponsive to affection	RB	22	08	30	.38	.03	26	08	33	.41	.04
	RG	18	14	33	.47	.05	18	01	20	.21	.05
	NB	05	<01	05	.05	.01	11	02	13	.15	.03
	NG	04	01	06	.07	.02	07	00	07	.07	.03
68. Self-conscious	RB	20	05	24	.29	.03	30	06	36	.41	.04
	RG	24	06	30	.36	.04	29	14	43	.58	.08
	NB	29	05	34	.38	.03	31	03	34	.37	.04
	NG	37	04	41	.46	.04	16	02	18	.21	.05
69. Selfish	RB	43	14	58	.72	.04	43	16	59	.74	.05
	RG	49	13	62	.76	.04	39	12	51	.63	.07
	NB	52	07	58	.65	.03	27	03	30	.33	.04
	NG	54	05	59	.64	.04	21	02	23	.25	.05
70. Little affection	RB	32	06	38	.44	.03	32	13	45	.58	.05
	RG	27	12	39	.51	.05	12	08	20	.27	.06
	NB	11	02	13	.15	.02	18	07	24	.31	.04
	NG	11	02	13	.14	.03	05	03	09	.12	.04

[a] RB = referred boys; RG = referred girls; NB = nonreferred boys; NG = nonreferred girls. For CBCL, RB and NB=333 each; RG and NG=230 each; for C-TRF, RB and NB = 211 each; RG and NG = 92 each.
[b] SE = standard error of the mean.

APPENDIX F

Item	Group[a]	CBCL % 1	% 2	% 1+2	Mean	SE[b]	C-TRF % 1	% 2	% 1+2	Mean	SE[b]
71. Little interest	RB	19	03	23	.26	.03	21	03	24	.27	.03
	RG	17	03	20	.23	.03	18	02	21	.23	.05
	NB	11	02	12	.14	.02	18	02	20	.23	.03
	NG	08	01	09	.10	.02	02	03	05	.09	.04
72. Little fear	RB	24	20	44	.63	.04	18	17	35	.52	.05
	RG	30	14	44	.58	.05	13	09	22	.30	.07
	NB	29	14	43	.57	.04	16	04	19	.23	.03
	NG	30	10	40	.50	.04	08	00	08	.08	.03
73. Shy, timid	RB	35	11	47	.58	.04	28	04	32	.36	.04
	RG	37	11	47	.58	.04	41	09	50	.59	.07
	NB	27	04	31	.35	.03	30	08	37	.45	.04
	NG	36	04	40	.43	.04	24	05	29	.35	.06
74. Sleeps little-CBCL Not liked-C-TRF	RB	21	20	41	.61	.04	34	08	42	.50	.04
	RG	21	17	39	.56	.05	20	02	22	.24	.05
	NB	10	05	15	.20	.03	15	<01	16	.16	.03
	NG	14	07	20	.27	.04	08	00	08	.08	.03
75. Smears BM-CBCL Overactive-C-TRF	RB	07	08	15	.23	.03	30	30	60	.90	.06
	RG	11	08	19	.27	.04	23	13	36	.49	.07
	NB	01	<01	02	.02	.01	19	06	25	.31	.04
	NG	<01	00	04	<.01	<.01	07	02	09	.11	.04
76. Speech problem	RB	14	20	34	.54	.04	16	12	27	.39	.05
	RG	13	19	32	.51	.05	22	13	35	.48	.07
	NB	09	03	13	.16	.02	09	06	15	.20	.04
	NG	06	01	07	.07	.02	04	03	08	.11	.04
77. Stares	RB	20	14	33	.47	.04	30	08	38	.46	.04
	RG	21	04	26	.30	.04	28	09	37	.46	.07
	NB	11	01	11	.12	.02	22	05	27	.32	.04
	NG	08	00	08	.08	.02	16	02	18	.21	.05
78. Stomachaches	RB	18	02	20	.23	.03	02	00	02	.02	.01
	RG	18	04	22	.26	.03	03	01	04	.05	.03
	NB	08	<01	08	.08	.02	03	<01	04	.04	.02
	NG	10	01	11	.12	.02	02	01	03	.04	.03
79. Shifts between sad-excite-CBCL Overconforms-C-TRF	RB	17	13	30	.43	.09	08	01	09	.10	.02
	RG	32	21	53	.74	.14	15	02	17	.20	.05
	NB	17	02	19	.21	.03	10	00	10	.10	.02
	NG	13	04	17	.22	.03	02	00	02	.02	.02
80. Strange behavior	RB	19	11	30	.41	.04	12	08	20	.28	.04
	RG	19	11	30	.42	.05	07	05	12	.17	.05
	NB	05	01	05	.06	.01	02	03	05	.08	.03
	NG	03	<01	03	.04	.01	02	02	04	.07	.03

[a] RB = referred boys; RG = referred girls; NB = nonreferred boys; NG = nonreferred girls. For CBCL, RB and NB=333 each; RG and NG=230 each; for C-TRF, RB and NB = 211 each; RG and NG = 92 each.

[b] SE = standard error of the mean.

APPENDIX F

		CBCL					C-TRF				
Item	Group[a]	% 1	% 2	% 1+2	Mean	SE[b]	% 1	% 2	% 1+2	Mean	SE[b]
81. Stubborn	RB	32	31	63	.93	.05	43	28	71	.99	.05
	RG	40	28	68	.96	.05	50	18	68	.87	.07
	NB	46	12	58	.70	.04	28	09	36	.45	.04
	NG	50	09	59	.67	.04	28	02	30	.33	.05
82. Sudden mood change	RB	42	22	64	.85	.04	34	25	58	.83	.06
	RG	40	27	66	.93	.05	33	21	53	.74	.08
	NB	25	03	28	.32	.03	17	04	21	.26	.04
	NG	24	03	27	.30	.03	13	01	14	.15	.04
83. Sulks a lot	RB	29	10	39	.49	.04	26	10	36	.46	.05
	RG	28	15	43	.58	.05	35	08	42	.50	.07
	NB	11	02	14	.16	.02	15	05	20	.25	.04
	NG	19	02	20	.22	.03	14	02	16	.18	.05
84. Talks, cries in sleep-CBCL Teases a lot-C-TRF	RB	34	13	47	.59	.04	30	14	45	.59	.05
	RG	30	17	47	.64	.05	21	09	29	.38	.07
	NB	26	04	30	.34	.03	14	04	18	.22	.04
	NG	26	04	30	.33	.04	08	00	08	.08	.03
85. Temper	RB	36	33	69	1.03	.04	30	29	59	.89	.06
	RG	40	37	77	1.13	.05	34	18	52	.71	.08
	NB	46	14	59	.73	.04	18	07	24	.31	.04
	NG	42	13	54	.67	.05	21	04	25	.29	.06
86. Too concerned with neatness	RB	25	11	36	.47	.04	08	03	11	.14	.03
	RG	24	17	41	.58	.05	12	03	15	.18	.05
	NB	18	05	23	.29	.03	06	01	07	.08	.02
	NG	20	07	27	.33	.04	07	00	07	.07	.03
87. Fearful	RB	16	05	21	.26	.03	16	03	19	.23	.03
	RG	21	07	28	.35	.04	17	07	24	.30	.06
	NB	18	02	20	.23	.03	10	<01	11	.11	.02
	NG	16	02	17	.19	.03	07	01	08	.09	.03
88. Uncooperative	RB	37	23	60	.83	.04	53	18	71	.89	.05
	RG	43	17	60	.77	.05	53	07	60	.66	.06
	NB	43	04	47	.52	.03	25	04	28	.32	.04
	NG	41	01	43	.44	.03	18	02	21	.23	.05
89. Underactive	RB	21	09	30	.39	.04	11	05	16	.21	.04
	RG	19	11	30	.42	.05	18	02	21	.23	.05
	NB	03	01	04	.05	.01	11	04	16	.20	.03
	NG	03	<01	04	.04	.01	05	03	09	.12	.04
90. Unhappy, sad, depressed	RB	14	03	17	.20	.03	31	07	37	.44	.04
	RG	23	04	27	.31	.04	39	07	46	.52	.06
	NB	05	01	06	.07	.01	12	02	15	.17	.03
	NG	06	<01	07	.07	.02	07	01	08	.09	.03

[a]RB = referred boys; RG = referred girls; NB = nonreferred boys; NG = nonreferred girls. For CBCL, RB and NB=333 each; RG and NG=230 each; for C-TRF, RB and NB = 211 each; RG and NG = 92 each.

[b]SE = standard error of the mean.

APPENDIX F

		CBCL					C-TRF				
Item	Group[a]	% 1	% 2	% 1+2	Mean	SE[b]	% 1	% 2	% 1+2	Mean	SE[b]
91. Loud	RB	32	18	50	.68	.04	31	18	49	.66	.05
	RG	33	10	44	.54	.04	30	12	42	.54	.07
	NB	33	06	39	.45	.03	15	05	19	.24	.04
	NG	26	06	32	.38	.04	07	00	07	.07	.03
92. Upset by new	RB	28	14	42	.56	.04	16	08	24	.31	.04
	RG	32	18	50	.69	.05	24	02	26	.28	.05
	NB	21	03	24	.26	.03	08	01	09	.10	.02
	NG	23	02	25	.27	.03	05	02	08	.10	.04
93. Vomits	RB	12	03	16	.19	.03	01	00	01	.01	.01
	RG	16	03	19	.22	.03	03	02	05	.08	.04
	NB	04	<01	04	.04	.01	01	00	01	.01	.01
	NG	02	00	02	.02	.01	00	00	00	.00	.00
94. Wakes often-CBCL Unclean-C-TRF	RB	21	19	40	.58	.04	09	04	12	.16	.03
	RG	25	16	41	.57	.05	11	03	14	.17	.05
	NB	19	03	22	.26	.03	04	02	06	.08	.02
	NG	18	05	23	.28	.04	00	00	00	.00	.00
95. Wanders away	RB	26	13	38	.51	.04	25	13	37	.50	.05
	RG	25	08	33	.41	.04	20	05	25	.30	.06
	NB	18	03	22	.25	.03	12	03	16	.19	.03
	NG	17	03	20	.23	.03	09	01	10	.11	.04
96. Wants attention	RB	29	36	64	1.00	.05	37	28	66	.94	.05
	RG	31	37	68	1.05	.05	43	25	68	.93	.08
	NB	46	26	72	.97	.04	22	06	28	.35	.04
	NG	43	31	74	1.05	.05	21	04	25	.29	.06
97. Whining	RB	42	35	77	1.12	.04	27	13	40	.53	.05
	RG	46	34	80	1.14	.05	46	11	57	.67	.07
	NB	52	10	62	.72	.03	21	04	25	.29	.04
	NG	50	16	66	.82	.05	26	04	30	.35	.06
98. Withdrawn	RB	27	13	40	.53	.04	30	07	37	.44	.04
	RG	28	12	40	.53	.05	34	03	37	.40	.06
	NB	08	<01	08	.08	.02	18	03	21	.24	.03
	NG	07	00	07	.07	.02	09	04	13	.17	.05
99. Worries	RB	23	06	28	.34	.03	23	05	28	.33	.04
	RG	23	02	25	.27	.03	17	10	27	.37	.07
	NB	13	01	14	.15	.02	12	01	13	.14	.03
	NG	13	<01	13	.14	.02	10	03	13	.16	.05
100. Other problems	RB	08	11	20	.31	.04	06	11	17	.27	.04
	RG	09	10	20	.30	.04	02	05	08	.13	.05
	NB	02	06	07	.13	.03	03	05	08	.13	.03
	NG	03	06	09	.14	.03	10	05	05	.11	.05

[a]RB = referred boys; RG = referred girls; NB = nonreferred boys; NG = nonreferred girls. For CBCL, RB and NB=333 each; RG and NG=230 each; for C-TRF, RB and NB = 211 each; RG and NG = 92 each.

[b]SE = standard error of the mean.

INDEX

Abramowitz, M. 62, 70, 143
Accreditation 38
Achenbach, T.M. . . . . . ii, iv, 1, 4, 30, 46, 48, 62, 64, 69, 72, 77, 82, 83, 96-99, 101, 121, 126, 130, 132, 133, 143, 146
Adoptive parents 134
Affective Problems . 31, 35, 51, 86, 90, 120
Age 84, 85, 102, 105
Aggressive Behavior . . 11, 44, 59, 62, 64, 70, 86, 98, 99
Algina, J. 62, 70, 144
Allen, H. 99, 145
Alley, A. 77, 83, 94-96, 147
Alpha 74, 83, 142
American Psychiatric Association . . . 9, 30, 139
Analysis of covariance (ANCOVA) 101
Anxiety Problems 31, 35, 46, 48, 50, 51, 120
Anxious/Depressed . 11, 44, 48, 50, 59, 70
Aoki, M. 97, 143
Archer, P. 39, 145
Arend, R. 30, 97, 149
Asperger's Disorder 30, 32
Assessment 125, 126
Attention Problems. . .11, 44, 59, 64, 70, 98
Attention-Deficit/Hyperactivity Disorder (ADHD) 30, 31, 32, 35, 46, 65, 120
Autistic Disorder 16, 30, 32, 126
Average length of phrases 142
Baby talk 141
Babysitters 134
Balla, D. 39, 148
Banez, G.A. 72, 144
Barrett, G.L. 75, 146
Base rates 124
Baseline 40, 51, 130
Bayley, N. 39, 51, 94, 95, 96, 99, 144
Bayley Scales of Infant Development . . . 39, 51, 92, 99
Beall, G. 61, 75, 148
Behar, L.B. 82, 144

Behavior modification plan 47
Behavior Checklist (BCL) 97
Benedict, H. 83, 144
Bérubé, R.L. 48, 96, 121, 130, 132, 133, 143
Best things about the child 1
Bias 135
Binns, H.J. 30, 97, 144
Bond, L.A. 82, 144
Book, J. 83, 147
Boomsma, D.I. 97, 99, 148
Borderline clinical range . . . 11, 14, 16, 31, 44, 65, 71, 86, 90
Bresnick, B. 39, 145
Briggs-Gowan, M.J. 97, 144
Browne, N.W. 58, 144
Bryant, D. 97, 148
Caputo, J. 75, 146
Caregivers 4, 56, 79, 141
Carson, D.K. 96, 146
Carter, A.S. 97, 144
Casework interviews 50
CBCL/4-18 97
Changes 38, 48, 136, 140
Chi-square 141
Child abuse 53, 121, 130
Child and family service 50
Child care workers 38, 134, 139
Christoffel, K.K. 30, 97, 144
Cicchetti, D.V. 39, 148
Clarke, R.A. 100, 144
Clinical range . . 14, 31, 32, 44, 65, 71, 86, 90, 138
Clinical interpretations 138
Clinical cutpoints 86
Cognitive functioning 127, 128
Cohen, B.M. 61, 75, 148
Cohen, J. 84, 86, 101, 116, 144
Comorbidity 35, 125
Compas, B.E. 72, 144
Computations 150
Computer-scoring 71, 137, 139

INDEX

Conduct Disorder (CD) 97
Confirmatory factor-analytic methodology (CFA) 57
Conover, N.C. 75, 145
Conrad, M. 135, 144
Constantine, N.A. 97, 148
Constantino, J.N. 100, 144
Construct validity 82, 96, 100
Content validity 82
Control condition 75, 132
Convergent validity 99
Correlational statistics 123, 141
Correlations 55, 140, 159, 160
Costello, A.J. 30, 75, 145
Criterion-related validity 83, 93
Crocker, L. 62, 70, 144
Cronbach, L.J. 74, 83, 96, 142, 144, 155, 157
Cross-cultural research 130
Cross-informant agreement 74, 78
Cross-informant comparisons . . . 32, 44, 48
Cross-informant correlation 46, 51, 77
Cross-informant differences 35
Cross-informant syndrome construct . 58, 59
Crowther, J.H. 82, 144
Cudek, R. 58, 144
Custody disputes 53
Cutpoints 14, 124, 137
Daycare providers . . . 31, 43, 50, 134, 141
Delayed language 4, 16, 96, 51, 124
Delliquadri, E. 72, 146
Demographic differences 84, 102, 105
Denver Developmental Screening Test . . 39
Depression 123, 130
Descriptions 1
Developmental delays 99, 126
Developmental evaluation 39, 51
Developmental level 99
Developmental measures 99
Developmental perspectives . . 121, 123, 126
Developmental service 39
Diagnosis . . iii, 31, 32, 38, 42, 97, 125, 126
Diagnostic and Statistical Manual of Mental Disorders 30, 139
Diagnostic formulations 43
Diagnostic process 38, 43
Direct observations 130
Direct Observation Form (DOF) 46
Disabilities . . . . iii, 1, 47
Discriminant analyses 92
Discriminant validity 99
Dodds, J. 39, 145
Dromi, E. 83, 145
DSM . . . . iv, 30, 31, 32, 38, 42, 83, 125, 126, 139
DSM-oriented scales . . . . . . iv, 38, 30-32, 35, 43, 46, 58, 65, 83, 118, 125, 126, 138, 139, 149, 154, 156, 158
Dulcan, M.K. 75, 145
Dumenci, L. . . . . iv, 30, 143
Dysthymic disorder 30, 31
Ear infections 16
Edelbrock, C. 30, 69, 75, 143, 145
Educational settings 43
Emde, R. 72, 148
Emotionally Reactive 11, 51, 53, 58, 59, 70, 117, 118
Epidemiology 124
Epidémiological research 90
Ethnic differences 39, 63, 84, 102, 105, 138
Etiological research 127
Etiology 72
Evans, W.R. 75, 145
Experimental intervention studies 129
Explanatory details 1
Exploratory factor-analytic methodology (EFA) 57
Externalizing 13, 58, 69, 86, 93, 97, 98, 100, 118, 150, 153, 155, 157, 159, 160
Factor analysis 55, 58, 69, 151
False negatives 71
False positives 71
Family assessment 136
Family doctor 39, 47
Family practice . . . . iii, 47
Family system 136

INDEX

Fathers 79, 99, 126, 138
Fears 46, 48
Fenson, L. 95, 145
Ferdinand, R.F. 30, 72, 145, 146
First-order factor analysis 69
Fleiss, J.L. 90, 145
Follow-up 37, 44, 47, 50, 51, 136
Forensic 53
Formal diagnosis 42
Foster parents 38, 134
Foster placement 50
Frankenburg, W.K. 39, 145
Fulker, D.W. 72, 99, 148
Gavin, W.J. 96, 146
Gender 39, 61, 62, 71, 79, 84, 85,
  102, 105, 142
Gender-specific cutpoints 142
Gender-specific norms 65, 67, 71
Generalized Anxiety Disorder (GAD) 30, 31
Genetic 55, 99, 100, 126, 130
Gent, C.L. 72, 146
Giovannelli, J. 72, 146
Goebel, P. 51, 148
Goodman, R. 99, 145
Graham, P.J. 82, 97, 147
Grandmother 13, 50
Grandparent 40
Gruber, C. 94, 95, 147
Hall, L. 96, 146
Hammen, C. 135, 144
Hampe, E. 75, 146
Hand-scoring 137, 149
Hay, D.F. 99, 145
Head Start 44, 46
Hearing loss 16
Heidish, I.E. 30, 146
Heinstein, M. 82, 145
Heritability 99, 126
High scores 139
HMO 47, 48
Hollingshead, A.B. 56, 145
Homecare providers 134
Howell, C.T. 77, 82, 97, 143
Howell, D.C. 72, 144

Illness 1, 4, 48
Imitation 141
Incidence 124
Infant-Toddler Social and Emotional
  Assessment (ITSEA) 97
Institute for Survey Research (ISR) . . 58, 64
Intake 37, 40
Interaction partners 4, 37
Internal consistency 74, 142
Internalizing 13, 58, 69, 86, 92, 93,
  97, 118, 150, 153, 155, 157, 159, 160
Intervals 39, 75, 129, 35
Interventions 37, 46, 50, 44, 48,
  97, 126, 128, 129, 132, 140
Interviews 1, 38, 40, 42, 135
Ireton, H. 39, 99, 145
Item 100 . . . . 136, 137, 149
"Jackknife" (cross-validation) 92
Kalas, R. 75, 145
Kappa 141
Kasius, M.C. 30, 146
Kazdin, A.E. 30, 146
Keenan, K. 72, 97, 146
Kelley, M.L. 97, 147
Kent, A. 96, 146
Klee, T. 95, 96, 146
Kohn, M. 82, 146
Kolen, M.J. 64, 147
Koot, H. 72, 97, 99, 146
Kraemer, H.C. 97, 148
Kumar, R. 99, 145
Language delays 99, 126, 141, 142
Language development 47, 94
Language Development Survey (LDS) . . 4,
  14, 47, 48, 51, 53, 65, 67, 77, 83, 93, 95,
  96, 99, 100, 124, 126, 127, 128, 142
Lavigne, J.V. 30, 97, 144
Length of phrases 67
Leopold, W.F. 83, 146
Lewis, M. 82, 143
Liability 38
Loehlin, J.C. 58, 146
Loney, J. 75, 146
Longitudinal 97, 98, 100, 140, 141

INDEX

Low birthweight 16, 97, 98
Low scores 138, 139
Machine-readable forms 136
Major Depressive Disorder 30, 31
Maternal depression 135
McCain, A.P. 97, 147
McCarthy, D. 99, 146
McCarthy General Cognitive Index 99, 146
Minnesota Child Development Inventory
   (MCDI) 99
McConaughy, S.H. . . . . . . ii, 72, 143, 146
Medical 43, 47, 48, 132, 133
Meehl, P.E. 96, 144
Mental health 39, 40, 56, 65, 84, 140
Mental retardation 126
Mesman, J. 72, 146
Milich, R. 75, 146
Miller, L.C. 69, 75, 146
Mills, A. 99, 145
Mothers 79, 99, 126, 138
Mouton-Simien, P. 97, 147
Mrazek, D.A. 99, 148
Mullen, E.M. 95, 147
Mullen Scales of Early Learning 95
Multi-word phrases 4, 14
Multiple informants 37
Multiple regression analysis 84
Murphy, D.L. 100, 144
Myringotomy tubes 128
National Institute of Child Health and
   Development (NICHD) 61, 77
National Survey . . . 31, 56, 67, 69, 77, 99
Nelson, K. 83, 147
Neurological dysfunction 16
Noble, H. 75, 146
Non-referred children 60, 65, 71, 83,
   84, 101, 137, 155, 157, 159, 160
Norm-referenced 70
Normal 86
Normal range 13, 65, 71, 90
Normative samples . . . 13, 37, 58, 60, 61,
   62, 64, 65, 70, 71, 84, 122, 138, 153
Norms 58, 65, 67, 137
Nurse practitioners 47, 48
Observations 42, 136
Odds ratio 96, 141
Oppositional Defiant Disorder (ODD) . . 30,
   32, 35, 97
Oppositional Defiant Problems 31, 32,
   35, 46, 65, 86, 93, 120
Other problems 137, 149, 150
Outcomes . . . 38, 39, 44, 48, 126, 128, 129
Parent surrogates 1, 31, 40
Parental bias 131
Parental characteristics 130, 132
Parent's perceptions 42
Parents 1, 31, 40, 42, 44
Pawlby, S. 99, 145
Pediatric psychologists 47
Pediatrician 39, 47
Pediatrics iii
Pellegrini, D. 135, 148
Percentile 11, 13, 14, 16, 31, 62,
   64, 70, 71, 122
Pervasive Developmental Disorders (PDD)
   32, 121, 126
Pervasive Developmental Problems 32,
   86, 90, 93, 118
Petersen, N.S. 64, 147
Peterson, D.R. 69, 147
Phares, V.S. 72, 144
Phenotypic characteristics 99
Phrase development 16
Phrase length 67
Pickett, R.M. 71, 148
Play sessions 136
Population studies 124
Practical applications 37
Prediction 97
Preschool 43, 134
Preschool Development Inventories 39
Prevalence 38, 105, 124
Prevention 121
Previous scales 117
Profiles 11, 13, 16, 31, 32, 71,
   126, 127, 137, 139, 149
Psychiatrists 30, 139
Psychiatry iii

INDEX

Psychoactive medications 121
Psychologists 30, 139
Q correlations 40, 83
Randomized assignment 129
Rauh, V. 97, 143
Raw scores 13, 62, 122, 138, 140, 155
Reading skill 1, 40, 135
Reassessment 39, 75, 136
Receiver Operating Characteristics (ROC)
 analyses 71
Reece, S. 96, 146
Referral Status . . 83, 85, 86, 101, 102, 104
Referred children 71, 83, 84,
 101, 137, 155, 157, 159, 160
Region 63
Regression analyses 127, 140
Relative risk odds ratios 79, 90
Reliability 74, 75, 76, 77
Rescorla, L.A. . . . . . . ii, iv, 4, 30, 77, 83,
 95, 96, 100, 123, 143, 147
Research 121
Respondent 63
Reynell, J. 94, 95, 96, 147
Richman, N. 82, 97, 147
Richters, J.E. 135, 147
Risk factors 16, 90
Roberts, M. 75, 146
Robins, L.N. 75, 149
Robinson, J. 72, 148
Rolf, J.E. 82, 144
Rosenbaum, D. 30, 97, 144
Rosman, B.L. 82, 146
Ruffle, T.M. 48, 143
Sakoda, J.M. 61, 75, 76, 79, 84,
 101, 148
Sampling procedures 124
SAS Institute 92, 122, 148
Schmitz, S. 72, 99, 148
School-age forms 39, 44, 123, 140
Schmucker, G. 99, 145
Scoring templates 137
Scoring 136
Screening 37, 121
Second-order factor analysis 69

Separation Anxiety Disorder (SAD) . 30, 31
Serotonin 100
Service delivery 38
Severity 35
Shapiro, H. 39, 145
Sharp, D. 99, 145
Shaw, D. 72, 146
Short forms 136
Sleep Problems 11, 13, 35, 48, 50, 59,
 70, 99
Social desirability 42, 135, 139
Socioeconomic status (SES) 1, 39, 56,
 63, 84, 85, 102, 105
Somatic Complaints . . .11, 59, 63, 64, 70, 90
Somatic Problems 35
Spanish 1, 51, 77, 95, 141
Sparrow, S. 39, 94, 95, 148
Special education 56, 84
Special educators 38
Specific Phobia 30, 31
Spiker, D. 97, 148
SPSS 122, 148
Stability 74, 79, 80
Standard scores 13, 62, 122, 123
Standard error of measurement 140,
 156, 158
Statistical analyses 122, 123, 138, 140
Stegun, I.A. 62, 70, 143
Stelzer, S.C. 95, 148
Stevenson, J. 97, 147
Stomachaches 43
Strengths 38, 43, 53
Strengths and Difficulties Questionnaire . . .99
Stress 130, 132
Stringfield, S. 82, 144
Structural models 127
Structural modeling 123
Subjective judgments 135
Support programs 48
Swets, J.E. 71, 148
Syndromes . . . . iv, 11, 13, 16, 43,
 55, 58, 59, 90, 99, 117, 138, 149, 151, 153,
 155, 157, 159, 160

INDEX

T Scores 13, 14, 16, 31, 62, 64, 65, 70, 122, 138, 140, 150, 155, 159, 160
Taxonomic research 125
Taxonomy 125, 126
Teacher's Report Form (TRF) . . . 82, 99, 140
Teachers 4, 16, 31, 56, 79
Teachers' ratings 99
Temperament 127
Templates 139, 149
Test-retest attenuation effect 75, 129
Tests 136
Testing 4
Tetrachoric correlations 57, 151
Therapeutic alliances 38
Therapy 48
Third party payment 38, 125
Thorndike, R.L. 95, 148
Thwing, E.J. 99, 145
Toddler Behavior Screening Inventory (TBSI) 97
Total Problems 14, 56, 58, 69, 83, 86, 90, 92, 93, 96-99, 104, 118, 137-139, 149, 150, 153, 155, 157, 159, 160
Trainees 38, 134
Translations 130, 131, 135
Traumatic experiences 127
Truncation of T Scores 62, 122, 138, 140
Twin studies 99
Unanswered items 137
Validity 82, 84
van den Berg, H. 30, 146
van den Oord, E.J.C.G. 97, 99, 148
van der Valk, M.A. 99, 126, 148
Verhulst, F.C. . . 30, 72, 97, 99, 130, 146, 148
Vineland Adaptive Behavior Scales . . 39, 94
Vocabulary 14, 16, 67, 94, 95, 100, 141, 142
Wakschlag, L.S. 97, 146
Walsh, B. 72, 146
Warda, M. 51, 148
Website 9, 121
Wechsler, D.C. 72, 96, 148
Weiss, S.J. 51, 148
Wilson, P. 51, 148
Windows® software 32
WISC-R 96
Withdrawn 11, 51, 59, 70, 90, 93, 98
Wiznitzer, M. 72, 145
Zahn-Waxler, C. 72, 148
Zimmerman, I. 95, 148